Thriving Beyond Sustainability

*Pathways to a
Resilient Society*

ANDRÉS R. EDWARDS

NEW SOCIETY PUBLISHERS

Cataloging in Publication Data:
A catalog record for this publication is available from
the National Library of Canada.

Cover design by Diane McIntosh.
Cover images © iStock : leaves - Aleksander Trankov;
butterfly - David Hillerby

Printed in Canada by Friesens.
Third printing September 2013.

Paperback ISBN: 978-0-86571-641-4

Inquiries regarding requests to reprint all or part
of *Thriving Beyond Sustainability* should be addressed to
New Society Publishers at the address below.

To order directly from the publishers,
please call toll-free (North America) 1-800-567-6772,
or order online at newsociety.com

Any other inquiries can be directed by mail to:

New Society Publishers
P.O. Box 189, Gabriola Island, BC V0R 1X0, Canada
(250) 247-9737

New Society Publishers' mission is to publish books that contribute
in fundamental ways to building an ecologically sustainable and just
society, and to do so with the least possible impact on the environment,
in a manner that models this vision. We are committed to doing this
not just through education, but through action. This book is one step
toward ending global deforestation and climate change. It is printed on
Forest Stewardship Council-certified acid-free paper that is **100% post-
consumer recycled** (100% old growth forest-free), processed chlorine free,
and printed with vegetable-based, low-VOC inks, with covers produced
using FSC-certified stock. New Society also works to reduce its carbon
footprint, and purchases carbon offsets based on an annual audit to ensure
a carbon neutral footprint. For further information, or to browse our full
list of books and purchase securely, visit our website at: newsociety.com

NEW SOCIETY PUBLISHERS
www.newsociety.com

MIX
Paper from
responsible sources
FSC
www.fsc.org
FSC® C016245

Advance Praise for *Thriving Beyond Sustainability*

Andrés Edwards has given us a comprehensive, up-to-date, and highly inspiring guide to the pioneering initiatives and practices of individuals, organizations, and communities from around the world who strive to create a future that is ecologically sustainable and socially just. It is thoroughly researched, deeply contemplated, and yet eminently practical. I warmly recommend it to anyone concerned about the future of human civilization.

— Fritjof Capra, Author,
The Web of Life and *The Hidden Connections*

For those of you who have given up, who believe that making environmental change is too hard or too late, this book is not for you. For those ready to be inspired and energized, read this book right away. Edwards's latest book is chock-full of examples of real solutions, advanced by real people all over the globe — solutions that can build a lasting path towards sustainability.

— Annie Leonard, Author, *The Story of Stuff*

From sustainability to resilience is the theme of Andrés Edwards's new book...it is an inventory of grounded hope, practical inspiration, and achievable visions...exactly the kind of thinking, work, and doing that will bring civilization to safe harbor.

— David W. Orr, Author, *Down to the Wire*

Andrés Edwards is a walking database of information on efforts to create sustainable societies, and his enthusiasm for the promise of sustainability is infectious. Read *Thriving Beyond Sustainability* and your belief in the prospects for human survival — no, human "thriveability" — will brighten dramatically!

— Gary Gardner, Senior Researcher, Worldwatch Institute

Peppered with examples, *Thriving Beyond Sustainability* presents a delectable feast of people, communities, companies, and countries thriving by reducing energy and water use, waste, and cost.

— David Blockstein, Senior Scientist,
National Council for Science and the Environment

Thriving Beyond Sustainability challenges us to move from using a deficit model for thinking about sustainability to using a natural and human abundance approach to thinking about how society will thrive. Edwards provides the reader with both principles and examples from throughout the world. He gives concrete suggestions for action and provides an annotated resource list that supports taking actions. This is a welcome addition to the growing sustainability literature.

— Paul Rowland, Ph.D., Executive Director,
Association for the Advancement
of Sustainability in Higher Education.

Thriving Beyond Sustainability is simply a must-read. It offers a concise, insightful and deeply thoughtful overview of the most hopeful and important emergent trends and ideas driving the global sustainability movement. You will also find an eminently readable book that has shelf life. Edwards is sophisticated, and his nuanced analysis and discernment could not be more timely as green goes mainstream and everyone wants to know: What do we do?

— Kenny Ausubel, Co-CEO and Founder of Bioneers

Thriving Beyond Sustainability captures the spirit of the people and organizations finding solutions that are creating a brighter future for all. In this important book, Edwards presents engaging stories about the positive impact that leaders are making in transforming their communities through green building, energy, agriculture and green business practices among others. A fabulous resource for those interested in learning about the challenges and opportunities before us.

— David Johnston, Author,
Toward a Zero Energy Home and *Green Remodeling*

Edwards covers a breathtaking swath of world-changing stories, frameworks and tools that are essential knowledge for the sustainability advocate. You can't help but feel optimistic after reading this book.

— Adam Werbach, Global CEO, Saatchi & Saatchi S

To my parents and siblings,

with gratitude

~

Contents

Cultural Indicators | *Tibetan Nomads* | *Balinese Water Temples*
Inuit Traditional Knowledge | *The Kogi: Guardians of the Planet*
The Value of Traditional Knowledge | *The Extinction of Languages*
Building Community | *Taking Action*

Transition Initiatives | *Sustainability Street*
Salmon Nation | *Regional Climate Plans*
National Initiatives: Sweden and New Zealand
International Environmental Plans | *Glocalization Reframed*
Taking Action

The New Bottom Lines | *The Drivers*
Implementing Nature's Strategies | *The Trilogy*
Growth, Consumption and Pollution | *Creating New Alliances*
Mission-Based Enterprises | *A New Role for Civil Society*
Blue Chip Companies Turn Green | *Tax Shifting*
Providing Tools and Metrics | *Building New Business Models*
Taking Action

New Design Approaches and Objectives
Design Tools and Frameworks
Building Green Homes, Towns and Cities

Acknowledgments

The idea for this book emerged while I was in the midst of writing *The Sustainability Revolution*. At that time I realized I could illustrate the sustainability principles by sharing the stories of the people and organizations undertaking this important work. But in the interest of concluding my research within my timeline, that aspect was left for another time — and another book. So here it is!

Much has changed since the publication of my last book. The field of sustainability is changing at lightning speed and I have counted on the guidance and insights of scores of friends and colleagues. They have collectively helped me focus on the essential points and have shared their subject expertise to ensure accuracy and relevance.

I would like to thank Gary Gardner, Rick Medrick and Linda Steck for their unwavering commitment to reviewing the entire manuscript. Despite their hectic schedules, their suggestions strengthened the "string" of the narrative and made the "pearls" (examples) more cohesive and integrated with the body of the work. Because of the broad topic areas, numerous colleagues assisted me in reviewing particular sections of the text. For this part of the work, I am indebted to: Debra Amador, Robert Z. Apte, Elizabeth J. D. Baker, Spencer Beebe, T. J. Blasing, Steve Bushnell, Gretchen Daily, Adam Davis, David Eisenberg, Will Elkins, Tom Fookes, John Garn, Pam Hartwell-Herrero, Christopher Heald, Stacey Iverson, Warren Karlenzig, Rebecca Klein, Mark Lakeman, Kory Lundberg, Susan Minnemeyer, Dave Rapaport, Bill Reed, Mark Samolis, David Schaller, Bill Schmidt, Rand Selig, Howard Silverman, Amelia Spilger, Mark Stefanski, Geof Syphers, Doug Tompkins, Marjorie van Roon, Kim Vicariu, Don Weeden, Paul Westbrook, Karin Widegren and Bob Willard. Their help in clarifying specific sections of the book is greatly appreciated.

Another important aspect of this book was researching and selecting the photographs. The assistance and perseverance of people from a wide range of organizations throughout the world helped me identify and retrieve high-resolution photographs that encapsulate the initiatives described in the text. I would like to thank those who were instrumental in securing the photos: Niles Barnes, Samuel M. Beebe, Kelly Blynn, Eden Brukman, Zoey Burrows, Joseph P. Campbell, Joel Catchlove, Jason Cox,

Andrew Cuneo, Allison Deines, Danielle Engelman, Alan Ereira, Jim Estes, Dan Forman, Rikin Gandhi, Jackie Goneconti, Lasse Hejdenberg, Jamie Henn, Stacey Iverson, Mindee Jeffery, J. Stephen Lansing, Shavonne Lee, Stephanie Mohan, Carolina Morgado, Jennie Organ, Mary Paris, Frank Ryan, Emily Schlickman, Bill Schmidt, Rajesh Shah, Mark Steele, Lee Wakechon, Ruth Ann Wedel and Will Wilson. Special thanks go to Cheetah Conservation Botswana, Marin Farmers Markets and Tanzania Mission to the Poor and Disabled (PADI).

Over the years my research and ideas about sustainability have evolved through the exchange of views with friends and colleagues. I would like to thank the following for their openness to discussing topics of common interest: Tam Beeler, David Blockstein, Jana Boring, Josiah Caine, David Caploe, Geoff Chase, Lindsey Corbin, Kayla Cranston, Bruce Dickinson, Erik Dunmire, Elizabeth Durney, Shelley Flint, Tom Fookes, Pete Gang, Marya Glass, Nicky Gonzalez Yuen, Bruce Hammond, Randy Hayes, Trathen Heckman, Richard Heinberg, David Johnston, Bruce King, Miriam Landman, Jack Lin, Michele McGeoy, Charles McGlashan, Nancy Metzger, Ramsay Millie, Carol Misseldine, Mutombo Mpanya, Michael Murray, Jim Newell, Greg Newth, Pramod Parajuli, James Pittman, Susan Pridmore, Jeffrey Reynolds, Chris Schmidt, Tom Sebastian, Paul Sheldon, John Shurtz, Brian Staszenski, Mark Stefanski, Tom Tamblyn, Andrea Traber, Scott Valentino, Sim Van der Ryn, Judy Walton, Nils Warnock, Duane Warren, Barbara Widhalm and Mark Woodrow.

My work has been enriched through my affiliation with the people from the following organizations, which are making positive changes at the local and regional levels: Cascade Canyon School, the Environmental Education Council of Marin, Environmental Forum of Marin, Marin Green Schools Alliance, Prescott College, the US Green Building Council's Redwood Empire Chapter and Pacific Regional Council and Sustainable Fairfax.

I would like to thank Chris Plant, Judith Plant, EJ Hurst, Ginny Miller, Sue Custance and the team at New Society Publishers who have done a fabulous job designing and producing my work and bringing to the mainstream the ideas of countless other authors committed to a better future. I am especially indebted to Ingrid Witvoet and Diane Killou of New Society Publishers for their editorial skills that helped focus and synthesize the message of this book.

With sincere appreciation and gratitude I would like to thank my wife Rochelle and our children Naomi, Easton and Rylan for sharing their unique spirits with me on our collective journey.

Foreword

I've just returned from Denmark, where hopes for a historic worldwide agreement to bring global warming under control went down in, well, flames. The Copenhagen conference was dispiriting in every way — the great powers refused to listen to the small nations, to civil society, to scientists. They signed their own meaningless document — no timetables, no targets — and jetted back to DC and Beijing.

Or rather it was dispiriting in every way but one. In the years since the Kyoto meeting of the late 90s, a huge groundswell has formed across the planet. Every kind of person was on hand — activists, entrepreneurs, people working locally, regionally, in business, in the arts. There's a critical mass out there — it just hasn't coalesced yet into something powerful enough to challenge the status quo.

With this fine book, Andrés Edwards gives some idea of how that might happen. It offers example after example of what is already working and could be brought to scale. And with its SPIRALS framework and its rhetoric of thrive-ability, it offers some sense of how that scaling-up might happen.

After Copenhagen we're faced with the fact that our leaders will not solve this problem for us. We're going to have to do it, one place and one country and one planet at a time. Let's get to work.

— Bill McKibben,
December 2009

Introduction: Drawing a Collective Map of Earth Island

If you save the living environment, you will automatically save the physical environment. Omit the living and you lose them both. Our relationship to the rest of life can be put in a nutshell: The biosphere is richer in diversity than ever before conceived. Biodiversity is being eroded. If we continue this way, it is estimated that we will lose half the plants and animal species (on land) by end of century. That loss will inflict a heavy price in wealth and spirit.

— E. O. WILSON

We do not need magic to change the world, we carry all the power we need inside ourselves already: we have the power to imagine better.

— J. K. ROWLING

The sustainability revolution is nothing less than a rethinking and remaking of our role in the natural world.

— DAVID W. ORR

WHEN DUTCH MARINER Jacob Roggeveen first landed on Easter Island in the South Pacific on Easter Sunday in 1722, he encountered a denuded, eroded landscape of about 64 square miles. Easter Island had a few thousand inhabitants and hundreds of tall stone statues known as *moai*, representing the islanders' high-ranking ancestors. Historians and archeologists have since pieced together Easter Island's decline from an advanced, complex society to one that destroyed its forests and marine life. They have concluded that its population was decimated by famines, slave raids, epidemics and civil war. Similar to the collapse of the Anasazi culture of North America, the Mayan culture of Central America and the Tiwanaku culture of South America, the Easter Island culture, in the words of author Jared Diamond, committed "unintended ecological suicide — ecocide" by destroying its natural resources.[1] The collapse of Easter Island's society has often been seen as a microcosm of what may lie in store for modern civilization if its social and ecological systems continue their precipitous decline. However, a brighter outcome for humanity could be on the horizon.

Over 8,000 miles from Easter Island in the North Sea lies another island: the windswept Danish island of Samsø, with about 40 square miles and 4,100 permanent residents. Unlike Easter Island, Samsø Island symbolizes a story of hope and action. In 1997 Samsø won a Danish government competition for its plan to shift from its reliance on fossil fuels to 100 percent renewable energy sources. The residents, known as Samsingers, launched a renewable energy program that has attracted the world's attention. Over the last decade, Samsø's wind turbines, solar panels, biomass projects and district heating systems, owned either individually or collectively by Samsingers, have made its communities fossil-fuel free and renewable energy exporters to mainland Denmark. In the process, the island has cut its carbon footprint by 140 percent. As community leader Soren Harmensen says, "We are not hippies. We just want to change how we use our energy without harming the planet or without giving up the good life."[2]

The stories of Easter Island and Samsø Island highlight divergent destinies for the future of the world's civilization — our Earth Island. One is marked by overconsumption, ecological decline and social chaos while the other is built on the inspiration and self-determination of individuals committed to making a difference in the world. Samsø, which historically was a meeting place for Vikings, comes from the word "samle," meaning "to gather." The Samsingers' actions allow us to witness the remarkable possibilities that can emerge when a community gathers and unites with a common purpose and vision.

Every day on our Earth Island, with its 6.7 billion people, on average 5,000 children die from waterborne diseases (one every 15 seconds), over 70 species become extinct (one every 20 minutes), 85 million barrels of fossil-fuel-based oil are consumed and 23 million metric tons (about 28 pounds per person) of carbon dioxide are emitted by human activities into an already warming atmosphere.[3] Although the daily snapshot of Earth Island is indeed bleak, from isolated villages to major urban centers there are beacons of hope from thousands of large and small initiatives taking place.

This book draws a collective map of individuals, organizations and communities from around the world that are committed to building an alternative future that strives to restore environmental health, reinvent outmoded institutions and rejuvenate our environmental, social and economic systems. It is my intention to describe the emerging ideas and actions so that readers will gain a better understanding of the challenges we face and a determination to be part of the solutions. Each of us has an important role to play.

We begin to draw the contours of this map by exploring the value of Traditional Ecological Knowledge from indigenous societies including the Tibetans, Balinese, Inuit and Kogi. These cultures, which have survived for millennia, serve as a mirror to the world's peoples, reflecting practices that balance their well-being and that of the natural world. We then examine the flourishing of local efforts to become more self-reliant in energy, food, transportation and other areas. These efforts are being made by groups including Transition Initiatives in the UK and the US, Sustainability Street in Australia, Salmon Nation in the Northwestern US and ICLEI–Local Governments for Sustainability in conjunction with communities throughout the world.

Beyond initiatives at the local level, we turn to the greening of commerce. From start-up enterprises to well-established multinational companies, the transformation in commerce involves manufacturing goods and delivering services in ways that reduce environmental impact and emulate natural cycles. These alternative approaches strive to eliminate waste, to consider the full life cycle of manufactured goods — recycling products into new products at the end of their life — and to support individuals with socially-just employment opportunities. Along with the greening of commerce, we look at the transformation to green building practices. The shift to ecological design reduces the environmental impact of the built environment by reinventing regenerative design strategies, frameworks and tools that enhance natural systems and support the well-being of the people who live and work in our buildings.

We then chart the worldwide environmental conservation efforts aimed at restoring ecosystems in decline and protecting the Earth's biodiversity. These efforts range from protecting habitats at the continental scale, as in Australia's WildCountry Campaign, to identifying and protecting species, as in Conservation International's Biodiversity Hotspots program. In addition, we examine other mechanisms to protect habitats including land trusts, conservation philanthropy and financial tools such as Payment for Environmental Services, involving wetland mitigation and species banking programs.

Our Earth Island is experiencing five interrelated global trends: ecosystem decline, energy transition, population growth, economic disparity and climate change. These enormous challenges are converging, with potentially devastating consequences. We face an unprecedented crisis — and a unique opportunity for a brighter future.

The weight of these global challenges is lightened somewhat by the positive changes reshaping our world. The greening of college campuses, the explosion of farmers' markets and organic foods, the innovative green building standards, the push for renewable energy sources and the new green-collar jobs all point to a new economy. Worldwide collaborative efforts are encouraged by initiatives such as the new prize-philanthropy programs and open-source mechanisms.

Creating leverage points magnifies the positive impact of these efforts, which can then be replicated throughout the world. The bedrock of successful initiatives is captured by the SPIRALS framework, a set of criteria for thriveable initiatives that are Scalable, Place-making, Intergenerational, Resilient, Accessible, Life-affirming and involve Self-care. These criteria provide a compass to orient us to our new map.

Our journey through this landscape of possibilities calls for a change of perception. We must shift from merely sustaining to *thriving*. The transformation from sustainability to *thriveability* challenges us to expand our imaginations and create the future we want for ourselves and for future generations. Thriveability focuses on collaboration and abundance. The concept acts as a catalyst to motivate us to take action. It encourages us to step away from the notion that we are separate from nature and instead see ourselves as an integral part of natural systems. Rather than seeking to limit our impact by being "less bad," thriveability supports actions that regenerate natural systems and our quality of life. More significantly, thriveability embodies the innate qualities that define our humanity — our capacity for empathy, compassion, collaboration, playfulness, creativity, enthusiasm and love. These traits allow us to achieve remarkable feats in the face of adversity. In this spirit we can successfully confront our challenges and leave a positive legacy for future generations.

Instead of just sustaining ourselves through incremental improvements in our technological and social systems, thriveability calls for a vision based on possibilities for change, which, like our dreams and imagination, are limitless. This new thriveable future is one in which we show respect for ourselves, for our neighbors and for the limits of nature. The essence of thriveability is a belief in the capacity of the human spirit to collaborate in creating new possibilities for lasting solutions. This thriveable attitude shifts away from scarcity, loss and volatility and toward abundance, prosperity and equanimity. We must celebrate being part of the natural world and acknowledge that, in geological time, we are newcomers with much to learn.

In this spirit of humility, curiosity and imagination, we have an opportunity to redefine our relationship with the natural world. We recognize that greening the world begins by healing and greening our own lives. I hope that the information in this book, coupled with the creativity, courage and determination profiled in its stories, inspires readers to make meaningful changes that improve the lives of all species on our Earth Island.

ONE

Lessons from
Our Ancestors

Where is the wisdom we have lost in knowledge?
Where is the knowledge we have lost in information?
— T. S. Eliot

If you have knowledge, let others light their candles with it.
— Winston Churchill

To deal with the effects of our present predicament, which includes overpopulation, the energy crisis, loss of biodiversity and climate change, we can find lessons for industrial societies in our ancestors' relationship to the environment. Living close to nature, indigenous peoples learned to adapt to and coexist with other species and the land, gaining what scientists and anthropologists call Traditional Ecological Knowledge: an understanding of ecosystems and their interrelationships.

Traditional cultures can teach us about building resilient communities that can adapt to change. Thriving for millennia in habitats with limited resources and severe weather calls for a thorough understanding of the rhythms of natural systems and the creation of social structures that support long-term settlements. Traditional cultures remind us that we are dependent on healthy natural systems. Our modern urbanized societies still need clean air and water and healthy soil. Although natural systems are often masked in metropolitan areas and we spend most of our time indoors, these systems are at the root of our very survival. The impacts of climate change in the last decade serve as a powerful reminder that, as has been said, nature not only "bats last" but in fact "owns the stadium." Our stadium is not merely a venue visited seasonally for entertainment but is instead our permanent home planet.

Cultural Indicators

In conservation biology, bioindicators are plant, animal and microbial species and chemicals used to monitor the health of an ecosystem. For example, the changes in a species' population may serve as a bioindicator of the impact of pollution or other factors.[2] Cultural indicators passed on for millennia also monitor our ecosystems. These cultural indicators include understanding species migration, herbal medicines, agricultural practices, seasonal weather variations and networks for social organization and governance. This traditional knowledge complements our technological advances and will play an increasingly important role as we grapple with global challenges.

When we begin to understand that humans are not separate from nature but an integral part of the fabric of life, the significance of traditional cultures becomes more apparent. Protecting diversity extends beyond the biological to include the diversity of cultures. Living in proximity to the land, traditional cultures show us that humans are different from other species in our resourcefulness and dominance yet still dependent on the living systems essential for all species. These cultures demonstrate the foresight, resilience, adaptability and social systems that have stood the test of time. From them we can learn numerous lessons about how to integrate change and maintain values that serve for generations. We now turn to

---

Santa Fe "Living Treasures" Nears 25 Years of Honoring Community Elders

"Living Treasures" is a Santa Fe, New Mexico, program that is nearing a quarter century of honoring community elders who have generously served and inspired others over their lifetimes. Treasures include teachers, nurses, artists, writers, farmers, weavers, builders, dancers, physicians, naturalists, healers, pueblo governors, volunteers and people from many other walks of life. More than 170 Santa Fe Treasures have been honored since 1984. In 1997, portraits and excerpts from the interviews of the first 104 Santa Fe Treasures were compiled into a book, *Living Treasures: Celebration of the Human Spirit*. The Santa Fe organization has also developed a free how-to handbook for other communities interested in starting their own Living Treasures program.[1]

four traditional cultures whose stories illustrate different ways of living in balance with natural systems.

Throughout their histories, the Tibetan, Balinese, Inuit and Kogi cultures have integrated Traditional Ecological Knowledge into their lives and thrived in environments that range from tropical forests to mountain plateaus. Each of these cultures has devised ecological strategies that may seem primitive at first glance but have proven their resilience over time. Developing resilient systems is emerging as a key asset in our modern world. The loss of Traditional Ecological Knowledge, including the rapid extinction of native languages, diminishes the cultural diversity of the planet and erodes the knowledge base for living in balance with the natural world.

Tibetan Nomads

The plight of the Tibetans has usually been associated with human rights issues. These have been brought to international attention by His Holiness the Dalai Lama, Nobel laureate and the Tibetans' spiritual leader. Less attention has been focused on the environmental concerns and sustainability

Andrés R. Edwards

The Tibetan culture's traditional knowledge has allowed nomads to live in the harsh conditions of the Tibetan Plateau for millennia. Nomads maximize their resources by using the yak for milk, butter, meat, leather and wool. Here a yak herd grazes in a valley on the Tibetan Plateau, U-Tsang.

practices of the Tibetan people. Nomads and farmers have demonstrated their resilience and adaptability to extreme climate conditions as they live at an average elevation of over 15,000 feet on the Tibetan Plateau. The traditional Tibetan livelihood yields important insights about resource use, the cyclic patterns of animal migrations, weather and agricultural practices and their connections to governance. Living on the "roof of the world" on a plateau that is the source of Asia's major rivers and a lifeline to millions of people, Tibetans have historically thrived under challenging conditions. Tibet, referred to as the world's "third pole," also contains the largest ice fields outside the Arctic and Antarctic, and its melting glaciers provide an early warning of the impacts of climate change.[3]

Although Tibetan culture is known for its integration of Buddhism into all facets of life, its ecological practices stem from government directives and individual actions. Throughout Tibet's history its leaders, including the Dalai Lamas and regents, have issued decrees known as *tsatsigs* to protect the environment. In 1642 His Holiness the Great Fifth Dalai Lama Ngawang Lobsang issued the Decree for the Protection of Animals and the Environment. *Tsatsigs* were delivered to villages and discussed by village heads and officials and were displayed at every district office year round. In 1901, one of the *tsatsigs* issued by the Great Thirteenth Dalai Lama stated:

> From the first month of the Tibet calendar to the 30th of the seventh month, with the exception of tigers, leopards, bears, hyenas, rats and Rishu [no translation available], nobody will hurt, let alone kill, the different birds of the air, animals of the hills and forests, fish and otter of the water or air, no matter how big and small.[4]

Tibetan officials enforced the *tsatsigs* by sending government observers to local villages to make sure the laws were being implemented, and governors were directed to submit a report outlining how the *tsatsigs* were being carried out. In this way the Tibetan leaders ensured the enforcement and accountability of ecological protection measures, much like the modern Clean Air and Endangered Species Acts in the United States.

As Tibetan scholar Tenzin Atisha points out, the Tibetan ecological perspective went beyond government directives to individual actions. The Buddhist ethic, which promotes the sacredness of and reverence for all life, extended to individual farmers, who incorporated it into their own practices. When fields were newly seeded, farmers would not allow noisy activities, large crowds or monks and nuns, whose celibacy was seen as hindering the fertility of the crops.

Prior to 1959, when the Chinese took control of Tibet, nomads used a pasture-book system, which regulated the number of animals in the fields. The land, typically owned by aristocrats or monasteries, was divided into sectors for use at different times by nomads, who paid for the use of the land by offering meat, wool or butter to their landlords. This system protected the land from the overgrazing that affects many rural areas of the world,[5] ensuring the health of the livestock by protecting the "carrying capacity" of the fields upon which both the nomads and their herds depended for their survival.

Tibetan nomads and farmers once relied on barley as a staple in their diet. Because of its short growing season, good nutritional value and adaptability to harsh environments, barley was essential for Tibetans living in remote regions. It was roasted and ground to a powder known as *tsampa,* which could be eaten in powdered form or baked into bread. The various strains of barley gave Tibetans resilience in their crop yields and a reliable food source. Unfortunately, in the 1960s the Chinese introduced wheat monoculture that relied on fertilizers and was not suited to the harsh weather conditions, severely reducing crop yields and leading to malnutrition and famine. The Tibetan experience stands as a warning to our modern agricultural system that relies on monocultures dependent on petroleum-based pesticides and fertilizers.

An iconic symbol in Tibetan culture, the yak serves as a remarkable example of the interdependence of humans and the natural world. Much like the American bison in Native American culture, the yak provides Tibetan nomads with food, clothing, shelter, transportation and myriad tools for their livelihood. The nomads use yak hair to make their tents, cook the yak's bones and meat, drink its milk and eat yak cheese and butter. The traditional Tibetan black tent is usually about 30 feet square, seven feet high and suspended by two poles. The tent is made from yak hair, which is turned into thread and cloth and made into felt. The tightly woven tent fabric provides protection from the elements and its dark color absorbs sunlight during the cold winter months. The felt provides protection from snow and cold and is also used in overcoats, boot liners, saddle pads, bedding, hats and rugs.[6] The design principles inherent in the nomads' yak tent construction and its management of heat, sunlight and ventilation have applications for design of heating, ventilation and passive solar systems for our sophisticated high-performance buildings.

Unfortunately, the traditional knowledge from Tibetan nomads is being lost as the land comes under the forces of full-scale development. China's economic explosion in the last 30 years has severely undermined not only Tibet's biological diversity but its cultural diversity as well. Mega-development projects such as the Three Gorges Dam, which will be the world's largest hydroelectric power station when completed in 2011, have been criticized for their pollution, algal blooms, soil erosion and threats to wildlife. The 1,956-kilometer Qinghai-Tibet railway from Golmud to Lhasa, which opened in 2006, will undoubtedly affect the Tibetan culture through increased immigration and Chinese settlements. Although environmental measures, including overpasses for animal migrations, have been taken, the full ecological and cultural impacts of the world's highest railway have yet to be determined.

The massive "outward" technological advancements and cultural changes occurring in China stand in stark contrast to the "inner" growth in the Tibetan culture. The Tibetan environmental ethic stems from their Buddhist religion in which individuals seek not only their own enlightenment but also to help others and, in the process, end suffering. This path supports altruism and compassion toward all life on earth. In gauging the intrinsic value of the Tibetan culture, noted scholar Robert A. Thurman states:

[Tibet] is a culture of inestimable value to us, as a mirror image of ours, as extremely inward as we have been extremely outward. It may contain precious keys with which we can rediscover planetary equilibrium, restoring spiritual sanity to those maddened by extreme materialism. Its life or death is our life or death. It lives underground at home, in open air only in exile. We must protect it, nurture it and patiently wait for all concerned to rediscover its jewel-like value and need for special treasuring.[7]

Tibet's inward spiritual focus provides a valuable alternative to the outward, consumer-oriented cultures of the developed countries. The Tibetan environmental ethic, which is spiritual rather than material, may also serve as a useful model for our individual actions and public policies.

Balinese Water Temples

The rich spiritual and pastoral traditions of Tibet are echoed by the cultural traditions of the Indonesian island of Bali, where farmers have developed renowned irrigation systems. The traditional farming practices on Bali have evolved over a thousand years. The island's agricultural tradition involves a ritual-based system of irrigation, pest management and planting schedules. At the heart of Balinese irrigation for the terraced rice paddies lies a system of water temples administered by *subaks*, or irrigation cooperatives, which manage the water resources. The Balinese water temples highlight the intergenerational practices for resource use. But, as we'll see, the introduction of modern technology, including the Green Revolution's hybrid crops, is a warning to modern society of the negative consequences of sidelining cultural practices for more "efficient" measures.

The irrigation system is an intricate network of water temples that diverts water at different elevations to irrigate the rice paddy fields. Farmers meet at temples to discuss the condition of their fields and their pest situation. They coordinate their planting schedule according to the indigenous calendar known as the *tika*, which regulates the irrigation schedule for

J. Stephen Lansing

Pura Tirtha Empul, a Balinese temple, encloses sacred springs that provide water for several *subaks*, or irrigation cooperatives, downstream. *Subaks* that receive water from the temple's springs bring offerings of a small portion of their harvest to the temple's annual festival at the full moon of the fourth month of the Balinese calendar. *Subaks* illustrate the value of traditional knowledge passed through generations.

numerous farms in a watershed. This system ensures benefits to all farmers by synchronizing water allotment to manage pests. When fields are planted simultaneously, pests have an abundance of food and crop damage is minimized; when the fields are laid fallow, pests have limited food options and therefore little impact on the harvest. This system of synchronized planting has proven its efficacy over modern agroindustrial methods based on pesticides and fertilizers. Farmers show gratitude for their harvests through prayers and offerings at the water temples. Farming practices form an intricate web of religious, social and technological relationships.

Starting the 1960s, the water temple system was abandoned when the Indonesian government adopted the Green Revolution's strategies to feed the country's growing population by introducing new varieties of rice and growing practices. Priests who administered the water temples were no longer in charge of irrigation and planting schedules. Although Bali's volcanic soil is naturally rich in nutrients, farmers were encouraged to purchase seeds and agrochemicals, known as "technology packets." Farmers stopped their traditional cyclical planting schedules in favor of year-round planting. Initially there was a 50 percent increase in rice production, but the yields rapidly dwindled. Farmers became dependent on pesticides, fertilizers and agricultural machinery for seeding and harvesting. In addition, the use of hybrid rice varieties resulted in the loss of self-generating seeds. The Green Revolution led to yield losses due to water shortages and infestation by rats, insects and other plant pathogens, some of which became resistant to pesticides.[8] The fertilizers also killed wildlife, depleted soil fertility, polluted the coastal areas and damaged the coral reefs with algal blooms.[9]

In the 1980s Balinese farmers petitioned their government to return to traditional farming practices, and anthropologist J. Stephen Lansing began to research the role of water temples in Balinese rice production. Lansing and fellow ecologist and computer scientist James Kremer developed computer simulation models showing how effective the Balinese water temple system with its synchronized planting had been in providing a resilient system yielding adequate harvests while controlling pests. This system proved to be far more effective than the "technology packets" and other strategies implemented by the Green Revolution. The lessons learned from the resilience of the Balinese farming methods will become increasingly relevant as rural communities throughout the world experience the severe effects of climate change.

Lansing's subsequent research showed that the water temples organized over time and that no Great Designer was involved in putting the system in place. Lansing and Kremer's work was finally acknowledged by the Asian Development Bank, and the wisdom of traditional farming practices was validated by the Balinese government when it encouraged farmers to re-turn to their water temple system.[10] The Balinese self-organized irrigation systems are quite distinct from our modern industrial farms and illustrate the value of local knowledge gained over generations. However, while rec-ognition of the value of Bali's traditional farming methods has had a posi-tive impact, the government continues to promote high-yield rice strains and fertilizers that damage Bali's ecosystem.

Inuit Traditional Knowledge

From the finely crafted Balinese irrigation systems, we turn to the north polar region, where Inuit knowledge of their environment is under siege from the impacts of climate change. The Inuit culture represents the Earth's cultural "canary in the coal mine" as the warming climate is forcing numer-ous Inuit communities to abandon their settlements because of disappear-ing permafrost. In other instances, coastal Inuit villages are suffering from the disappearance of ice that protected them from winter storms. These are early warnings of what lies ahead for other coastal communities expected to experience climate change.

The following Inuit hunting story underscores the way cultures build their traditional knowledge based on their understanding of predator/prey relationships and the role of humans within this context.

> An Eskimo hunter once saw a polar bear far off across flat ice, where he couldn't stalk it without being seen. But he knew an old tech-nique of mimicking a seal. He lay down in plain sight, conspicuous in his dark parka and pants, then lifted and dropped his head like a seal, scratched the ice and imitated flippers with his hands. The bear mistook his pursuer for prey. Each time the hunter lifted his head the animal kept still; whenever the hunter "slept," the bear crept closer. When it came near enough, a gunshot pierced the snowy si-lence. That night, polar bear meat was shared among the villagers.[11]

The Inuit people who inhabit the arctic regions of Alaska, Canada, Rus-sia and Greenland have traditionally survived by gathering grasses and berries as well as fishing and hunting mammals, including seals, whales, walruses, muskoxen, caribou and polar bears. Similar to other native cultures in harsh environments, the Inuit have perfected tools including kayaks, *umiags* (large, open wooden boats), dog sleds, knives (made from walrus ivory) and shelters including the igloo, sod house and driftwood shelters. Wood, bone and soapstone also play a central role in their rich tradition of arts and crafts.[12]

Learning about the ecological knowledge of traditional cultures involves effective oral interviewing methods, which often lead to surprising insights. In their research into the migration patterns of beluga whales in the North Pacific, Henry Huntington and Nikolai Mymrin performed "semi-directive" interviews to spark a discussion with individuals or groups. By allowing the discussion to arise spontaneously, Huntington and Mymrin explored topics they may not have anticipated. Groups of Inuit discussed the impact of ice, wind, weather and predators on belugas. When the discussion turned to beavers, the researchers, though at first confused, allowed the group to elaborate and then discovered the connection between beavers and belugas: a burgeoning beaver population increases the number of beaver dams, which damage the salmon spawning sites and reduce the salmon population, a key food source for the belugas.[13] The sharing of the connections linking beluga whales, beavers and salmon underscores the value to modern scientists of obtaining knowledge gained over generations.

Inuit culture is witnessing firsthand the impact of the Earth's warming. Reduced sea ice, breakup of ice sheets, earlier onset of the spring season, reduced wildlife populations and reduced permafrost are just a few of the signs appearing in the north polar regions. Inuit knowledge of the variations of snow and ice formation, for example, includes names for the specific snow and ice conditions essential for gauging the ability of ice to support the weight of a person, kayak, sled or dog.[14] The traditional knowledge of native peoples such as the Inuit can play a critical role in complementing our search for viable solutions.

Traditional knowledge is often dismissed as unscientific and anecdotal because it is qualitative rather than quantitative and can be enmeshed in spiritual beliefs, but its strength lies in its endurance over millennia. The Inuit, as well as thousands of other traditional cultures, have managed not merely to survive but to thrive by adapting their way of life to environmental changes over time. Through observation, they have developed pattern recognition useful in understanding animal health, migrations and seasonal weather changes. The longevity of their settlements and adaptability to changing conditions serves as a contrast to our fast-paced, material-based culture. However, the exchange of knowledge runs both ways, and there are aspects of modern society's medical, educational and agricultural expertise that could benefit the Inuits' well-being. In the field, this exchange will occur as scientists involve native peoples in the planning and interpretation of research projects.

The Kogi: Guardians of the Planet

One of the most isolated tribes on Earth, the Kogi of South America, sends a warning of the irreparable ecological damage modern society is causing to their homeland. The predicament of the Kogi tribe in Colombia brings

Alan Ereira, Tairona Heritage Trust

Arregoces, his wife, three daughters and a son are members of the Kogi tribe living in the highlands of Colombia. Arregoces is a leading intermediary with the Colombian government and a defender of traditional Kogi values. The Kogi have highlighted the environmental impact of modern society, which they call the Younger Brothers.

to light the importance of maintaining a spiritual connection with the natural world and preserving the integrity of natural systems. The Kogis' close connection to the natural world highlights the vast chasm that exists between humans and nature in modern society. The Kogis' message to us in the modern world, known to them as the Younger Brothers, is to stop destroying the natural world. This call brings to the forefront the devastating impact of an economic system based on resource extraction.

Deep in the Sierra Nevada de Santa Marta mountains on the Caribbean coast of northern Colombia live the Kogi, a unique indigenous tribe that was never conquered by the Spaniards. The Kogi, along with the Arhuaco, Wiwa and Kankuamo tribes, form the Tayrona civilization, which today numbers approximately 45,000.[15] The Kogis' extraordinary worldview, which incorporates the power of the human spirit and human interdependence with the natural world, has endured for centuries and has only recently been revealed to the world.

Home for the Kogi lies in the stunning biodiversity of the Sierra Nevada mountains. These mountains encompass an 8,000-square-mile area that includes the world's highest coastal mountain range, the 18,942-foot Sierra Nevada massif, whose peaks lie only 25 miles from the shore near the Equator. The wide range of elevations supports tropical and alpine ecosystems that include coral reefs, mangroves, desert, tropical and cloud forests, alpine tundra and snow-covered peaks. There are over 3,000 species of plants and 628 bird species. There are also 120 species of mammals, including red howler monkeys, giant anteaters, white-lipped peccaries and red-crested tree rats.[16]

Within this rich biological region, the Kogi have managed to survive by planting crops at various elevations — manioc, corn, sugarcane and pineapples in the lowlands and potatoes and onions in the mid-level regions, where they also graze cattle. Unfortunately, the Kogis' survival is threatened by the destruction of their forests by banana and palm plantations. They have been forced to move to higher elevations, thus limiting their farming production and endangering their survival. Their homeland has also been infiltrated by drug cartels that use the land to grow coca, by guerilla and paramilitary forces and by the Colombian army. In addition, the mountain snowpack and glaciers have been melting over the past decades because of climate change, adversely affecting the ecology of the region. As are the Inuit, the Kogi tribe is experiencing firsthand the devastating impacts of climate change through glacier melt.

Noticing changes over several decades, the Kogi priests, or Mamas, decided to come out of isolation in 1991 and declare their warning to the world. They see themselves as the Elder Brothers who live in the Heart of the World and have a responsibility to maintain a balance with nature. We in the developed world are the Younger Brothers who are unwittingly destroying the planet out of ignorance of our interdependence with natural systems. As the Mamas point out:

> Because Younger Brother is among us,
> Younger Brother is violating
> The basic foundation of the world's law.
> A total violation.
> Robbing.
> Ransacking.
> Building highways,
> extracting petrol,
> minerals....
> Younger Brother thinks,
> "Yes! Here I am! I know much about the universe!"
> But this knowing is learning to destroy the world,
> to destroy everything,
> all humanity.[17]

The Mamas envision the world as our Mother — a living organism we are damaging through deforestation, mining and development practices.

> The Mother is suffering.
> They have broken her teeth
> and taken out her eyes and ears.
> She vomits,
> she has diarrhea,
> she is ill.
> If we cut off our arms, we can't work,
> if we cut off our tongue, we can't speak,
> if we cut off our legs, we can't walk.
> That is how it is with the Mother.
> The Mother is suffering.
> She has nothing.[18]

At the heart of the Kogi belief system is Aluna, the root of the soul and creativity. Aluna is also human thought and intelligence, a bridge between the human spirit and the world at large. It is the catalyst that ignites possibilities and provides forces responsible for birth, growth and fertility. Aluna is the Mother who represents the life force that engenders beauty in the world. The Kogi enter Aluna through deep thought and meditation, seeking the deeper interrelationships of natural systems. They understand the connections that underlie the fabric of life, which we often dismiss or do not see. In our modern society the Aluna or life force is often embodied in the character or "personality" of a place, which gives a building, a town or a location in nature its vitality. (See Chapter 4 for more details about the characteristics of place.)

We have achieved a great deal through our technological advancements, but we have disconnected from the life force that is at the core of our existence. In the Kogi creation story, humans are an integral part of the Earth, and we will therefore suffer the consequences of our actions. What we do to the Earth we do to ourselves, and for their sake and for ours the Kogi feel compelled to warn us about following this destructive path. We have the choice to listen or not.

The Value of Traditional Knowledge

The Tibetan, Balinese, Inuit and Kogi cultures possess traditional knowledge that forms part of the cultural DNA of the planet. This knowledge has been passed on from generation to generation through laws, stories, songs, folklore, rituals and art forms. Because their teachings are often embedded in belief systems, values, indigenous practices and specific places, Western scientists have had difficulty fitting the knowledge into the scientific process.

At a time of increasing interdependence among nations and the increasing need to devise better ways of living on the Earth, it would seem desirable to integrate traditional knowledge with Western science. Traditional knowledge has demonstrated its value in numerous areas, including understanding wildlife populations, biomedical information and the health of ecosystems, and points out the potential detrimental consequences of development. To effectively integrate traditional knowledge with science, we must first create a context that accommodates the profoundly different worldviews of native cultures and modern society. This would entail the protection of indigenous cultures so that they are included in and benefit from the scientific research.

Biopiracy and bioprospecting, which involve the appropriation of traditional knowledge and resources without proper compensation to indigenous cultures, demonstrate the need for measures to protect traditional knowledge, which means treating it as a cultural heritage, as an intellectual property right or as a human rights issue. The 1992 Convention on Biological Diversity (CBD) addresses this problem. As of 2006 the CBD had 188 signatories; the United States has signed but not ratified the CBD. The CBD states its intention to:

> respect, preserve and maintain knowledge, innovations and practices of indigenous and local communities embodying traditional lifestyles relevant for the conservation and sustainable use of biological diversity and promote their wider application with the approval and involvement of the holders of such knowledge, innovations and practices and encourage the equitable sharing of the benefits arising from the utilization of such knowledge, innovations and practices.[19]

In order to enforce the protection of traditional knowledge, including aspects of the CBD, the World Intellectual Property Organization (WIPO) set out to review the relevant issues and conducted fact-finding missions to 28 countries in 1998–1999.[20] Subsequently, WIPO's Intergovernmental Committee on Intellectual Property and Genetic Resources, Traditional Knowledge and Folklore (the IGC) developed provisions for the enhanced protection of traditional knowledge.

The current standards emerging from the work of WIPO and the CBD state that: (1) any policies regarding traditional knowledge must involve the participation of indigenous and local communities; (2) Free Prior Informed Consent from indigenous and local communities is required to access traditional knowledge and resources (including genetic resources); (3) indigenous and local communities are to determine the form of benefit sharing derived from traditional knowledge and the use by outside parties will be mutually agreed; and (4) in addition to property rights, indigenous peoples have rights to "intangible" heritage.[21] These guidelines are the first step in establishing a foundation to protect the rights of indigenous peoples and to give back to these cultures any benefits derived from their knowledge.

The human rights approach to the protection of traditional knowledge captured the world's attention in 2007 when the United Nations General

Assembly overwhelmingly adopted the Declaration on the Rights of Indigenous Peoples.

The declaration confirms:

> the right to unrestricted self-determination, an inalienable collective right to the ownership, use and control of lands, territories and other natural resources, their rights in terms of maintaining and developing their own political, religious, cultural and educational institutions along with the protection of their cultural and intellectual property.[22]

Although not a legally binding document, the Declaration on the Rights of Indigenous Peoples outlines an international commitment to the protection of indigenous cultures and their traditional knowledge. This protection is particularly applicable to wealth derived from natural resource extraction, as in the mineral-rich land in Tibet, and the biologically diverse regions of the tropics, such as the forests inhabited by the Kogi in Colombia.

The Extinction of Languages

Languages and the oral tradition are essential links in the survival of traditional knowledge and serve as an intergenerational thread. Language also identifies a people's culture and strengthens its endurance. Linguistic diversity is an integral aspect of the Earth's biodiversity that enriches the resilience of our planet's life-support systems. Thus, saving languages saves cultures, which in turn protects the biodiversity of the planet and our own well-being.

The extinction of the world's languages is accelerating largely unnoticed at an alarming rate. It is estimated that there are currently 5,000 to 6,700 languages in the world, and of these at least half will become extinct in the next 100 years. The loss of the Australian Aboriginal languages, for example, is estimated at one or more per year. In addition, 6,000 languages are spoken by only 10 percent of the world's population. Although indigenous peoples represent 4 percent of the world's population, they speak 60 percent of the world's languages. In the United States alone, the number of languages spoken has decreased from an estimated 300 in 1492 to 175 today. Presently, 90 percent of the world's population collectively speak about 100 of the most common languages. Similar to biological diversity, which is increasingly confined to isolated corners of the world, language diversity rests with indigenous peoples in remote regions.[23] Thus, the loss of languages goes hand in hand with the disappearance of traditional knowledge and the wisdom accumulated over millennia. The Earth's cultural diversity is diminished by the continuous loss of languages over time.

There is a remarkable correlation between ecological diversity and linguistic diversity in what Daniel Nettle and Suzanne Romaine term "biolinguistic diversity," the rich tapestry of plant, animal and human cultures. Many regions are threatened with both cultural and biological extinction. In many places where languages are disappearing, ecosystems are being threatened as well. In the Hawaiian Islands, for example, both the Hawaiian language, which is spoken only in these islands, and many of the biological species face extinction. Of the islands' 1,104 plant and animal species, 363, including the state flower and bird, are listed as threatened or endangered.[24]

Languages also provide important insights into the evolution of human expression and cultural heritage. Through language we learn about a culture's technological, cultural and artistic traditions. Devising strategies to preserve the world's languages must include the protection of ecosystems inhabited by indigenous people. For a language to thrive it must be spoken and transmitted from generation to generation. Continuity of language means continuity of culture, and many traditional cultures are on the brink of extinction.

There is also the need to archive existing languages. To this end, The Long Now Foundation's Rosetta Project, with support from the National Science Foundation, is building the Rosetta Digital Language Archive, which currently contains over 2,500 languages and is accessible through the Internet. The Rosetta Disk also provides a physical archive in the form of a sphere etched with over 15,000 pages of documentation about the Earth's languages.[25] The United Nations Educational, Scientific and Cultural Organization (UNESCO) and several nongovernmental organizations have created the Universal Declaration of Linguistic Rights to support linguistic rights including threatened languages. These and other efforts emphasize the significance of language diversity as a key to our global cultural heritage. These projects provide glimmers of hope in preserving for future generations what is left of the Earth's linguistic diversity.

Building Community

The Tibetan, Balinese, Inuit and Kogi cultures are links to our cultural legacy. Their stories, traditions and knowledge of their local environment provide clues for understanding our interdependence with nature. The diversity embodied in indigenous cultures may help us find ways to adapt to rapidly changing conditions. The integration of traditional knowledge and our modern scientific and technological innovations may provide the resilience we will need to meet our challenges and create lasting, vibrant communities.

The experiences of the Tibetan nomads, Balinese farmers, Inuit hunters and Kogi settlers represent the long-lasting, wide-ranging, collective, adaptable presence of humans on Earth. All indigenous peoples have the right to live in a world that respects their needs and aspirations and protects their land and cultural legacy. Modern society has an opportunity to share its own knowledge and benefit the lives of people in traditional cultures while being sensitive to their environmental and social concerns. In essence, the lessons from our ancestors are available if we engage with these cultures respectfully.

TAKING ACTION

➡ *Join an organization working on indigenous peoples' issues (see Organizations section in Resources).*

➡ *Learn about the cultural history of your home region.*

➡ *Learn about the natural history of your area and how the Earth provided for early dwellers.*

➡ *Volunteer at a local cultural history museum or center.*

➡ *Study the geology, hydrology and native flora and fauna of your area.*

➡ *Follow your family tree and learn about the land your ancestors inhabited; connect with local groups working on indigenous issues.*

➡ *Write an article for your local newspaper about the significance of protecting indigenous cultures.*

TWO

Going "Glocal"

And because a community is, by definition, placed, *its success
cannot be divided from the success of its place... its soils, forests,
grasslands, plants and animals, water, light, and air. The two
economies, the natural and the human, support each other;
each is the other's hope of a durable and a livable life.*
— WENDELL BERRY

*We can no longer import our lives in the form of food, fuel, and
fundamentalism. Life is homegrown, always has been. So is culture,
and so too are the solutions to global problems.*
— PAUL HAWKEN

As WE NEAR THE END of the fossil-fuel era, communities around the
world must reinvent themselves for the post-petroleum age. What are
the challenges in food production, housing, energy, education and transportation we will face in this transition? How can we design our dwellings,
villages, towns and cities to enhance our quality of life while providing
employment, education and health care and regenerating the planet's life-
support systems? More significantly, how do we capitalize on the benefits
of technology and design at the global level and infuse them into our local communities so that we can enjoy a thriveable future? These and other
questions are being addressed by visionary architects, developers, city
planners, urban designers and community leaders seeking alternative ways
of designing dwellings and energy, education, food and transportation systems as well as entire communities. There are glimpses of these new designs in communities ranging from Arcosanti in Arizona to Masdar in the
United Arab Emirates.

The term "glocalization" or "glocal" comes from the Japanese word
dochakuka, meaning global localization. This approach was first used by

Japanese economists and then popularized by sociologist Roland Robertson and Manfred Lange, former head of the Global Change Exhibition, in the late 1980s. The term encapsulates the "think globally, act locally" worldview. The glocal perspective recognizes that communities are linked to global systems through technologies such as the Internet, through natural resources including energy and food, through the economic ties of trade, labor and capital inflows, and through human impacts such as greenhouse gas emissions. Nevertheless, homegrown solutions are best suited for dealing with global issues facing communities. Because our global economic system can have a devastating impact on local livelihoods when it is oblivious to the needs of communities, we must protect and support the lifelines of local economies. We must find a balance between controlling our economic assets at the local level and benefiting from a world that is tightly interconnected and interdependent.

Glocal initiatives pay attention to the feedback loops in global/local interactions. This may include tracing the sources of economic investments in a local community, striving the keep financial investments in the community in order to create jobs and support local businesses or tracking how money circulates into and out of the community. Glocal initiatives recognize that the greatest impact is at the local level but that global factors may either support or hinder local objectives. Becoming aware of the impacts of the globalized economy at the local level is the first step in the "think globally, act locally" approach.

Community Voluntary Gas Tax
Used to Fund Bicycle Projects

A small group of citizens in the town of Goshen, Indiana, are taxing themselves an extra $0.50 per gallon of gasoline and giving the money to groups working to break the nation's oil addiction. The Gas Tax Club of Goshen has already donated more than $400 to a local bicycle club that is providing bicycle-powered curbside recycling, recycling secondhand bikes and advocating improved bike paths in the community. The voluntary tax organizers see the initiative as a way to be more mindful of how much gas they use and to turn the negative of their oil addiction into something with a positive benefit.[1]

An important aspect of a glocal perspective involves identifying a community's character or patterns and its place within the global economy. Place-making (discussed in Chapter 8), which recognizes a community's cultural traditions and ecological systems, plays an essential role in maintaining the long-term health and viability of a community. The initiatives that follow range in scale from local to international, yet they have a practical glocal approach that connects local actions with the global economic system.

At the local level, sustainable or "green" programs are sprouting across the globe in rural, suburban and urban settings and include relocalization efforts that aim to strengthen the economic and social fabric of communities. Programs such as Transition Initiatives in the United Kingdom and Sustainability Street in Australia are exploring how to transition to a post-petroleum age, rethinking solutions for food systems, transportation programs, energy security and social well-being.

At the regional level, Ecotrust, a nonprofit based in Portland, Oregon, uses "Salmon Nation" as a metaphor for residents of western coastal North America who share social and environmental values. Regional climate protection programs have developed partnerships focused on the challenge of curbing greenhouse gases. Examples are the Northeast Regional Greenhouse Gas Initiative in New England and the Western Climate Initiative in the western US states and the Canadian provinces of British Columbia, Manitoba, Ontario and Quebec.

On a national and international level, Sweden's energy and climate program, New Zealand's Resource Management Act (RMA) and ICLEI–Local Governments for Sustainability are large-scale initiatives targeted to meet the challenges of energy, resource consumption and climate change in local communities. Through a glocal approach, these initiatives are striving toward a thriveable future by strengthening the environmental, economic and social fabric of communities within the context of a global system.

Transition Initiatives

An exciting and innovative local program for the post-petroleum age involves the work of educator Rob Hopkins. In 2001 Hopkins taught a permaculture course at the Kinsale Further Education College in Kinsale, Ireland, a West Cork town with 7,000 inhabitants. This began the Transition Initiatives program. Concerned about the predicament of fossil-fuel dependence and climate change, Hopkins and his students explored how the community of Kinsale could move from high to low energy consumption. Their research studied energy use, food production, transportation, marine resources and tourism. They produced a pioneering final report, *Kinsale 2021: An Energy Descent Action Plan,* which provided a vision as well as practical steps for Kinsale's transition to the post-petroleum age. The plan was adopted by the Kinsale town council and is now viewed as a model glocal approach for communities worldwide.[2]

In 2005, Hopkins moved to Totnes in Devon, UK, and continued his work refining and implementing the Energy Descent Action Plan. This led to Transition Town Totnes, an energy descent strategy for Totnes that has since spread to over 30 communities in the UK and Ireland, Australia and New Zealand.[3] The Transition Towns concept highlights a critical aspect of cultural transformation that Hopkins refers to as the head, heart and hands of energy descent. As he points out:

> By the Head, I mean the concepts of peak oil, arguments for and against localisation as well as any historical examples that we can learn from. The Heart refers to exploring how to actually engage communities in a positive and dynamic way, how to use peak oil as a tool for empowerment rather than leaving people feeling helpless. This part of the exploration is about how to actually facilitate change, and the dynamics of cultural transformation. The Hands refers to the practical aspect, could the UK become self sufficient in food and how? How much well managed woodland would it take to heat a town with efficient CHPs [Combined Heat and Power]? Can local materials be used to retrofit houses?[4]

The Transition Initiatives model offers a framework for engaging local community members to effect change. The framework has 12 steps that, based on the experience of various towns, are essential for implementing community change. These steps are:

The 12 Steps to Transition[5]
1. **Set up a steering group and design its demise from the outset.** This step puts a core team in place to drive the project forward during the initial phases.
2. **Raise awareness.** This step identifies key allies, builds crucial networks and prepares the community for the launch of the Transition Initiative.

3. **Lay the foundations.** This step engages networks of existing groups and activists, and communicates that the Transition Initiative is designed to incorporate their previous efforts and future inputs.

4. **Organize a Great Unleashing.** This step creates a milestone to mark the project's "coming of age," moves it into the community, builds momentum to propel the initiative into the next endeavor and celebrates the community's desire to take action.

5. **Form working groups.** This step taps into the collective intelligence of the community by setting up small groups to focus on specific aspects of the process of developing an Energy Descent Action Plan.

6. **Use open space.** This step uses open-space technology as a tool to run highly effective meetings for Transition Initiatives.[6]

7. **Develop visible practical manifestations of the project.** This step creates practical, high visibility, noncontroversial manifestations of the project in the community; examples may include a community garden, a tree planting or a bus shelter.

8. **Facilitate the Great Reskilling.** This step offers training in a range of skills that have been lost over the past 40 years. It brings people together, builds networks and creates a "can do" attitude through one-to two-day courses.

9. **Build a bridge to local government.** This step cultivates a productive relationship with the local authority.

10. **Honor the elders.** This step involves doing historical research and conducting oral history interviews with the elders of the community to learn about the skills they used and their livelihood.

11. **Let it go where it wants to go.** This step recognizes that the process will inevitably go in unexpected directions. The facilitator's role is not to come up with all the answers but to act as a catalyst for the community to design their own transition.

12. **Create an Energy Descent Action Plan.** This step creates an Energy Descent Action Plan that is made up of the working groups' practical actions to increase community resilience and reduce the carbon footprint.

These 12 steps emphasize the importance of working within existing programs rather than supplanting them. Coalitions are formed among community members and a common vision results in tangible projects with successful outcomes such as an energy efficiency program for homes, a local biodiesel station or a farmers' market. Each of these programs calls for effective community organizing, with community members taking leadership roles.

The Transition Initiatives model underscores the importance of developing a cohesive community organizing program based on a community supported vision. Education, a knowledge base and technologies can then evolve. Transition Initiatives' glocal approach is a model for building resilient, thriving communities worldwide.

Sustainability Street

Similar to Transition Initiatives, Sustainability Street is a community development program designed to engage communities in sustainable living practices and initiatives. The Sustainability Street Approach (SSA) is led by Frank Ryan, an environmental educator, entrepreneur and founder of Vox Bandicoot, an Australian organization specializing in creating sustainability programs for community groups, schools, companies and government agencies. The Sustainability Street Approach, first piloted in 2000 in the

Local Sustainability Street villagers share the joy of worm composting at Brunswick Sustainability Street Village, Australia. Sustainability Street encourages residents throughout Australia to green their communities.

towns of Moreland and Wollongong, has since spread to over 200 communities throughout Australia. The success in Australia has sparked interest in China and the UK.

The Sustainability Street program is a grassroots method for people to learn about sustainable practices by teaching each other and their communities. The program encourages people to green their homes and join efforts to green their community. "Street" is a metaphor for the community at large.

People who participate in the SSA attend information workshops during a six-month training period. The sustainability training is organized into four stages: mulch (learn), sow (plan), grow (do) and harvest (teach). These stages ensure that knowledge is translated into action that inspires further change. A number of studies are underway to determine the effectiveness of the SSA program, and early outcomes indicate a reduction of water use, waste and energy/greenhouse gases by as much as 30 percent. In addition, local residents have initiated successful programs including gardens, water tanks and food co-ops. Residents have also shared their satisfaction in getting to know their neighbors.[7]

One of the key elements of the SSA training is discussion of the Eight Principles. These help participants understand the gravity of their ecological challenges and find the commitment to devise solutions.

The Eight Principles:[8]
1. Understand that biological diversity is the most precious of nature's gifts to us.
2. Spurn doom and gloom.
3. Imagine.... Imagine the future to be clean, green, and sustainable.
4. Avoid the "holier than thou" soap box.
5. Enjoy purposeful informality, build "social capital" and savor!
6. Celebrate the increasing number of good news stories — critical fuel for the journey.
7. Take baby steps and trust common sense!
8. See, and revel in, the enviro-links

These eight principles involve reexamining values and creating the strong social fabric essential for any initiative. The SSA also asks participants to reexamine their sense of self and their relationships to their neighbors, friends and relatives. These personal social connections create a tool for change based on trust among community residents. As one participant pointed out, "Sustainability Street will help us to get to a stage where we are comfortable saying hello to our neighbours and even strangers in our street. This is surely the definition of a strong community." Another mentioned, "It takes me 40 minutes to walk to the corner store now, so many hellos!" The community-based social marketing approach is effective because information comes from a personal source, such as a friend, instead of an organization.[9] In this way, knowledge is leveraged from the individual to the neighbors and beyond to outlying communities.

The Transition Initiatives and Sustainability Street programs are succeeding because their flexible frameworks support people coming together to learn and to devise solutions for social and environmental challenges. These programs create a trusting environment from which to imagine possibilities for a brighter future. As author and environmentalist Bill McKibben mentions, a good first step in the journey toward sustainability is to bake cookies, take them to your neighbors and get to know each other. Within this context, new working relationships with neighbors, government officials and business leaders emerge and changes at the local level begin to take shape. The glocal approach first builds personal relationships at the neighborhood level and then ties in connections to global issues.

Beyond local actions, there are numerous regional sustainability initiatives that emphasize geographic, ecological and cultural ties. In the western United States, Ecotrust's Salmon Nation and the West Coast Climate Plan are two programs that support a regional perspective. Both of these initiatives acknowledge the value of engaging regional stakeholders to develop strategies for protecting the region's natural heritage. They maintain a glocal perspective by keeping sight of local economic interests within a global context.

Salmon Nation

Spencer Beebe is the founder and president of Ecotrust, an environmental nonprofit in Portland, Oregon. As a strategy to capture interest in the natural heritage of the Pacific Northwest, he envisioned Salmon Nation: "a concept, a place, a set of values, a community, and a way of viewing the interrelationships between all of them."[10]

Since its founding in 1991, Ecotrust has developed a successful track record in implementing programs dealing with native communities, fisheries, forestry, food and farms within territorial boundaries marked by "anywhere Pacific salmon have ever run." Salmon Nation arose from the need to create a tangible, unifying concept for residents committed to protecting the identity of their home region. As an iconic species ranging from California to Alaska (and technically into Russia and Japan), the salmon symbolizes the natural and cultural heritage of this landscape. Salmon Nation invites people to join a larger vision rooted in this symbol. It challenges its "citizens" to reexamine their relationship to themselves, their neighbors and the natural world so that all can "live like we mean it," a commitment to go beyond surviving to build thriving communities based on rootedness, respect and interconnectedness. Salmon Nation's framework incorporates the following values that link everyday actions with cultural and biological systems.

What does Salmon Nation look like? The values:[11]
- Eventually, your neighbor's runoff becomes your tap water. We all live downstream.
- We live amidst the world's most productive forests. There is enough for everyone.
- Even the food you eat has a story. Know the story and help yourself.
- Each salmon is wired for its native stream. Our experience makes the difference.
- People have put down roots here for over 10,000 years. You are right where you belong.

The Salmon Nation values support a strong bioregional perspective. Citizens of this nation are encouraged to participate in decisions that determine the viability of its economy and its watersheds. Using natural systems as a mentor, they better understand how their interdependence with the natural world depends on the health of the watersheds for its survival, just as the salmon does. Through its alliance with ShoreBank Pacific, an American commercial bank providing capital to community development projects, Ecotrust offers the Salmon Nation card, an affinity or reward card supporting its programs throughout the bioregion. This is an example of the benefits of a glocal approach, where the established assets and reach of a financial institution are used to support the needs of local communities.

One of Ecotrust's best-known campaigns is the successful protection of the 800,000-acre Kitlope ecosystem inhabited by the Haisla Nation of

British Columbia, Canada. In the early 1990s analysts from Ecotrust identified the Kitlope as the world's largest remaining intact coastal temper-
ate rainforest, a region that had been sustainably harvested by the Haisla
people for generations. The West Fraser Timber Company offered to protect 250,000 acres of the forest in exchange for logging rights in the rest
of the ecosystem. They also offered to give the Haisla people all the logging jobs (valued at over $100 million) as well as training and equipment
finance. The Haislas' answer was no. As Haisla elder Cecil Paul pointed
out, "The Kitlope is my home, a bank to my people, and I will step back
from you no more. My blood will run in this river before you desecrate this
place. This place I will fight for." [12]

News of the Kitlope's intact ecosystem spread. Ecotrust's team members and allies, including Spencer Beebe, Ken Margolis and Erin Kellog,
helped establish two organizations geared to the Haislas' objective of preserving their ancestral lands. The first was the nonprofit Nanakila Institute,
aimed at facilitating the management of the Kitlope's natural resources.
The second was the Haisla Nation's Women's Society's Rediscovery Program, focused on engaging youth in their cultural traditions. As Ecotrust
laid the groundwork for an alternative economic model not dependent
on the destruction of the coastal forest ecosystem, new allies joined the
vision for a sustainably managed forest with a vibrant local economy. In a
goodwill gesture the West Fraser Timber Company, led by Hank Ketchum,
eventually relinquished its logging rights without requesting compensation, leaving the Kitlope to the joint management of the provincial government and the Haisla people. Ecotrust founder Spencer Beebe describes the
successful protection of the Kitlope as a "slow, patient, bottom-up, inside-
out effort we made with the Haisla." [13] The successful glocal approach for
protecting the Kitlope shows the benefit derived from Ecotrust's effort to
gain the trust of the local Haisla community in its strategy to protect the
land and its people from the impact of modern development.

The protection of the Kitlope and the unity of the Haisla were highlighted by the repatriation of the G'psgolox totem pole, a symbol of the
cultural traditions of the Haisla people. Originally carved in the 1870s, the
G'psgolox pole disappeared in 1929. In 1990 it was discovered in Sweden's
National Ethnographic Museum in Stockholm. The pole had been "sold"
by someone outside the Haisla community without their authorization.
Subsequent negotiations between Ecotrust and Swedish officials resulted
in an agreement in which a replica pole was carved for the Swedish mu-

seum and the original G'psgolox pole was returned in 2006 to Kitamaat Village in Haisla territory after nearly 80 years.[14]

The success of Ecotrust's Kitlope campaign and other regional programs supporting conservation economies has caught the attention of communities in other countries. Discussions are underway to explore setting up similar initiatives in northern Australia. The Salmon Nation concept underscores the significance of creating a powerful symbol that taps into the cultural and biological connections to our roots and our desire to make a contribution to the well-being of our region. Salmon continue to be used as a key sustainability indicator by groups such as Sustainable Seattle to evaluate their city's quality of life. Celebrating the salmon as an iconic species of the Northwest emphasizes the importance of identifying the character of a place in a way that resonates with its inhabitants.

Samuel M. Beebe, Ecotrust

Here youth are canoeing to Misk'usa, British Columbia, as part of a Salmon Nation project's ceremony repatriating the G'psgolox totem pole. An initiative of Ecotrust, based in Portland, Oregon, Salmon Nation brings stakeholders together to support a regional conservation economy for the Pacific Northwest.

Regional Climate Plans

The lack of national climate change leadership in the United States during the Bush administration spurred cities such as Portland, Seattle and San Francisco to take the lead in devising strategies for dealing with climate change. "Early adopter" states, such as New York and California, have developed statewide climate change initiatives that have grown into regional alliances, including the Northeast Regional Greenhouse Gas Initiative and the Western Climate Initiative. In the absence of a federal program, six midwestern states and Manitoba have launched the Midwestern Greenhouse Gas Reduction Accord. A closer look at California's initiative reveals the power of political leadership in confronting regional and global challenges.

On September 27, 2006 California's Governor Arnold Schwarzenegger signed the Global Solutions Warming Act of 2006, known as AB 32, the nation's first law to reduce greenhouse gas emissions. The bill outlines an aggressive timetable, in line with the provisions of the Kyoto Protocol, for emissions reduction targets. Schwarzenegger pointed out that "the debate is over. We know the science. We see the threat. And we know the time for action is now." [15]

As the 12th largest emitter of greenhouse gases in the world, California plays a significant role not only in emissions output but also as a world pioneer in environmental policies. Indeed, the world is watching to see how California implements its greenhouse gas reduction policies. AB 32 requires that by 2010 Californians reduce emissions to 2000 levels and that 20 percent of all power used in the state come from renewable resources. By 2020 California must reduce emissions to 1990 levels and by 2050 to 80 percent below 1990 levels. The latter target has also been set by the Obama administration for the US. [16]

In charge of administering AB 32, the California Environmental Protection Agency created the multiagency Climate Action Team to carry out the directives. The Climate Group, a nonprofit organization, is charged with promoting climate change issues in the private and public sectors, including tracking emissions reduction efforts in Fortune 500 companies. The strategies for meeting California's targets include initiatives in solar energy, biofuels, land use and transportation as well as educational programs and economic incentives. Preliminary estimates show that by 2020 California's climate strategies will create 83,000 new jobs and increase personal income by $4 billion. [17] To date, the state has approved a Scoping Plan aimed at reducing greenhouse gas emissions and measures such as the Low Carbon Fuel Standard and the Pavley Vehicle Standards, which address up to 40 percent of AB 32's goals. In 2009, Governor Schwarzenegger signed an executive order to increase California's renewable energy portfolio to 33 percent by 2020. [18] The targets highlight a glocal approach that emphasizes local employment opportunities within the context of greenhouse gas emissions goals at the state level.

On September 30, 2008, Schwarzenegger augmented the impact of AB 32 by signing SB 375, Senator Darrell Steinberg's anti-sprawl bill. SB 375 links greenhouse gas emissions reduction to land-use planning strategies that support pedestrian friendly, sustainable communities with alternative transportation systems and reductions in car travel. Steinberg said the measure "will be used as the national framework for fighting sprawl and transforming inevitable growth to smart growth."[19] The combination of AB 32 and SB 375 is an integrated glocal approach that likely will be emulated throughout the nation.

The climate change efforts in California have encouraged other states to set their own greenhouse gas emissions targets, such as the Western Climate Initiative (WCI). This initiative, launched in 2007 by the governors of Arizona, California, New Mexico, Oregon and Washington, aims to develop cooperative strategies to address climate change. The WCI now also includes Montana, Utah, and the Canadian provinces of British Columbia, Manitoba, Ontario and Quebec. Other US states, Mexican states and Canadian provinces have joined this initiative as observers with an eye to participating in the future.

In 2007 the WCI set a regional goal of reducing greenhouse gas emissions by 15 percent below 2005 levels by 2020.[20] WCI members are developing a multisector, market-based cap-and-trade mechanism for achieving these and future targets. Many members have also set their own greenhouse gas emissions targets. British Columbia, for example, has a target of 33 percent below 2007 levels by 2020 and 80 percent below 2007 levels by 2050.[21]

The WCI illustrates the momentum created when regional leaders come together with a common purpose. Another example of a regional cooperative effort is the New England Governors and Eastern Canadian Premiers Plan for emissions reductions. Similarly, the Northeast Regional Greenhouse Gas Initiative commits seven northeast states to a mandatory cap-and-trade program for carbon reduction from power plants from Maryland to Maine.

Regional climate change plans demonstrate the benefits of partnerships for dealing with challenges that spread across boundaries. These political leaders recognize that climate change is of paramount importance to their state's economy and their constituents' quality of life. In being proactive they hope to ensure a thriveable future. They have demonstrated their effectiveness in establishing implementation strategies that can serve as models for other regions. Nevertheless, these regional initiatives pale in comparison with the long-term effectiveness of comprehensive national plans. Sweden's energy and climate plan, New Zealand's Resource Management Act and ICLEI–Local Governments for Sustainability are national and international localized programs dealing with environmental issues.

National Initiatives: Sweden and New Zealand

Sweden and New Zealand are taking steps to make the transition to the post-petroleum age. This transition will give their citizens not only reduced carbon emissions but also greater domestic control of their energy supply. Eventually they hope to eliminate their dependence on unstable foreign energy sources. The leaders have outlined a national vision for energy independence based on local resilience.

In 2005, Swedish Prime Minister Göran Persson declared his nation's goal of becoming fossil-fuel independent by 2020. This would make Sweden the world's first oil-free nation. As Mona Sahlin, Sweden's minister of sustainable development, said, "There [will] always be better alternatives to oil, which means no house should need oil for heating, and no driver should need to turn solely to gasoline.... A Sweden free of fossil fuels would give us enormous advantages, not least by reducing impact from fluctuations in oil prices."[22]

In 2009, new government leadership in Sweden modified the former prime minister's oil-independence goals, announcing a new energy plan to increase the country's renewable energy production to 50 percent by 2020; make the nation's vehicles fossil-fuel independent by 2030; and have zero net emissions of greenhouse gases by 2050. Other countries striving for carbon neutrality, termed the Carbon World Cup, include Norway, New Zealand, Iceland, Costa Rica and the Maldives.[23] Sweden started a trend of working with local communities to make the nation energy-independent, a glocal approach setting an example for other nations to embrace.

To achieve its ambitious goal of carbon neutrality, the Swedish government received input from the Scientific Council on Climate Issues, the Climate Committee, the business sector and civil society. Sweden's path to a carbon-neutral economy has already made remarkable strides. Its population of 9 million receives about half its electricity from hydropower and the rest from nuclear power. Fossil fuels are used mostly in the transportation sector. Sweden's effective strategy of diversifying its energy sources and implementing energy efficiency has paid off: the use of oil has dropped from 70 percent of the total energy supply in 1970 to about 30 percent in 2009. Renewable energy consumption has increased from 34 percent in 1990 to 44 percent in 2007. The district heating sector, powered mostly by biomass, accounts for about 40 percent of the heating market. By 2020 the government plans for a 40 percent reduction in its greenhouse gas emissions, with half the country's energy to come from renewable sources. Sweden has reduced its greenhouse gases by over 9 percent since 1990 while increasing its GDP by about 48 percent (1990–2007).[24] These achievements demonstrate the ability of national policy to facilitate and accelerate work at the local level.

Creative solutions for weaning Sweden off oil include seizing opportunities that provide an alternative to business as usual. One example is the production of biogas from liquor. The high price of alcohol in Sweden lures people to drive to Germany and Denmark, where liquor is less expensive. However, the Swedish "personal use" rule limits liquor for personal consumption and creates a surplus of confiscated liquor: 55,000 liters of spirits, 294,000 liters of beer and 39,000 liters of wine in one year. Rather than pouring the liquor down the drain as had been the practice of customs officials, they are now turning it into biofuel for use by buses, taxis and

Lasse Hejdenberg

"Amanda," a Swedish biogas train that began service in 2005, is powered by animal byproducts, alcohol, fat and industrial food waste such as chocolate, milk and yogurt. Committed to increasing the country's renewable energy production to 50 percent and reducing greenhouse gas emissions by 40 percent by 2020, and to having zero net greenhouse gas emissions by 2050, Sweden is leading the world by example.

garbage trucks. Even a train, running between Linkoping and Vastervik, is one of the first in the world to be powered by biogas.[25] This example points to the value of reexamining existing policies and imagining how we can redeploy our resources.

In 2007 New Zealand's Prime Minister Helen Clark announced her nation's intention to commit to 90 percent renewable electricity by 2025. In addition, Clark outlined a target for reducing by half the per capita emissions from transportation by 2040. She also set a goal of a net increase in forest area of 250,000 hectares by 2020. As Clark pointed out in her address to the nation, "Sustainability is a key competitive advantage. In today's global marketplace consumers are increasingly concerned about ethical and environmental issues, and the carbon footprint of products and services is becoming an issue. To protect our markets and our nation's reputation, we need to act preemptively."[26] New Zealand's leaders have seized on the economic advantages of reinventing their economy for resilience and thriveability.

These targets are backed by New Zealand's track record of innovative environmental programs. At the core of New Zealand's successes lies its government's green plan, the Resource Management Act (RMA), adopted in 1991. One of the world's model green plans, it focuses on watersheds rather than on political boundaries. It supports sustainable management of resources and accounts for the social and environmental costs of economic development. The RMA was created with the input of environmental groups and New Zealand's indigenous people, the Maori, who make up 15 percent of the country's population of 4 million.[27] The RMA's glocal perspective successfully integrates the needs of local communities with policy objectives at the national level.

Through an immigration cap of 45,000 per year and a growth rate of 0.91 percent, New Zealand's population is expected to reach 5.5 million in 2015 and stabilize thereafter. Since tourism ranks as the top source of revenue, New Zealanders are aware of the significance of protecting their natural heritage. To this end, the RMA balances economic viability and environmental protection. In addition, New Zealand supplies 98 percent of its wood needs through its managed plantation forests, its third largest source of export revenue. The RMA has also implemented a freshwater quality management program; promoted sustainable dairy farming practices through the Commodity Levies Act of 1990; developed a national packaging waste reduction strategy through the Packaging Accord 2004;

established the Permanent Forest Sink Initiative to allow landowners to establish forest sinks and obtain Kyoto Protocol-compliant emissions units; and developed an emissions reduction agreement to coincide with an emissions trading scheme.[28]

One of New Zealand's most progressive green initiatives is in the Lake Taupo catchment area in the North Island's Waikato region. As the country's largest lake, with a surface area of 238 square miles, Lake Taupo annually draws over 1.2 million tourists to the lake and nearby communities.[29] The need for a comprehensive green plan prompted the residents to develop the 2020 Taupo-nui-a-Tia Action Plan (2020 TAP). A collaborative effort over three years, it presents 12 values identified by the community as essential for the health of the lake and its surrounding areas:[30]

- Clear water
- Diverse plants and animals in lakes and rivers
- Foreshore reserves
- Geological features
- Good trout fishing
- High quality inflowing water
- Outstanding scenery
- Recreational opportunities
- Safe drinking water
- Safe swimming
- Weed-free lake
- Wilderness areas

Using these values as guidelines, the 2020 TAP identifies over 130 threats and devises strategies for prioritizing and reducing them. The threats are subdivided into categories including ecosystem health, human health and quality of life.[31] The 2020 Joint Management Group, with members of the central and local government agencies, the Tuwharetoa Maori Trust Board and the Lakes and Waterways Action Group, is responsible for each of the actions. This group represents a unique alliance of stakeholders and has been instrumental in the success of the program and the creation of a model for future sustainable development plans.

Nearly 70 percent of the actions identified in the 2020 TAP are being implemented, resulting in the reduction of nitrogen input to the lake from farms and urban areas, improved stormwater management, protection of Ngati Tuwharetoa values and a review of the Regional Pest Management

Strategy. Although numerous challenges remain, such as boat sewage and wastewater disposal in the lake, the 2020 TAP stands as a practical plan for managing development pressures in this tourist destination.[32] The 2020 TAP's glocal perspective maintains a link between national policies and local initiatives aimed at improving the quality of life of the residents.

International Environmental Plans

Beyond the scope of national initiatives such as Sweden's energy and climate plan and New Zealand's RMA lie international environmental plans. These involve treaties, legislation and agreements among governments that share a common vision for their citizens, their private and public sectors and industry. These plans are creating new international mechanisms for solving environmental problems beyond political boundaries. The European Union's green plan and ICLEI–Local Governments for Sustainability are such initiatives. Both provide frameworks for local programs under the umbrella of international policies. This approach is key in an increasingly integrated world where many communities lack the expertise and resources to implement local green plans.

As the European Union (EU) has grown from 6 to 27 countries, environmental and energy security concerns have played an increasing role in its vision. In 2000 the Lisbon European Council set the EU a goal of becoming "the most competitive and dynamic knowledge-based economy in the world, capable of sustainable economic growth with more and better jobs and greater social cohesion."[33] This lofty goal has since had to be reconciled with the environmental, economic and social pressures of a rapidly expanding EU.

The Netherlands has historically inspired the EU with its innovative green plan, the Netherlands' National Environmental Policy Plan (NEPP). More recently, the European Commission has built upon the Netherlands' experience and adopted an integrated approach to energy security and climate change. Because of the EU's dependence on oil imports, it has set a goal of reducing energy consumption by 20 percent by 2020. This target would reduce costs by €100 billion annually and eliminate 780 million tons of CO_2 every year. In addition, meeting this target would increase the EU's economic competitiveness, provide jobs, support innovative technologies and improve the quality of life for European citizens.[34]

Another initiative supported by the EU involves the life cycle of products. The EU Directive on Restriction of Hazardous Substances (RoHS) restricts manufacturers from producing electronic equipment that contains hazardous substances such as lead, mercury and cadmium. This directive is aimed at reducing the volume of the wastestream and its impact on regional landfills and local environmental health. The responsibility is put on the manufacturer to take back its products and recycle them at the end of their useful life. This legislation provides an incentive for manufacturers to design products with a cradle to cradle approach. This international agreement is having an impact in communities struggling to reduce their wastestreams.

The private sector is also taking significant steps to reduce the ecological footprint, particularly in densely populated urban areas. For example, in 2009 Cisco Systems, a leader in Internet networking equipment and management tools, launched its Intelligent Urbanisation initiative. In collaboration with Metropolis, an association of over 100 of the world's largest cities, Cisco hopes to promote technologies for sustainable development. Its Urban Leadership Academy is designed to develop new transportation technologies, pollution reduction strategies and collaborative tools for connecting cities to reduce traveling and associated carbon emissions. WebEx and TelePresence are examples of pilot projects in the state of Karnataka, India, and Incheon City, Korea. As Cisco's chief globalization officer Wim Elfring points out, "Cities that are run on information will transform the quality of life for citizens, drive economic growth and improve city services and management. Particularly in these tough economic times, cities that use the network to accelerate and multiply their infrastructure investments will be those who not only survive but thrive and lead into the future."[35]

ICLEI is one of the most successful international programs embracing a glocal approach. Founded in 1990 as the International Council for Local Environmental Initiatives, ICLEI emerged from a United Nations sponsored conference, the World Congress of Local Governments for a Sustainable Future, attended by over 200 local government officials from 43 countries. ICLEI's membership has since grown to more than 700 cities, towns and counties representing over 300 million people. Its international campaigns, including Cities for Climate Protection, involve working with local governments to build awareness of CO_2 emissions, to create action plans with CO_2 reduction targets and to monitor results. ICLEI's campaigns incorporate a "five-milestone" structure: (1) establish a baseline; (2) set a target; (3) develop a local action plan; (4) implement the local action plan; and (5) measure results.[36]

ICLEI has successfully supported alliances of local governments, businesses and nonprofits worldwide to find solutions to the challenges of climate change. By connecting the lessons learned from its work with hundreds of communities to the needs of local cities, ICLEI lends a glocal perspective to global issues. ICLEI USA, for example, will work with the Clinton Foundation and Microsoft to develop a web-based tool for global standard accounting and software to allow cities to share data on greenhouse gas emissions. In this way there will be an internationally recognized standard for evaluating city programs for greenhouse gas reductions. In association with the US Green Building Council and the Center for American Progress, ICLEI is also developing the STAR Community Index. Planned for launch in 2010, this tool is designed to help local governments plan, track and measure their sustainability programs. Similar to the US Green Building Council's Leadership in Energy and Environmental Design (LEED') building standard, the STAR program will have a tiered system.

ICLEI has tapped into the strength of alliances that complement its core mission and has a strong training and support program, Regional Capacity Centers, organized throughout the US to coordinate its program offerings. In essence, ICLEI is a glocal infrastructure making a difference in the climate crisis. Working with 375 local governments, representing 25 percent of the US population, it has achieved over 23 million tons of greenhouse gas emissions reduction, over 43,000 tons of smog reduction and over $535 million of savings in energy and fuel costs.[37]

ICLEI's success in working with local communities is mirrored by other sustainable community initiatives. The US Green Building Council's LEED for Neighborhood Development (LEED-ND) rating and certification program, launched in 2009, is becoming a widely accepted standard for sustainable communities interested in green building, new urbanism and smart growth. Another city program is Climate Resilient Communities, which assists cities with their response to hazards from global warming. Communities 21 is aimed at establishing healthy communities. SustainLane's US City Rankings, launched in 2005, compares green initiatives from various cities. Warren Karlenzig, the creator of the SustainLane US City Rankings methodology, wrote a landmark book in 2007, *How Green is Your City?* US City Rankings is now recognized by mayors and government agencies as a standard for measuring environmental impacts and quality of life in cities throughout the US. Karlenzig's research analyzes the connection between sustainability and glocalization.[38] This type of city ranking may expand to urban regions throughout the world and could encourage residents and government leaders to adopt glocal measures supporting local quality of life and local economies while addressing global sustainability issues.

Glocalization Reframed

Communities from small villages to large cities are grappling with economic, social and environmental pressures that call for place-based, glocal solutions using local resources and regional networks. For example, the communications revolution, led by wireless technologies and the Internet, provides communities with information about "best practices" that assist in modeling and implementing sustainable policies and programs. Regional and international organizations, in turn, can establish the foundation for local initiatives. In this way, the "think globally, act locally" approach is taking root with the active participation of local stakeholders and the support of partners with a global reach.

Local, regional, national and international initiatives point to the importance of civil society's involvement in making change. Individuals who are motivated by the desire for the well-being of their families and the economic vitality of their towns often initiate actions that catch the ear of local leaders. Whether the actions are inspired by the symbolism of a native salmon species or a bold greenhouse gas reduction target, their goals are the health, safety and thriveability of their local communities.

TAKING ACTION

➡ *Join an organization working on global/local issues in your home region, such as food, energy, water, waste, transportation or education (see Organizations section in Resources).*

➡ *Do a neighborhood audit to determine who has skills and who has needs; create a neighborhood alliance that builds connections.*

➡ *Meet your neighbors and develop strategies for resource conservation (energy, water, waste) at the individual, family and community level.*

➡ *Stay abreast of regional and national issues and their connections to the local level.*

➡ *Join your local Chamber of Commerce and suggest ways to promote sustainability initiatives.*

➡ *Attend your local town council, planning commission, water district and waste board meetings and engage your elected officials on issues of concern to you.*

➡ *Calculate your ecological footprint and explore ways of reducing it.*

THREE

Greening Commerce

Our personal consumer choices have ecological, social, and spiritual consequences. It is time to re-examine some of our deeply held notions that underlie our lifestyles.

— DAVID SUZUKI

We need to move from capital markets based on consumption and extraction to capital markets based on restoration and preservation. You can call the new markets values-driven, but I would say that they are just getting down-right practical. It's just recognizing that where we are in history, we have to behave differently if we want to survive — much less live by higher ethical standards.

— WOODY TASCH

EVERY DAY, news of businesses "going green" permeates newspapers, magazines, television programs and the Internet. Whether a large firm declares a greenhouse gas reduction goal, a small start-up develops a new solar technology or a nonprofit launches a local organic food program, the green wave of commerce is upon us. This wave includes for-profits, nonprofits, government agencies, trade associations and special interest groups. What are the trends that are shaping this new commercial landscape? Are organizations adapting to the changes? What are the challenges and opportunities for commercial enterprises? These questions reflect a transformation that involves reexamining the values and purposes of commercial enterprises in the emerging green economy.

Commerce is the most influential force on the planet. It is also responsible for a great deal of the environmental destruction caused by "business as usual." Reinventing the way we design, manufacture and deliver products presents an opportunity to reverse this destruction. Decisions made by consumers, organizations and government agencies will lay the groundwork for a thriveable future as public awareness pushes business to take greater environmental and social responsibility.

To eliminate waste, green commerce requires manufacturing processes with a cradle to cradle approach. Designs that emulate natural systems will use nontoxic, biodegradable materials. Significantly, businesses are discovering that going green is good not only for public relations but also for their bottom line. Detailed information about companies' practices and the ingredients in products ranging from sunscreen to shampoo is available from such resources as blogs, social networking sites and GoodGuide. With a level of information that was never available in the past, companies that avoid full disclosure run the risk of a public-relations backlash.

The New Bottom Lines

A milestone in the business community's change toward more thriveable practices was the concept of the triple bottom line. In 1994, John Elkington, founder of the business consulting firm SustainAbility and author of *Cannibals with Forks,* enlarged the horizon of business interests beyond the traditional bottom line by including environmental and social concerns in a new triple bottom line. These concerns, which had been treated as mere

Retail Products Beginning to Carry Carbon Intensity Labels

A bag of Walkers potato chips in the UK now sports a label stating that the 34.5 gram bag also "contains" 75 grams of carbon dioxide. The 75 grams is a calculation of the amount of gas released into the atmosphere as a result of making that amount of product, from growing the potato to packaging and distributing the finished chips. A handful of companies in the UK are now working with the Carbon Trust to put carbon footprint information on their products. In addition to supermarket giant Tesco, others embracing the labeling partnership with Carbon Trust include J Sainsbury, Marks and Spencer and Cadbury Schweppes. All of the companies that the Carbon Trust has worked with on labels have found that they could make energy savings as a result of what they discovered during the process — cutting their costs as well as their carbon output.[1]

"externalities," moved to the forefront of sustainable business practices. As Andrew Savitz, author of *The Triple Bottom Line,* suggests, "A sustainable business ought to be able to measure, document, and report a positive ROI [return on investment] on all three bottom lines — economic, environmental, and social — as well as the benefits that stakeholders receive along the same three dimensions."[2] The triple bottom line concept has also been described as people (social), planet (environmental) and profit (economic).

Theo Ferguson, founder and executive director of Sustainable Ventures, a nonprofit citizen advocacy organization, introduced the concept of an integrated bottom line, which merges the financial, environmental and social costs and benefits into a single balance sheet rather than three separate ones. Some members of the business community welcome this integration since it allows them to focus on one bottom line. It also makes sustainability's relevance to the "real" bottom line more evident.

The Drivers

Although we may not yet have a firm grasp of what a sustainable corporate enterprise looks like, innovative companies are experimenting with production and service models. The trends driving innovation include: a move toward globalization, expanded communications, greater interdependence and a demand from stakeholders for accountability. The first three drivers contribute to the impact of the fourth, which is the main driver for sustainable business practices. While in the past environmental and social concerns were raised by nonprofits and scientists, now customers, investors, bankers and insurers are demanding action. They see the connection between a company's bottom line and environmental issues such as the price of carbon. Sustainability is shifting from a green issue to a mainstream issue.

The move toward globalization can be seen in the accelerated pace of international trade agreements at the bilateral, regional and global levels. The World Trade Organization (WTO), created in 1995, governs trade rules among nations and has paved the way to international trade by opening economic markets worldwide. From the WTO have grown numerous regional free-trade agreements including the North American Free Trade Agreement, Asia-Pacific Economic Cooperation and the Middle East Free Trade Area Initiative. At the national level, scores of countries have set up bilateral free trade agreements. Currently the United States has over a dozen free-trade agreements, either established or pending approval by

Congress, with countries such as Australia, Chile, Oman, Singapore and Korea. These agreements have opened economic opportunities to developing counties but have questionable benefits for local economies.

As these agreements are implemented, transnational companies compete on the world stage with their goods and services. Competitive pricing of labor and raw materials has created global supply chains and production methods that leave local economies vulnerable to international price fluctuations. Social justice, safety and environmental concerns have also been raised by groups concerned about weak regulations by governments of developing countries. Public opposition to the globalization trend has been expressed during trade negotiations, including the WTO ministerial conference of 1999, where thousands made their voices heard in the "Battle of Seattle." The International Forum on Globalization has rallied 60 organizations in 25 countries to promote "equitable, democratic, and ecologically sustainable economies."[3] These and other organizations have concerns about protecting social justice and the environment in the movement toward global commercial agreements.

Globalization has been facilitated in part by the communications explosion. The worldwide growth of the Internet has changed business manufacturing methods, service models and marketing strategies. There were over 108 million websites in 2007, 1.3 billion e-mail users in 2008, 2.1 billion cell phones as of 2005 and 1.7 billion television sets in 2005.[4] Add to these the constant news, information and programming and you have a marketing deluge. The Internet, for example, makes it possible for companies to work around the clock by e-mailing files to offices abroad to prepare by the next morning.

The communications explosion has also made possible a high degree of customization in products and services. For example, one can now order online a computer with the desired components and then track its manufacturing process until it arrives at its destination. Similar customization programs are available for products ranging from sneakers with embroidered names to cars with special features. However, although communications technologies have transformed the business climate, there remains a digital divide between developed and developing countries in their access to the Internet and other tools.

The viral marketing qualities of the Internet can also spread ideas for social change. Paul Hawken's *Blessed Unrest* highlights the impact of the Internet in mobilizing people around the world to common causes. In

2007, for example, Annie Leonard produced a 20-minute animation, *The Story of Stuff*, describing the impact of production and consumption patterns.[5] In the first week after its release, *The Story of Stuff* was viewed online by 100,000 people around the world. In the first six months it was seen by two million people and in its first year it reached nearly five million viewers. It continues to grow in popularity. *The Story of Stuff* website has been translated into ten languages, and many of its viewers have committed to reducing waste in their communities. Similarly, an online spelling game, FreeRice, donates money to buy ten grains of rice for the hungry for each correctly spelled word. Launched in October 2007 as an initiative of Poverty.com, in the first month FreeRice donated a billion grains of rice, enough to feed 50,000 people for one day. By March 2009, the website had raised over 60 billion grains of rice, enough to feed three million people for a day.[6] These initiatives show the power of the Internet, which individuals can use to bring global awareness and action to environmental causes.

In our globalized, media-saturated world, interdependence plays a role in commerce. Organizations rely on reciprocal relationships with marketers, suppliers, vendors, distributors, regulators and numerous others in the production and distribution of their products and services. Dell, for example, which on an average day sells about 150,000 computers, works with 400 companies in North America, Europe and Asia. The interactions required to order a laptop over the telephone or on the Internet and have it customized, built and delivered a few weeks later rely on a manufacturing process of thousands of production and communications links.[7] Similarly, the Ford Motor Company has over 2,000 vendors supplying it with parts or services for its automobiles.[8]

Beyond manufacturing circles, the interdependence of businesses, municipalities and nongovernmental organizations is spawning numerous public/private, nonprofit/for-profit partnerships. County planning and development departments, for example, rely on research from environmental nonprofits to formulate development policies. Local municipalities form alliances with businesses to promote green-collar training programs for inner-city youth. Foundations encourage nonprofits with similar missions to work together when applying for grants in order to increase their scope and impact. These partnerships are redefining the commercial sector to include the expertise of a wider range of players.

Globalization, communications and interdependence contribute to what Andrew Savitz calls the Age of Accountability in which "everyone knows your business, has an opinion about it, and feels that he or she has the right to express that opinion and try hard to change your behavior."[9] Accountability speaks to the responsibility of corporations to go beyond their shareholders to include their stakeholders. Increased information about corporate activities and the demand for transparency have the running of companies under scrutiny.

Stakeholders' questions go to the heart of an organization's mission. They balance financial gain, environmental responsibility and social equity issues. As John Elkington points out, "Now instead of just focusing on issues such as the pay packet of 'fat cat' directors, new questions are being asked. For example, what is business for? Who should have a say in how companies are run? What is the appropriate balance between shareholders and other stakeholders? And what balance should be struck at the level of the triple bottom line?"[10] These questions, coupled with public pressure for increased transparency, are spurring corporate leaders to reassess their companies' operations and priorities and to design new strategies that serve both shareholders and stakeholders.

Implementing Nature's Strategies

In their search for the integrated bottom line, business leaders are beginning to manage their organizations with the understanding that the economy is dependent on the biosphere, not the other way around. Our economy depends on Earth's life support systems that provide us with clean air and water, healthy soil and nutrients, making possible the production and delivery of goods and services. This shift in perception is essential for building a thriveable economy.

The ecological systems often referred to as nature's services include pollination, erosion prevention, water filtering, soil fertilization, game habitats, pest control and wildlife corridors (see Chapter 5). Nature's services, which have evolved over 3.8 billion years, can serve as guiding principles for our industrial system. The field of biomimicry explores how nature can serve as a model, measure and mentor. Architects, fabricators and manufacturers can imitate nature's designs and processes. Examples include solar cells based on the leaf, building designs and ventilation systems modeled on termite mounds and adhesives based on the glue secreted by blue mussels.

Janine Benyus, a biologist and leader in the biomimicry field, says we have to slow down, observe closely and ask the right questions: What would nature do? How is this done in nature at ambient temperature with no waste? The challenges, currently being studied through Biomimicry Affiliate programs at the Universidad Iberoamericana in Mexico City, the Ontario College of Art and Design in Toronto and Arizona State University in Tempe, may include devising new food and energy production methods, building organically-based shelter structures and selecting new materials or health treatments.[11] Green commerce is raising possibilities for reinventing how we live on the planet.

The Trilogy

Thriveable business practices also are based on nature's principles. Three concepts promoted by designer Bill McDonough and entrepreneur Paul Hawken are cradle to cradle (a complete life-cycle approach that regenerates itself), waste equals food (waste from one system is food for another) and solar income (using the sun's energy to sustain the planet). As Hawken suggests in *Blessed Unrest,* "The trilogy of concepts — cradle to cradle, waste equals food, and stay within current solar income — lays out the basic tenets of the greening of industry and elimination of pollution, waste and toxins."[12]

These concepts focus on the primary issues that begin at the design phase, move through the manufacturing process and "end" with the product's life as the beginning of a new cycle. Through education, consumers can more easily find information about products in order to make informed decisions about their purchases.

The cradle to cradle approach mimics nature's life cycles. Like decaying leaves that become nutrients for organisms in the soil and thereby replenish the tree, cradle to cradle products are designed to maintain their material integrity as they are recycled into new products at the end of their useful life. While our current cradle to grave manufacturing is an open-loop system in which discarded products end up in landfills, the cradle to cradle model supports a closed-loop system.

The cradle to cradle model is related to the notion that waste equals food. In nature there is no waste: nutrients support metabolic processes. The compost from decayed plants, for example, provides food for living plants. In the manufacturing sector, industrial ecology sites such as Kalundborg, Denmark, mimic these processes. Excess heat and material from a power plant, a water treatment plant, a refinery and a biotech company are reused. For example, closed-loop systems use surplus steam from the power plant to heat 3,500 local homes; sludge from a fish farm's water treatment plant as fertilizer for a farm; and sulfur dioxide from a power plant mixed with calcium carbonate to produce gypsum for a plasterboard factory.[13]

The concept of solar income means relying on renewable energy sources rather than on fossil fuels. Compared to the environmental impact of limited, polluting sources of oil and natural gas, the benefits of clean, renewable energy from sources such as wind, the sun and biomass are obvious.

Companies engulfed by growth, consumption and pollution can adapt their production methods to mimic natural processes. Gregory Unruh, a leader in technological innovation, says that businesses emulating Earth's biosphere can focus on using fewer raw materials, "upcycling" and leveraging platforms.[14] All living things are produced from 4 of the 100 elements: carbon, hydrogen, oxygen and nitrogen. Green companies seek to use fewer materials and materials that can be easily recycled. For example, fabric manufacturer Designtex hired Bill McDonough and Michael Braungart to create environmentally safe fabrics. They began by reviewing Ciba Geigy's inventory of chemicals. Out of 7,962 textile chemicals, only 38 met their criteria and were selected to build an organic, environmentally friendly fabric line. It became an award-winning financial success.[15]

In downcycling, a product at the end of its life is recycled into a lesser grade product, which merely delays its journey to a landfill. By contrast, in upcycling the integrity of materials is maintained and they are reused in a higher value product. Car manufacturers such as BMW and carpet tile producers such as Shaw are implementing upcycling strategies that support a cradle to cradle model of production.

Leveraging platforms is a concept taken from nature, where it is seen in the multiple uses of the building blocks that support biodiversity. In industry, companies achieve a competitive advantage by relying on platforms that adapt to many uses. Software manufacturers, for example, use computer operating systems that evolve over time; auto manufacturers rely on basic frame designs that can be adapted for various models; architects design modules that can vary with occupant use and climate conditions.

Extended producer responsibility or take-back laws place responsibility for recycling on the manufacturer. In 2008, for example, Texas required computer manufacturers to take back desktops, laptops, monitors, keyboards and mouse devices at no cost to consumers. In addition, the

Texas Commission on Environmental Quality requires computer retailers, including Internet-based enterprises, to sell only equipment for which the manufacturers have a recovery plan.[16]

The European Union's Waste Electrical and Electronic Equipment Directive requires manufacturers to take back appliances and electronics at the end of their useful life. Similar take-back laws are in place in Canada, Brazil and Japan, covering a range of appliances such as televisions, computers, washing machines, air conditioners and refrigerators. The EU's End of Life Vehicles Directive has extended the take-back concept into the automotive industry by influencing automakers to design vehicles with a cradle to cradle approach.[17] These programs are reinventing how we build and dispose of products to minimize environmental impacts.

Growth, Consumption and Pollution

Economic growth, consumption and pollution challenge our assumptions about business activities. Until the recent upheaval in the world's markets, the economic growth of the past several decades had been rapid and relentless. As author and environmental leader Gus Speth pointed out, "Of the hundred largest economies in the world, fifty-three are corporations. Exxon alone is larger than more than 180 nations. In 1970 there were seven thousand multinationals; by 2007 there were at least sixty-three thousand. These sixty-three thousand companies directly employ about ninety million people and contribute a quarter of the gross world product."[18] These statistics illustrate how companies have perfected extracting raw materials and making and delivering their products and services on a global scale.

The worldwide economic crisis that erupted in 2008 has provided an opportunity to reassess the repercussions of a commercial system devoid of ties to the environment, where multinational conglomerates treat the environment as a mere "externality." As *New York Times* columnist Thomas L. Friedman asks, "What if the crisis of 2008 represents something much more fundamental than a deep recession? What if it's telling us that the whole growth model we created over the last 50 years is simply unsustainable economically and ecologically and that 2008 was when we hit the wall — when Mother Nature and the market both said: 'No more.'"[19] This crisis brings up fundamental questions such as: What is the role of growth in commercial ventures? What type of growth is necessary for a thriving economy: quantitative (gross domestic product), qualitative (quality of life) or perhaps none?

As Bill McKibben reminds us, our current economic growth model is associated with environmental decline, limited happiness and social inequality. In the US between 1997 and 2000 the top 1 percent of wage earners claimed more of the "real national gain" than the bottom 50 percent.[20] On a worldwide scale, the richest 1 percent of people (50 million households), with an average income of $24,000 per capita, earn more than the 60 percent of households (2.7 billion people) at the bottom of the income distribution. In terms of global income, 84 percent of the world's population receives only 16 percent of its income.[21] These statistics underscore the gap created by our global economic model. This gap affects political stability and highlights the importance of social justice in the greening of commerce.

There is not enough energy or raw material to sustain the world's economic growth at the current rate. The Global Footprint Network's research shows that our world's ecological footprint has tripled since 1961. By 2006 the world's footprint exceeded its ability to regenerate resources by 25 percent. In addition, the steady decline of the planet's biodiversity, including the loss of one third of the Earth's vertebrate species since 1970, indicates the limits of the Earth's ability to support hyperconsumption. To maintain the North American standard of living would require three to five Earths.[22] The United Nation's Millennium Ecosystem Assessment states that human activity "is putting such strain on the environment that the ability of the planet's ecosystems to sustain future generations can no longer be taken for granted."[23] This rate of growth on a global scale is unsustainable from both the social and the environmental perspectives.

The growth-dependent economic system we have built has led to a cycle of consumption. Thomas Friedman describes it:

> We have created a system for growth that depended on our building more and more stores to sell more and more stuff made in more and more factories in China, powered by more and more coal that would cause more and more climate change but earn China more and more dollars to buy more and more U.S. T-bills so America would have more and more money to build more and more stores and sell more and more stuff that would employ more and more Chinese.... We can't do this anymore.[24]

In the US this lifestyle manifests itself in larger homes consuming more electricity and generating more waste, with the size of new homes going up 50 percent since 1970, electricity consumption rising 70 percent and solid waste increasing 33 percent. Since 1994, 80 percent of the new homes are exurban with over half the lots being ten acres or more.[25] The question that arises is: Has this growth made us happier? Numerous studies have looked at the relationship between income and happiness. There seems to be a threshold of $10,000 per capita. Below this, money is correlated with happiness as basic necessities are taken care of, but beyond this there is no connection. McKibben states that "money consistently buys happiness right up to $10,000 per capita income, and that after that point the correlation disappears.... A sampling of *Forbes* magazine's 'richest Americans' has happiness scores identical with those of the Pennsylvania Amish and only a whisker above those of Swedes, not to mention Masai tribesmen."[26] How do we get off this growth-induced treadmill and use our resources more wisely? Some firms are experimenting with new ways of greening commerce.

Creating New Alliances

Given the limitations of the present growth trajectory, some companies are turning toward better ways of managing natural resources and giving back to their employees and communities. Patagonia, for example, launched a Common Threads Garment Recycling program, which encourages customers to return worn out recyclable garments for reuse. This program shows the firm's commitment to the cradle to cradle concept. In addition, Patagonia cofounded The Conservation Alliance, which supports environmental organizations that together have saved 34 million acres of wildlands and prevented or removed 14 dams.[27] Shaw, a leading carpet tile producer, has developed a process that separates the backing from used carpet tiles for reuse in new carpet products. Shaw takes responsibility for the life cycle of its products, reducing the impact on landfills.

Numerous environmental and community-based initiatives encourage progressive companies to give to local nonprofits and merchants. In 2002, Patagonia's founder Yvon Chouinard and Craig Mathews, owner of Blue Ribbon Flies, launched 1% For The Planet, which asks its member companies to contribute 1 percent of their sales to select nonprofit environmental organizations. To encourage alliances between the for-profit and nonprofit sectors, members contact environmental groups directly. As of 2008, 1% For The Planet had been responsible for $42 million in environmental donations. More than 1,000 member companies in 37 countries have given over $12 million annually to almost 1,700 environmental groups worldwide.[28]

These companies are expanding the concept of profit for themselves and their shareholders to include supporting the aims of a civil society.

The Interra Project has designed a financial mechanism that supports local economies and quality of life through transactions with local merchants. Interra's leaders include the founder of Odwalla, Greg Steltenpohl, the founder of Visa International, Dee Hock, and the founder of Elf Technologies and SmartChannels, Jon Ramer. Each purchase gives cardholders cash rewards and provides donations to local nonprofits and schools. Begun in Boston in 2006, Interra's Community Card programs have since expanded to Ohio and the Puget Sound area in Washington State. The Interra model aligns consumers' purchasing power with a values-based economy.

Mission-Based Enterprises

CEOs are increasingly undertaking socially responsible ventures. Numerous nonprofit organizations are establishing alliances, guidelines and standards for companies committed to going beyond profits to generating social value in their operations. These nonprofits include Business for Social Responsibility, Social Venture Network and B Lab's B Corporation. Two US companies that use a mission-based, whole-systems approach to commerce are Massachusetts' Dean's Beans Organic Coffee Company and Vermont's Seventh Generation. A family-owned enterprise, Dean's Beans is a fair-trade, organic, kosher coffee roaster with a commitment to "peaceful social change and environmental stewardship."[29] Founded in 1993 by Dean Cycon, Dean's Beans is a leading voice in the coffee industry's fair-trade policies and practices. As the coffee roaster points out, "It's not that hard to roast coffee, but it's another matter to confront the poverty, inequity and ecological impact that has been endemic to coffee since the early days.... we are using the vehicle of business as a force for positive, peaceful change in our confused world, not as a vehicle to gain wealth at the expense of others."[30]

Dean's Beans' People-Centered Development initiatives in a dozen countries involve grassroots projects that focus on necessities such as fresh water, employment and health care. In Nicaragua, for example, Dean's Beans teamed up with the Polus Center, a Massachusetts nonprofit, to set up a café that employs local people. The income supports a clinic for prosthetic limbs and therapy for villagers maimed by land mines from past civil conflicts. Additional projects include supplying water buffaloes to Sumatran coffee farmers to fertilize the soil and control weeds; reforesting degraded lands in the Peruvian Andes; providing villagers in Papua New Guinea with hand-powered coffee depulping machines; and establishing a revolving loan fund to build wells in Ethiopia. The last is a program that would have cost a large development organization $40,000. Dean's Beans accomplished it for $8,000 by establishing a direct partnership with farmers and local groups.

The firm's environmental commitment shows in other ways. The company uses recyclable bags for packaging, preventing a million plastic bags from reaching landfills. Their Carbon Neutral Initiative has yielded a 23 percent reduction of CO_2 since 2005 despite a business growth of 14 percent. In their Reforestation Off-set Initiative in Peru, farmers have planted 80,000 trees that upon full maturity will reduce annual CO_2 emissions by 1,792 metric tons, over 17 times the company's annual CO_2 emissions.[31]

Dean's Beans' success is quite unconventional. Over the past decade, its sales have grown almost 500 percent.[32] This growth is described by Cycon's business philosophy: "To me growth is the outcome of a good business; it's not the goal." Instead of creating a formal marketing plan, Dean's Beans relies on a "passive guerilla" approach based on word of mouth, product demonstrations, speaking appearances and giveaway promotions at high-profile national events.[33] In 2007 Dean's Beans also joined the United Nations' Global Compact, an international corporate responsibility initiative, to share its best practices with other companies worldwide. Dean's Beans shows how a small enterprise can improve the social and environmental aspects of its commercial ventures.

Seventh Generation's environmental approach has earned it recognition as a leader in corporate social responsibility issues. A privately held company founded by Jeff Hollender in 1988, Seventh Generation produces numerous household products such as biodegradable, vegetable-based cleaning and laundry products and recycled, chlorine-free paper towels, napkins, facial tissues, diapers, training pants and trash bags. Seventh Generation uses post-consumer recycled materials, has eliminated toxins from its products and is pioneering the use of a third party to certify that its products are chlorine-free.[34] Seventh Generation also uses its packaging to educate customers about reducing environmental impacts, and a recent software program, available to mobile phones, allows customers to understand product labels while making purchasing decisions.

Seventh Generation gets its name from the Great Law of the Iroquois Confederacy, which states, "In our every deliberation, we must consider the impact of our decisions on the next seven generations." To this end, the firm is committed to a holistic, long-term approach in its business practices, "offering people varied avenues to express their idealism, passion, and commitment to causes larger than themselves at every point along our supply chain from suppliers and partners to shareholders, customers, and our own employees."[35]

Seventh Generation's commitment to becoming a transparent company came to the forefront when in 2007 media reports surfaced that one of its liquid dishwashing products contained the carcinogenic chemical 1,4-dioxane. Learning from past errors of not including stakeholders, Hollender points out their key step: "to share our trials and tribulations with everyone who wanted to weigh in, express concerns, ask questions, and challenge our progress." The dioxane mishap spurred the company to recognize the importance of opening a public dialog with its customers and partners as it grapples with business challenges. For example, it decided to engage its customers through its website as it seeks naturally derived pigments for dyes in its diapers. As Hollender says, "Transparency is not a state of being: it's an endless process of becoming."[36] Hollender's decision is setting a standard for consumer relations in green commerce.

In 2008 Seventh Generation established a partnership with Walmart and its four Marketside stores in Arizona. Though originally opposed to Walmart's policies, Hollender recognized the retailer's commitment to and progress in reducing its environmental impact. In the spirit of transparency he shared his views with his customers, stating, "Whether it's climate change, health-care reform, or natural-resources depletion, we can't take on the world's challenges without Walmart and its tens-of-thousands of partners and suppliers. At this point, we now believe that we can have a bigger impact by partnering with Walmart than by shunning it."[37] This alliance shows Hollender's and Seventh Generation's adaptability and vision. Seizing these opportunities, which initially might be viewed as selling out, may in the long term prove to have a positive impact not only for Seventh Generation but also for the planet.

Seventh Generation has achieved sales in excess of $100 million with fewer than 100 employees. In 2008 its sales grew by 50 percent over the previous year and it was the brand leader in every category. It reduced its greenhouse gas emissions 34 percent from 2005 to 2007, with a goal of reducing them 80 percent by 2050. It has also established an annual corporate giving program donating 10 percent of its pretax profits.[38]

In its effort to go beyond selling products, Seventh Generation partnered with Greenpeace in 2006. Together they launched the Change It program aimed at college students interested in training for social and environmental activism. The five-day training has inspired students from across the US to return to their communities and effect change. Examples include convincing the University of Vermont to stop purchasing toilet paper from old-growth trees and lobbying New York Representative Michael Arcuri to support global warming legislation. These programs go beyond Seventh Generation's earnings and strive to promote the well-being of future generations.

Dean's Beans and Seventh Generation represent a whole-systems business approach that extends beyond their products and services into improving the lives of people and communities. Bill Fishbein points out that "you can sell the highest quality product, pay the highest price for it, pay for the environmental and social value and you can still earn a profit."[39] Dean Cycon and Jeff Hollender are pioneering strategies to achieve these commercial and social goals.

Beyond individual firms are programs that benefit society at large. At the national level, the Chicago Climate Exchange (CCX) provides a market mechanism and trading system for greenhouse gas reduction. Richard Sandor from Sustainable Performance Group founded CCX in 2003. The 400 members make a legally binding commitment to reduce greenhouse gas emissions and trade their right to pollute. Members include large companies such as DuPont, Sony and Ford, municipalities such as Chicago, Oakland and Melbourne, educational institutions such as Michigan State and Tufts University and trade organizations such as the National Farmers Union. CCX's reach is expanding internationally as farmers in India have entered the carbon trading market through their use of biogas. In 2008, CCX members traded 23 million tons of carbon emissions, up from 10.3 million tons in 2006. Companies are rapidly joining CCX because of the savings through carbon reduction strategies; they are also taking proactive steps in anticipation of impending US government regulations. In addition, as CCX members US companies gain a competitive advantage overseas, particularly in the European markets, where they need to comply with regulations. Although CCX works as a voluntary market, significant greenhouse gas reduction in the US calls for a mandatory carbon cap. The American Clean Energy and Security Act, introduced by Democratic representatives Henry Waxman and Ed Markey, was passed by the House of

Representatives in June 2009. It is a landmark step that set the reduction of greenhouse gas emissions at 17 percent below 2005 levels by 2020 and 83 percent below 2005 levels by 2050.[40]

A New Role for Civil Society

As commerce rides the green wave, alliances are forming between business and civil society. In the Sierra Nevada region of California, Lucy Blake, a rancher and MacArthur Fellowship winner, spearheaded the formation of the Sierra Business Council (SBC) in 1994. SBC has since developed a model for rural communities to come together "to secure the social, natural, and financial health of the Sierra Nevada for this and future generations." As a nonprofit working with 700 businesses, agencies and individual members, SBC's efforts affect 26,000 citizens in 200 rural communities through community planning projects, conservation efforts, leadership training and sustainable business practices.

SBC developed the Sierra Nevada Wealth Index to understand the assets of the region and make appropriate business and policy decisions. Going beyond monetary worth, the Index uses data from 60 indicators to evaluate the social, natural and financial capital of the region. Similarly, ecological economist Mark Anielski developed the Genuine Wealth model, described in *The Economics of Happiness: Building Genuine Wealth*, which also taps into ways of measuring well-being and economic progress. This approach provides communities with a tool to make decisions that support the quality of life residents wish to protect. As the SBC Wealth Index suggests, "Our wealth is our total capital — social, natural, and financial — and our investment strategies must reflect this reality. Only by monitoring trends in all three forms of capital and taking full account of those trends in our investment decisions will we be able to build the wealth of our communities for ourselves and our descendants."[41] This view of a region's economy is a model for other rural communities to follow in developing alliances that benefit all residents.

While the Sierra Business Council provides a business network for rural residents, the Business Alliance for Local Living Economies (BALLE) has created one for urban areas. It began in 2001 when Philadelphia restaurant owner Judy Wicks wanted to buy from local and fair-trade food suppliers, and it has since evolved into an international network of business entrepreneurs. With a current membership of 15,000 entrepreneurs in the

US and Canada, BALLE strives to build strong local economies. "When enterprises are locally rooted, human-scale, owned by stakeholders, and held accountable to the rule of law by democratically elected governments, there is a natural incentive for all concerned to take human and community needs and interests into account. When income and ownership are equitably distributed, justice is served and political democracy is strong. When needs are met locally by locally owned enterprises, people have greater control over their lives...."[42] BALLE's approach supports the power of local businesses when owners have a stake in their community.

BALLE's living economy principles include: building communities through local exchange; decentralized business ownership; citizens' support of local businesses; investors who support a "living return" rather than a maximum return on their investments; media free from corporate control; and independent locally owned businesses that support stakeholders. BALLE emphasizes the benefits of basing economic decisions on values beyond financial profit. The BALLE model, similar to Transition Initiatives in Chapter 2, seeks to "think local first" by identifying local assets in natural, social and economic capital including raw materials, labor and financing.

FLOW is a nonprofit organization established by educator Michael Strong and Whole Foods Market cofounder and CEO John Mackey. FLOW is dedicated to "liberating the entrepreneurial spirit for good and focusing it on creating sustainable peace, prosperity, and happiness for all, in our lifetime." These ideals are matched by a network of programs for entrepreneurs including Accelerating Women Entrepreneurs, Conscious Capitalism and Peace Through Commerce. FLOW's principles and values are: cultivate human flourishing; practice nonviolence and radical tolerance; embrace freely chosen, mutually beneficial solutions; and criticize by creating. FLOW challenges members to step outside traditional business practices and envision a future of possibilities. Its members support each other's work through ongoing Activation Circles, gatherings in cities including New York, San Francisco and Austin. By combining ideas, community and action, the FLOW network promotes the positive impact of entrepreneurial endeavors.[43]

SBC, BALLE and FLOW illustrate a new kind of grassroots force. They are greening the commercial landscape by shining a light on the ecological, social and economic "blind spots" of traditional companies. They are creating small entrepreneurial networks with holistic initiatives.

Blue Chip Companies Turn Green

Large companies are also changing to sustainable practices for economic reasons. Reports of large companies "going green" are rampant, and the shift is increasing public awareness of sustainability. This has had a ripple effect on suppliers, who are changing their own business practices. Some of these firms adopt science-based sustainability frameworks such as The Natural Step, while others incorporate green practices that fit their corporate culture. The sustainability initiatives of five corporations — DuPont, Whole Foods Market, Swiss-Re, Fireman's Fund and Walmart — include strategies that reduce environmental impacts, promote social well-being and increase economic savings.

Founded in 1802 as a gunpowder manufacturer, DuPont has diversified into numerous areas, supplying products to the agriculture, construction, transportation and communications sectors. Through the original work of Paul V. Tebo and more recently that of sustainability officer Linda Fisher, the company's sustainability initiatives have achieved a reduction of 72 percent in their global greenhouse gas emissions since 1990. In addition, DuPont has reduced its carcinogen emissions by 92 percent since 1990, and in 2005 its global energy consumption was 6 percent lower than in 1990 despite a 40 percent growth in production.[44] These award-winning achievements support DuPont's core values: safety and health, environmental stewardship, respect for people and ethical behavior.

DuPont's goal of zero waste and emissions is communicated to every employee through the concept of "felt leadership." Mike Hewitt, vice president for Global Workplace Safety Practice, states that "leadership is not only about driving revenue and contributing to shareholder value — it is about helping preserve and protect an organization's most valuable resource — its employees." Some of felt leadership's principles are: be relentless about time with people; recognize your role as teacher/trainer; and behave and lead as you desire others to do.[45] These principles inspire DuPont's employees to align themselves with their firm's vision.

Similarly, Whole Foods Market has led in environmental practices in the food sector. Consistently ranked by *Fortune* magazine as one of America's 100 best companies to work for, Whole Foods is transforming the food industry. From the opening of its initial store in Austin in 1980, cofounder and CEO John Mackey has expanded Whole Foods Market to become one of the world's leaders in natural and organic foods, with over 270 stores in the US, Canada and the UK.[46] Its "Whole Foods, Whole People, Whole

Planet" philosophy describes the interdependence of humans and the environment. Whole Foods' core values are: selling the highest quality natural and organic products available; satisfying and delighting its customers; supporting team member excellence and happiness; creating wealth through profits and growth; and caring about its communities and the environment. These values emphasize the relationship of food, customers and communities.

Michael Pollan's challenge to Whole Foods' business practices in his book *The Omnivore's Dilemma* began a series of web-posted "open letter" exchanges between CEO Mackey and Pollan. This dialog highlights the challenges of supporting local organic food at a global scale, raising issues such as corporate farming, the definition of "local" farms and the treatment of farm animals. Their discourse educated the public about the organic food industry and brought positive changes to Whole Foods Market's operations and the industry at large. Some of the new practices at Whole Foods, due in part to the public scrutiny of its business practices, include hiring an animal-compassionate field buyer; focusing on acquiring more local products; establishing a $10 million annual budget to promote local agriculture; supporting local farmers' markets; and educating the public about locally produced products.[47] Whole Foods Market's transparency and interactions with stakeholders show how the age of accountability has come to life through the Internet.

Whole Foods' impact in the food sector is matched by Swiss Re's commitment in the insurance world. As the world's second largest global reinsurer, with 10,000 employees in 30 countries and revenues of $24 billion, Swiss Re is leading the way with its climate change strategies. Because Swiss Re was aware of the increasing financial risk for insurers resulting from climate change, such as severe hurricanes, tornados, droughts and floods, it made a commitment to incorporate climate change into its long-term risk-management strategy. Swiss Re states: "Our actions are based on the premise that it is in the interest of our shareholders, clients and employees, the wider stakeholder community and society in general to tackle this issue. Furthermore, we believe that companies can make an effective contribution by developing the numerous business opportunities which climate change has created, or will create in the future."[48] This is not the traditional position of an insurance company, but insurers bear the brunt of claims from natural disasters, which are often augmented by climate change.

Swiss Re's climate change programs include: advancing the understanding of inherent risks in climate change and communicating them to clients, employees and the public; developing products and services that deal with climate change issues; and reducing its own carbon footprint. Swiss Re has research programs on the economic impact of climate change and shares the findings with its shareholders. The firm also engages in climate change initiatives. In 2007 it began the Climate Adaptation Development Programme, which in its initial phase aims to provide financial protection against drought conditions for 400,000 people in Africa.[49] Such innovative insurance programs rely on creative financial mechanisms. One example is weather-based derivatives, in which buyers bet on the severity and timing of future heat waves or cold snaps, allowing farmers to buy insurance protection against these natural events.[50] These programs illustrate the firm's proactive stance on climate change issues.

As a member of the Chicago Climate Exchange, Swiss Re also invests in companies supporting carbon reduction. One of these is IdleAire, which provides hook-ups for trucks at highway rest stops, enabling drivers to turn off their engines. Swiss Re reduced its own carbon footprint by more than 25 percent between 2003 and 2007, and offset the remaining emissions through certified emissions reduction certificates. Swiss Re aims to maintain its carbon neutrality and increase its internal contribution to 30 percent by 2013.[51] These achievements underscore the importance of establishing ambitious initiatives in a traditionally conservative industry.

Swiss Re's concern with climate change in Europe is mirrored by Fireman's Fund Insurance Company's focus on green insurance. In 2006 the Allianz subsidiary Fireman's Fund introduced the first green insurance policies for commercial clients. These were marked by a premium discount for clients that use the US Green Building Council's LEED rating system and coverage for upgrading buildings with green materials and Energy Star rated equipment and for buildings with efficient performance. In the event of a loss, Fireman's Fund covers the extra cost of recycling the debris rather than sending it to a landfill. It also provides commercial clients with a hybrid upgrade endorsement, which replaces standard vehicles with hybrids.

In 2008 Fireman's Fund became the first US insurer to offer green insurance to homeowners. They gave Green Upgrade coverage to policy holders who currently own a house that is LEED for Homes rated, including a 5 percent discount on their premiums. The green insurance program also covers home policy holders who plan to rebuild using the LEED rating system. Again, Fireman's Fund is in the vanguard of the green insurance field. Since 2001, Fireman's Fund has reduced its own water consumption by 40 percent and its energy consumption by 35 percent and has diverted 77 percent of its solid waste from landfills.[52]

Walmart has made a similar shift to sustainable practices. Though at first glance Walmart's green efforts might be suspect, given criticisms of its business practices in wages, workers rights and employee health care, their effect on the retail sector is enormous. With annual sales of over $400 billion in 2008, it is the largest corporation in the world. Since 200 million Americans (two out of three) shop there regularly and 89 percent shop there once a year, Walmart's impact is undeniable and it is able to play a proportional role in sustainability.[53] Walmart's commitment to leadership in sustainable practices is marked by three goals: to be supplied 100 percent by renewable energy, to create zero waste and to sell products that sustain our resources and environment. Walmart hired environmental activist Adam Werbach to lead its efforts. He had been the youngest president of the Sierra Club at 23 and founder of Act Now Productions, a sustainability consulting division of Saatchi & Saatchi.

Walmart's approach, known as Sustainability 360, involves incorporating sustainable practices with suppliers, employees, customers and communities. Using a few stores as laboratories to test energy-saving technologies, Walmart has created high-efficiency stores that are 20 percent more energy efficient than its Supercenter stores. It aims to have every new store be 25 to 30 percent more energy efficient than those built in 2005. In a pilot phase in 2007, the company installed solar power in 22 locations in California and Hawaii. Walmart's interim benchmarks include making its existing stores 20 percent more efficient by 2015, its new stores 30 percent more efficient by 2012 and its truck fleet 25 percent more efficient by 2011 and 50 percent more efficient by 2018. From 2005 to 2009 Walmart achieved a 38 percent increase in its US fleet efficiency.[54]

Walmart set a long-term goal of zero waste by 2025 and a mid-term goal of reducing waste by 25 percent by 2008; from February 2008 to January 2009, more than 57 percent of the waste generated by Walmart and Sam's Club stores was redirected from landfills. Working with 60,000 suppliers, Walmart aims to reduce its overall packaging by 5 percent by 2013, a target that will remove 213,000 trucks from the road and save 67 million gallons of diesel fuel per year. Individual suppliers are streamlining their production processes and Walmart is developing new tools such as a packaging scorecard to evaluate suppliers' sustainable practices. For example, by working with one toy manufacturer to reduce packaging on 16 items, Walmart used 230 fewer shipping containers to distribute its products, which saved about 356 barrels of oil and 1,300 trees.[55] Expanding these resource-saving initiatives across its product lines will have far reaching impacts throughout the manufacturing sector.

At the personal level, Walmart's work with Adam Werbach created the Personal Sustainability Project, which encourages each of the 1.3 million Walmart associates to bring sustainability to the individual level. Associates are asked to take a physical, emotional, financial or spiritual step known as a Personal Sustainability Practice (PSP) that makes them happy and supports their communities and the Earth. A PSP Sustains the planet; Makes you happy; Affects the community; is Repeatable; and Takes visible action. These SMART actions may include losing weight, exercising, recycling, biking to work, eating healthy foods or changing light bulbs to CFLs and LEDs. As a voluntary grassroots program, PSP uses the train-the-trainer model, with managers and associates training their peers at their stores. In six months the program spread to over 4,500 Walmarts and Sam's Clubs in the US, and in the first year 500,000 Walmart associates adopted and maintained a PSP.[56] Since the inception of the PSP in 2006, nearly 20,000 associates have quit smoking; collectively, employees have lost more than 184,000 pounds, walked, biked or swum over 1.1 million miles, created over 16,000 Idea Groups that support each other's PSPs and recycled over three million pounds of plastic. In 2008, the PSP program expanded to Brazil, Canada and Japan.[57]

The commendable green strategies implemented by DuPont, Whole Foods Market, Swiss Re, Fireman's Fund, Walmart and other multinational corporations raise questions. What is the impact of large green corporations on local communities? What are the costs and benefits to the vitality of local economies and to the quality of life of residents? How does a Walmart impact initiatives such as the Sierra Business Council, BALLE and FLOW? The localization movement shows the importance community members place on maintaining local economies supported by local merchants. While programs such as Walmart's PSP indicate that because of their scale green corporations are making positive changes in lives and the environment, the larger issues related to their impact on local communities calls for reexamining the balance between global and local economies.

Tax Shifting

One of the most powerful tools for reducing the environmental degradation that often results from commercial activities is tax shifting or restructuring. Taxes are shifted from what we want, such as income and healthy communities, to what we do not want, such as air and water pollution. Lowering income taxes and increasing taxes on activities that damage the environment, such as coal, oil and natural gas extraction, would provide an economic incentive to reduce environmentally destructive actions. Tax shifting has yet to be widely adopted in the US for greening commerce.

European countries have already implemented tax shifting schemes. In Germany, for example, a program started in 1999 shifting taxes from labor to energy has accelerated the country's world leadership in renewable energy production, creating 82,100 jobs in wind energy by 2006, expected to increase by another 60,000 jobs by 2010. Similarly, Sweden has shifted $2 billion from income to ecologically damaging actions primarily through vehicle and fuel taxes, and other countries such as Italy, Spain and the UK are following suit.[58] The UK has implemented a congestion charge for motorists driving into London as a way to reduce pollution and traffic and to encourage the use of public transportation.

In addition to shifting taxes, a shift in subsidies would also change economic incentives. In 2006, a study of US federal energy subsidies showed $74 billion in subsidies, with oil and gas receiving $39 billion, coal $8 billion and nuclear power $9 billion. Shifting these government subsidies, called "perverse" subsidies, toward building efficiency, weatherization measures and renewable energy sources such as solar, wind, geothermal and tidal would generate new jobs and reduce environmental degradation.[59]

Currently the marketplace ignores the ecological costs of producing, for example, gasoline from petroleum or energy from coal-fired power plants. In the case of coal, these costs include medical expenses for miners, habitat destruction, water pollution from mining and acid rain from coal plants. For gasoline the true costs range from military expenditures to secure shipping lanes from the Middle East to health costs from breathing polluted air. An estimate by the International Center for Technology Assessment placed the indirect costs of gasoline at approximately $12 per gallon. In 2006, the Centers for Disease Control and Prevention estimated the indirect costs of smoking cigarettes, including medical treatments and lost worker productivity, at $10.47 a pack.[60]

One way to address the inconsistency between the true costs and what our current economic model considers "externalities" is through an eco-tax, such as a gasoline or carbon tax that encourages a shift away from fossil fuels to renewable sources of energy. Among the innovative alternative programs suggested by Peter Barnes, Robert Costanza, Paul Hawken and David Orr is an Earth Atmospheric Trust, a mechanism for a global cap-and-trade system for all greenhouse gases. As emissions permits are auctioned and greenhouse gases are stabilized, revenues would be deposited into the trust. Fifty percent of the revenues from auctioning the permits would be distributed to all people on Earth through an annual per capita payment ($71 to $285 per year) and the rest would be used to restore the atmosphere, encourage technological and social innovations and manage the trust.[61] The Earth Atmospheric Trust provides an insight into the environmental, social and economic aspects of the new green economy.

Providing Tools and Metrics

Numerous nonprofits and government agencies have stepped up to provide guidance, tool kits, resources and certification programs to help the business community implement sustainable practices. Ceres, a coalition of investors, environmental organizations and public interest groups, developed the Global Reporting Initiative, which has become an international standard used by 1,200 companies to assess their progress in environmental, social and economic performance.[62] Green America (formerly Co-op America), a nonprofit membership organization, has a screening process for businesses to join its National Green Pages Directory. Natural Capitalism Solutions, a nonprofit working to educate government and business leaders on sustainability issues, offers the *Climate Protection Manual for Cities* and the *Climate Protection Manual for Businesses,* two frameworks for implementing climate protection programs.[63] Assessment tools such as Sun Microsystems' OpenEco.org carbon footprint tool and The Climate Group's *The Business Guide to the Low Carbon Economy: California* are designed to meet the demand for methods of reducing environmental impacts. Municipalities have also created green business certification programs. The Bay Area Green Business Program in the San Francisco Bay region developed a framework in 1997 for improving environmental performance, now used by over 1,000 businesses and public agencies in the nine surrounding counties.[64] All these tools are facilitating thriveable practices for greening commerce.

Building New Business Models

Companies operating in the traditional business model, oblivious to their social and environmental responsibilities, continue to focus on maximizing profits and return on investments for their shareholders. Their non-traditional competitors, however, are taking a much broader view that embraces ecological and social concerns as opportunities for economic savings and long-term viability.

New business models are taking root, marked by alliances of nonprofits, for-profits, government and industry. An example is member-owned retail cooperatives such as Canada's Mountain Equipment Co-op, which sells outdoor gear exclusively to its members. Another is the credit union Vancity, which provides financial services with a commitment to corporate social responsibility. To give to communities, enterprises are reinventing the way business is structured. The Tata Group from India has a core value stating, "What comes from the people goes back to the people many times over."[65] As innovators in the business sector implement strategies aligned with natural systems, new jobs and industries will flourish that will regenerate the biosphere while promoting employment opportunities that support social justice. These win-win scenarios are an encouraging sign for the greening of commerce.

TAKING ACTION

➡ Invite colleagues to a brown-bag lunch and discuss green initiatives for your workplace.

➡ Design and implement a sustainability assessment for your workplace.

➡ Review your workplace sustainability policy. If there isn't one, develop one with your colleagues.

➡ Research sustainability organizations that are in alignment with your workplace's mission. Make the case for joining them.

➡ Contact your congressional representative and advocate for tax shifting or take-back policies.

➡ Join a local green business program. If none exists, start one.

➡ Connect with organizations working on responsible consumption and social justice issues.

FOUR

Regenerative Design

*My working assumption is that we are here as local-Universe infor-
mation gatherers. We are given access to the divine design principles
so that from them we can invent objectively the instruments and
tools that qualify us as local-Universe problem solvers in support
of the integrity of an eternally regenerative Universe.*

— BUCKMINSTER FULLER

Green building is not about buildings — it is about people.

— SANDY WIGGINS

THE GREEN WAVE that is changing how we grow food, conduct business and produce and consume energy is also affecting how we design,
build and inhabit buildings and communities. Green building concepts
and design strategies are being used in the retrofitting of existing structures and the construction of new ones at the residential, commercial and
community levels.

The environmental, social and economic impacts of buildings are un-
deniable. Buildings provide cultural and historical links to our traditions.
Since they affect energy consumption, materials, waste and water use,
they also present opportunities for reducing environmental degradation
and enhancing our lives. Urban residents spend an estimated 90 percent
of their day indoors. Green building design can emphasize indoor spaces
that are aesthetically pleasing and healthful and promote human interactions. Green buildings still rely on their occupants to save energy, water
and waste by turning off appliances and office equipment and opening and
closing windows, for example. These actions, multiplied by millions, can
greatly reduce environmental impacts.

Green building designs are expanding the emphasis from the efficiency
of a single building to include the efficiency and synergy of surrounding
buildings. When strategies for energy saving, water conservation and waste

reduction are implemented across a neighborhood, economies of scale can be significant. Greenhouse gas emissions, food consumption and transportation needs are all considered part of our ecological footprint. This holistic approach connects buildings to land use planning, reminding us that people, not buildings, are the focus of the green building movement.

Given the statistics on environmental impact, the arrival of green building is timely. In the United States, buildings account for 72 percent of electricity consumption; 39 percent of primary energy use; 14 percent of potable water use; 30 percent of waste output (including 136 million tons annually of construction and demolition debris); and 38 percent of all carbon dioxide emissions.[2] Globally, buildings use 30 to 40 percent of all energy.[3] These numbers highlight the opportunities for using environmentally friendly architectural designs to create the places where we live and work.

New Design Approaches and Objectives

Conventional building practices are based on cheap energy sources and on materials associated with considerable waste. These practices are giving way to holistic and efficient design strategies. The integrated design approach, for example, incorporates seemingly unrelated aspects of design to achieve high-performance buildings with multiple benefits. In the early phase, the integrated design team may include the owner, architect, electrical and mechanical engineers, lighting designer, interior designer and landscape designer. Their brainstorming sessions or "design charrettes"

Termite Mound Design Lets African High-Rise Go Without Air Conditioning

The Eastgate Development in Harare, Zimbabwe, has been modeled on the design of self-cooling termite mounds, allowing it to function comfortably without conventional air conditioning. The building draws fresh air in from the ground floor, pushes it with fans to the core and then allows fresh air to replace hot, stale air, which rises and exits through exhaust ports on the ceilings of each floor. The building uses less than 10 percent of the energy of a conventional office tower of similar size, saving management $3.5 million annually on air-conditioning costs.[1]

can spark creative solutions to design challenges. Early in the integrated design process, the team articulates project objectives. All stakeholders participate so that project objectives, building materials, systems and assemblies are explored from different perspectives. Architect Sim Van der Ryn points out that "everyone is a designer."[4]

Social ecologist Stephen Kellert builds on the integrated design model with restorative environmental design. The goal of restorative environmental design is to "achieve a more harmonious relationship between people and nature in the built environment [through two basic objectives]: (1) to reduce the adverse effects of modern design and development on natural systems and human health, and (2) to promote more positive contact between people and nature in the built environment."[5] Kellert refers to the latter as positive environmental impact design, or biophilic design.

The first objective is to reduce the environmental impact of architectural design with lower energy, water and materials use; minimum site disturbance; minimum pollution and waste; and enhanced indoor environmental quality. Architect Bill McDonough and chemist Michael Braungart call this "eco-efficiency," or "being less bad" — that is, finding ways to lessen the human impact on the environment through technological solutions and reduced use of natural resources.

The second objective, promoting a positive environmental impact through biophilic design, celebrates our connection and contribution to the natural world. McDonough and Braungart call this "eco-effectiveness," in which design "replenishes, restores and nourishes the rest of the world."[6] For example, buildings can generate more energy than they consume, produce food, support diversity through sustainable landscaping and be aesthetically pleasing. For Kellert, biophilic design includes both organic and vernacular, or place-based, design. Organic design, coined by architect Frank Lloyd Wright, refers to design elements such as natural lighting, ventilation, views and shapes and forms that elicit a connection with the natural world. Vernacular design is what landscape architect Frederick Law Olmsted and biologist René Dubois called "spirit of place."[7] It recognizes the cultural history and the human and environmental characteristics of a place. Restorative environmental design supports the interactions of people, buildings and nature, moving beyond being "less bad" to nourishing the environment and ourselves.

Numerous ecodesigners support the idea of regeneration, which integrates natural and social processes. John T. Lyle, landscape architect,

scholar and founder of the Center for Regenerative Studies, added to restorative environmental design to create regenerative design, which "provides for continuous replacement, through its own functional processes, of
the energy and materials used in its operation. Energy is replaced primarily by incoming solar radiation while materials are replaced by recycling
and reuse." Regenerative design calls for a minimum use of fossil fuels
and nonrenewable resources and embraces a shift "from a simple, highly
mechanized technological base to one of great complexity, rooted in natural processes."[8]

Whole systems designer Bill Reed, a partner with Regenesis, applies
the principles of regeneration to Regenerative Development. He "starts
from a radically different perspective—human environments and activities can and should be engines of positive evolutionary change for all living
systems. The path begins with Place."[9] Regenerative Development en-
hances the quality of ecosystems and human settlements by improving the
ecological, cultural and economic health of a place. Humans must be co-
developers with the evolving natural systems. Rather than merely reducing
ecological degradation, Regenerative Development improves the health of
habitats, the strength of social networks and the depth of a community's
historical roots. This perspective is the essence of thriveability: enhancing
natural systems and supporting flourishing social networks. The approach
recognizes the interdependence of humans and nature and the mutual
benefits of conscious, responsible, codeveloping interactions.

Regenerative strategies are based on understanding a place's unique
patterns: geologic, climatic, migratory, social, economic and historical.
The character of a place is communicated through its stories and cultural
traditions. A human being's character has intellectual, emotional, physical
and spiritual dimensions. The data about a place or person give us bits of
information but the "whole" remains fragmented.

Proponents of Regenerative Development understand that a place encompasses a web of relationships. Ecological relationships include drainage, climate, wildlife and vegetation; social relationships are historical,
ethnic, artistic and cultural; economic relationships include employment
and fiscal health. Rather than treating these as distinct elements, Regenerative Development identifies the threads that link them. It examines the
ecological processes of a given site and its "spirit of place" through conver-
sations with community members. *Who* a place is with its unique characteristics is more significant than *what* a place is. Regenerative Development

discovers the ecological and social history of a place and suggests possibilities for design solutions attractive to the community.[10]

The New Urbanism movement reflects this sense of place. The movement was founded in 1993 by urban designers Peter Calthorpe, Andrés Duany, Elizabeth Plater-Zyberk, Stefanos Polyzoides and Daniel Solomon. The Congress for the New Urbanism fights urban sprawl, environmental degradation and the loss of walkable neighborhoods, wildlands and farmland. It stands instead for compact, pedestrian-friendly, mixed-use neighborhoods with transportation alternatives. As the Charter of the New Urbanism states:

> Neighborhoods should be diverse in use and population; communities should be designed for the pedestrian and transit as well as the car; cities and towns should be shaped by physically defined and universally accessible public spaces and community institutions; urban places should be framed by architecture and landscape design that celebrate local history, climate, ecology, and building practice.[11]

Examples of New Urbanism developments in the US include the towns of Seaside, Haile Plantation and Celebration in Florida and Stapleton in Colorado. In the UK, New Urbanism principles have been advocated by organizations such as The Council for European Urbanism and The Prince's Foundation for the Built Environment. European New Urbanist projects include Alta de Lisboa in Portugal, Jakriborg in Sweden, Heulebrugge in the Netherlands and Fonti de Matilda in Italy.[12]

Complementing New Urbanism's ideas for urban centers, the Principles of Intelligent Urbanism (PIU) are a guide for city planners: balance with nature, balance with tradition, appropriate technology, conviviality, efficiency, human scale, opportunity matrix, regional integration, balanced movement and institutional integrity. The PIU grew from guidelines established by the International Congress of Modern Architecture, using Josep Lluis Sert's work at Harvard University's urban design department.[13] The structure plan for the city of Thimphu, Bhutan, for example, incorporates key PIU principles in its development guidelines. These include protecting the ecosystem of the Thimphu Valley; preserving Thimphu's religious and cultural heritage through its gateways, chortens (shrines) and sacred sites; and establishing an urban corridor for essential transportation links. This comprehensive design approach could change the standard planning process for cities around the world.

The Smart Growth movement focuses on minimizing sprawl by restricting urban growth to city center areas. Smart Growth also supports alternatives to the detached housing model. Rather than communities dependent on automobiles and government-subsidized infrastructures such as highways and electricity, it proposes walkable, bike-friendly communities that include mixed land uses. Regenerative Development, New Urbanism and Smart Growth are redefining the interface of buildings, people and nature. These movements support thriving human interactions while enhancing natural systems.

Design Tools and Frameworks

The emergence of green building tools and frameworks has increased sustainable building practices. One organization transforming the building industry is the US Green Building Council (USGBC), a nonprofit with over 20,000 member organizations. In the last five years its membership has grown nearly 500 percent and by 2009 it had over 28,000 commercial LEED projects (over 7.1 billion square feet) participating in its programs in all 50 states and in 91 countries.[14] It was founded in 1993 by former developer David Gottfried, who sought an alternative to the environmental impacts of conventional building practices. The USGBC's LEED Green Building Rating System has become an industry standard for environmentally friendly buildings.

LEED uses a credit point system to evaluate key elements of a building project such as site selection, water and energy efficiency, materials and indoor environmental quality. Depending on the extent of green building practices used, projects that fulfill the LEED criteria receive a Certified, Silver, Gold or Platinum level designation. LEED has influenced a range of sectors including new and existing commercial buildings, homes, neighborhoods, schools, healthcare facilities, retail stores, commercial interiors and core and shell structures. Numerous city and state governments have also adopted the LEED standard for their public buildings.

The success of LEED in the US has been extended through the World Green Building Council. Over a dozen established and emerging green building councils are participating in Australia, Brazil, Canada, India, New Zealand, Japan and the United Arab Emirates. The wide adoption of the LEED standard reflects the realization by the building industry that sustainable building practices have environmental, social and economic benefits. Green buildings are more economical to operate and provide more healthful, welcoming and productive spaces for their occupants. International acceptance of the LEED standard signals that the ideal time for a flexible, adaptable building standard is when there is a global awareness of the need for economy in building.

Although the success of the LEED standard is transforming the building industry, rather than focusing on the learning process some have focused on "LEED cramming" to obtain certification. They have abandoned the intent of the standard, which is to promote creative design solutions. The LEED rating system is a knowledge base, a point of departure from which to discover ways of designing environmentally friendly and livable buildings. It has revolutionized the marketplace by changing the way we approach design. In addition to LEED, the California-based Build It Green's GreenPoint Rated system provides third-party verification for green building measures for new and existing homes and multifamily construction. Other green building standards include Canada's industry-based Green Globes, Australia's Green Star, the United Kingdom's BREEAM, Hong Kong's BEAM, Italy's Protocollo ITACA and Japan's CASBEE.

To stretch the boundaries of green building practices, in 2006 visionary architect Jason F. McLennan and the Cascadia Region Green Building Chapter of the USGBC introduced the Living Building Challenge. Its goal is "to define the highest measure of sustainability attainable in the built environment based on the best current thinking — recognizing that 'true sustainability' is not yet possible." [15] The performance-based Living Building Challenge has 16 prerequisites for certification.

The challenge has six performance criteria: site design, materials, energy, water, indoor environmental quality and beauty and inspiration. Prerequisites include: 100 percent of energy from renewable sources; 100 percent of water from captured precipitation or re-used water; and 100 percent of wood certified by the Forest Stewardship Council or salvaged. The Living Building Challenge, a program of the International Living Building Institute, has raised the bar for the building industry, and several projects are vying to meet the challenge. Among the first projects to achieve the Living Building Challenge certification are the Tyson Living Learning Center in Eureka, Missouri, and the Omega Center for Sustainable Living in Rhinebeck, New York.

Omega Institute for Holistic Studies

The 6,200-square-foot Omega Center for Sustainable
Living in Rhinebeck, New York, is one of the first carbon-
neutral green buildings to achieve both LEED Platinum and Living Building Challenge certifications. The
building purifies wastewater with a filtration system
known as the Eco-Machine, which relies on the natural
processes of plants, bacteria, algae, snails and fungi.

In the spirit of the Living Building Challenge, architect and founder of
the nonprofit Architecture 2030 Edward Mazria launched the 2030 Challenge to reduce global greenhouse gas emissions. It asks architects and
builders to design new buildings to use 50 percent of the fossil-fuel energy
they would normally consume and to renovate existing buildings to use 50
percent of their normal fossil-fuel energy. The timetable for fossil-fuel energy reduction for new buildings is 60 percent in 2010; 70 percent in 2015;
80 percent in 2020; 90 percent in 2025; and carbon neutral by 2030.[16] The
2030 Challenge has been unanimously accepted by the US Conference of
Mayors and by scores of nonprofits, trade organizations and municipalities.

Recognizing the importance of ecological literacy for the design education community, Mazria created the 2010 Imperative. The plan has two
paths. Path A requires that by 2008 design studios incorporate strategies to
reduce or eliminate the need for fossil fuels, and by 2010 ecological education should be completely incorporated into the design curriculum. Path B
requires the curriculum goals of Path A as well as a carbon-neutral campus

by 2010. This goal would be achieved through sustainable design strategies and renewable energy sources, including onsite renewable power and the purchase of renewable energy credits. Mazria's efforts have brought to the forefront the importance of setting goals with measurable benchmarks.

In addition to the Living Building Challenge, the 2030 Challenge and the 2010 Imperative, the US Environmental Protection Agency and the US Department of Energy's Energy Star program has been a force for encouraging energy conservation. Started in 1992 as a voluntary labeling program for computers and monitors, Energy Star has since expanded to appliances, office equipment, new homes and commercial and industrial buildings. Energy Star helps consumers make wise decisions in choosing energy efficient appliances, which saved consumers an estimated $19 billion in 2008 alone.[17] Energy Star is an example of a government-initiated environmental program that has anticipated the needs of the marketplace and evolved as the marketplace has transformed.

The European Passive House (Passiv Haus) standard is geared to designing very efficient building envelopes to reduce energy consumption. Conceived in 1990 by the University of Lund in Sweden and the German Institute for Housing and the Environment, this voluntary standard is spreading to countries in Europe and to the United States.[18]

Materials evaluation tools and standards help consumers and industry professionals determine the environmental impacts of various products. Product standards include industry-based labels such as the Carpet and Rug Institute's CRI Seal, multisector labels such as Scientific Certification Systems' Environmentally Preferable Product (EPP) and third-party programs such as GreenSeal. Two prominent product standards that incorporate broad perspectives are MBDC's Cradle to Cradle Certification and the Pharos Project. Initiated by Bill McDonough and Michael Braungart's firm McDonough Braungart Design Chemistry, the Cradle to Cradle Certification Program emphasizes environmental chemistry and materials flows management.

The cradle to cradle philosophy is a closed-loop approach where "biological nutrients" (biodegradable materials) and "technical nutrients" (materials that remain in closed-loop manufacturing systems) are fully recycled and reused. The cradle to cradle framework evaluates a product's environmental and human health characteristics, material reutilization, energy production, water quality and social responsibility. Similar to the LEED standard, the Cradle to Cradle Certification recognizes Basic, Silver,

Gold and Platinum levels. It has certified products including office furniture, fabrics, packaging materials and diapers.

The Pharos Framework is an open-source, third-party approach to materials evaluation. The Pharos Lens is a guide for evaluating a material's environmental and social performance. Its three main categories or "wedges" are health/pollution (the material's impact on human health and environmental damage); environment/resources (conservation of natural resources, habitat destruction and waste issues); and social/community (employment, safety and equity issues). The Pharos Label evaluates a product's manufacturing process and use of raw materials, compares it with other products in its class and encapsulates the information on an identifiable ecolabel.[19] The combination of the Pharos Lens and Pharos Label provides the public with a framework for evaluating the impact of materials. The originators of the Pharos Project welcome public participation to augment the scientific data gathered on materials and products. This third-party approach broadens the framework's appeal to consumers while strengthening the evaluation criteria.

The inclusive aspect of the Pharos Framework is expanded in the LENSES (Living Environments in Natural, Social, and Economic Systems) tool, developed by the Institute for the Built Environment. LENSES is a process and metrics tool that examines the built environment through three "lenses": the Foundational Lens, looking at broad sustainability principles such as stewardship, interdependence and social justice; the Built Environment Lens, focusing on 12 elements that interact with buildings such as water use, energy use, education and land use; and the Flows Lens, describing resources that flow in and out of buildings, including people, money, ideas, light, heat and waste. LENSES provides a dynamic way to view buildings within their broader economic, ecological and social context, a "beyond the building" perspective that integrates people and their activities with the built environment.[20]

Building Green Homes, Towns and Cities

New "best practices" illustrate the evolving nature of green building strategies, which are being applied in single buildings, villages and towns and city and national projects. At the residential level, communities are establishing green building and energy efficiency guidelines to help homeowners build new homes or remodel existing ones in environmentally sound ways. Whether it is the LEED for Homes, Energy Star or the Green-

Point Rated system, these guidelines are shifting the mental model from "business as usual" to approaches that consider human health, resource conservation and the interdependence of buildings and their surroundings. Michelle Kaufmann Designs builds modular green homes at a factory and delivers them to selected sites. Projects like this are a more affordable alternative to traditional building practices, particularly in expensive real estate markets.

In the commercial sector, Texas Instruments (TI) faced a challenge in the design and construction of its new semiconductor plant. Desiring to build near its headquarters in Dallas, Texas, TI needed an economical design that would offset the construction costs of building in the US rather than overseas. By enlisting a team of architects and engineers with "outside the box" thinking, TI was able to eliminate an entire floor, drastically reducing construction and operating costs. In addition, new piping, air circulation and passive solar techniques eliminated mechanical systems and improved water and energy efficiency.

As Paul Westbrook, TI's sustainable development manager, notes, "Green building is not necessarily about producing your own power with windmills and solar panels. It's about addressing the consumption side with really creative design and engineering to eliminate waste and reduce energy usage — it's the next industrial revolution." The factory was built for 30 percent less per square foot than a conventional facility and is expected to save more than $4 million per year, including a 20 percent energy reduction, 35 percent water use reduction and 50 percent emissions reduction. The plant was awarded LEED Gold certification, making it the first LEED Gold wafer plant in the world. TI has continued to utilize LEED for new projects. The Phase V building recently added to TI's Baguio City site in the Philippines was awarded LEED Silver certification. It is the first LEED certified project of any type in the Philippines.[21]

According to the Global Ecovillage Network, there are over 400 ecovillages throughout the world, including more than 100 in the US.[22] A pioneering effort in the design of green residential communities is Village Homes, encompassing 225 homes and 20 apartment units on a 70-acre site in Davis, California. Construction began in 1975 and continued through the 1980s. Designed by Judith and Michael Corbett, Village Homes incorporates sustainable design features including passive solar design, swales that naturally control stormwater drainage and open spaces. A study of Village Homes found that residents knew about "forty neighbors compared with seventeen in the standard development and had three or four close friends in the neighborhood, compared with one in the control group."[23]

The design of Village Homes encourages a sense of community. Based on a homeowners' association, Village Homes has a low turnover and a strong resale value for its residences. Other green residential communities are emerging in urban regions from Los Angeles to Cairo and in rural areas throughout the Americas, Europe, Africa, Asia and Oceania. These communities have become desirable because they fill a need for living environments that encourage human interactions and shared resources. Residents are going beyond just "getting by" and embracing the benefits that support a thriving community.

One Planet Living was formed as a collaborative between the Bioregional Development Group, based in the UK, and the World Wildlife Fund. Its purpose is to design and build model thriveable communities in six countries across five continents including Portugal, the UK, the US, China, Australia and South Africa. Its aim is for the communities to be replicable and to demonstrate their ten principles:

One Planet Living Guiding Principles[24]

1. **Zero Carbon:** Our climate is changing because of human-induced build up of CO_2 in the atmosphere.
2. **Zero Waste:** Waste from discarded products and packaging creates disposal problems and squanders valuable resources.
3. **Sustainable Transport:** Travel by car and airplane is contributing to climate change, air and noise pollution, and congestion.
4. **Local and Sustainable Materials:** Destructive resources exploitation (e.g., in construction and manufacturing) increases environmental damage and reduces benefits to [the] local community.
5. **Local and Sustainable Food:** Industrial agriculture produces food of uncertain quality, harms local ecosystems, and may have high transport impacts.
6. **Sustainable Water:** Local supplies of freshwater are often insufficient to meet human needs, due to pollution, disruption of hydrological cycles, and depletion.
7. **Natural Habitats and Wildlife:** Loss of biodiversity [is] due to development in natural areas and over-exploitation of natural resources.
8. **Culture and Heritage:** Local cultural heritage is being lost throughout the world due to globalisation, resulting in loss of local identity and knowledge.

9. **Equity and Fair Trade:** Some in the industrialised world live in relative poverty, while many in the developing world cannot meet their basic needs from what they produce or sell.

10. **Health and Happiness:** Rising wealth and greater health and happiness increasingly diverge, raising questions about the true basis of well-being and contentment.

BedZED

One Planet Living has completed its signature community, the Beddington Zero Energy Development, or BedZED, in the UK. It is now building Mata de Sesimbra near Lisbon, Portugal, and Sonoma Mountain Village in Rohnert Park, California.

Marcus Lyon, BioRegional Development Group

The Beddington Zero Energy Development, or BedZED, a One Planet Living initiative, contains 100 homes as well as community facilities and workspaces. As Britain's first carbon-neutral eco-community, BedZED is a model for green communities in other parts of the world.

Completed in 2002, the Beddington Zero Energy Development community is located in Wallington. It was developed by the Peabody Trust, with Bill Dunster Architects and the BioRegional Development Group. As Britain's first carbon neutral ecocommunity, BedZED's primary objective is to create a net-zero fossil energy development, in essence a carbon-neutral community using 100 percent renewable energy. BedZED comprises 100 homes as well as community facilities and workspaces for 100 people. Some of the residences were designed for sale, some for shared ownership and others as affordable housing units.[25]

Built on reclaimed land, BedZED's passive solar design emphasizes energy conservation, rooftop gardens, natural light, renewable energy through photovoltaic panels and wastewater recycling. The buildings use recycled or reclaimed materials including sustainably harvested wood. They have thick insulation to create a high thermal mass envelope to store heat during the day and release it slowly at night. Space heating for the units absorbs heat from the sun, from occupants and from daily activities including cooking. Power and hot water heating are generated from a small heat and power plant that utilizes tree waste as its energy source.

BedZED's transportation plan encourages walking, bicycling, carpools and public transit. Residents use shared ZEDcars, which have access to numerous charging stations onsite and in the Sutton town center. By 2012 BedZED aims to reduce its fossil fuel consumption by 50 percent and to have up to 40 electric vehicles powered by photovoltaic panels.[26] BedZED taps into community resources that enhance the quality of life for its residents.

Greensburg

The sustainable building plan for the city of Greensburg, Kansas, emerged from catastrophe. On May 4, 2007 a Force 5 tornado ripped a two-mile swath of destruction through the city, leveling 95 percent of its structures and killing 11 people. Recovering from this tragedy, Greensburg established the goal of becoming the first city in the US to set a LEED Platinum level of green construction for all its new city-owned buildings. It hoped to serve as a model sustainable rural community.

Soon after the tornado, Greensburg residents, "blessed with a unique opportunity to create a strong community devoted to family, fostering business, working together for future generations," adopted The Greensburg Sustainable Comprehensive Plan. The planning process involved hundreds of citizen stakeholders, architects, planners and city staff. Community leaders set up a Public Square process involving hearings in four sectors: government, business, education and health and human services. Greensburg GreenTown, a community-owned nonprofit organization, was established to help residents and merchants embrace green practices in the rebuilding of their city of 1,389 residents.

GreenTown offers residents information and materials about green building and green living and technical assistance with green building strategies. Greensburg residents had made clear that they did not want to

The tornado that devastated Greensburg, Kansas, on May 4, 2007 set the stage for residents to rebuild. The town committed to developing a model green community by building all of its city-owned structures at the US Green Building Council's LEED Platinum level. Here is the eastern facade of the 5.4.7 Arts Center, the first LEED Platinum building in Kansas. It boasts three wind turbines, a solar area, geothermal heating and cooling, recycled materials, a green roof, rainwater collection and native landscaping.

rebuild what they had in the past but wanted instead to create a progressive community for the future. Citizens' groups set goals covering community, family, prosperity, environment, affordability, growth, renewal, water, health, energy, wind and the built environment.[27] In 2009, Greensburg GreenTown and the US Green Building Council's Cascadia Region Chapter began a competition whereby teams will design, build and prove the performance of affordable homes that meet all the requirements of the Living Building Challenge.

Växjö

The vision for Greensburg as a model green community has been attained in the city of Växjö, Sweden. Situated in southern Sweden with 80,000 inhabitants, Växjö's environmental actions date back to the 1970s, when the city's lakes fell victim to pollution caused by local industry and unsustainable agricultural practices. Växjö then set out to become one of Europe's greenest cities, its success confirmed by its winning the Sustainable Energy Europe Award in 2007. Currently more than 50 percent of Växjö's energy comes from renewable sources, primarily from a district heating system that uses biomass such as wood waste from the local lumber industry.

Växjö has a target of reducing its per capita carbon emissions by 50 percent by 2010 and 70 percent by 2025, compared to 1993. By 2006 it already had achieved a 30 percent reduction in per capita carbon emissions to 7,125 pounds, far below the US average of about 20 metric tons and the EU average of 10 metric tons per capita. Växjö uses ethanol and biogas vehicles and has improved the efficiency of its taxicabs by using a satellite navigation system that alerts drivers to their nearest pick-up location. This technology has resulted in a 20 percent reduction in total driving distance. Drivers also take an "ecodriving" course to learn energy-efficient driving techniques.[28]

Växjö's success stems from a campaign involving educational and technological solutions. Växjö's mobility office, for example, aims to change residents' attitudes toward transportation options by promoting the financial, health and environmental benefits of using bicycles. Växjö has also introduced energy-saving street lights, bicycle paths, its district heating and cooling technologies and residential biomass boilers. These green measures have reduced energy consumption by 30 percent.

Växjö manages its natural resources with the same diligence as its financial resources, using an ecological accounting system or ecoBudget that tracks environmental factors. Växjö's ecoBudget oversees three areas: consumption and waste, water and nature conservation and transport and energy. The ecoBudget first establishes an environmental budget, then implements measures to achieve its targets and finally monitors its results by balancing the annual environmental account. Växjö's annual economic and ecologic budgets identify key indices that are reviewed twice a year. The accomplishments of the budget targets are illustrated on the account with a smiling, indifferent or sad face.[29] Växjö's approach to sustainability measures and manages environmental, social and economic links. The ecoBudget and other accounting tools are now being adopted by other municipalities throughout the world.

Masdar City in Abu Dhabi aims to become the world's first zero-carbon, zero-waste, car-free city. The Chinese village of Huangbaiyu has been designed as an experimental model green living community. The German suburb of Vauban, outside Freiburg, and Quarry Village near Oakland, California, are experimenting with car-free communities.[30] Green city projects, examples of thriveable communities, are arising on many continents.

Integrating Design and Living Systems

Individuals with commitment and courage are leading the search for new ways of envisioning the built environment. Their vision is based on the natural cycles characteristic of a region's geographic features and on cultural traditions. They seek to leap from merely improving efficiency in construction to reinventing the way we design our communities and our interactions with each other and nature. Focusing on energy, water and materials is akin to resharpening a knife; eventually the blade disappears. Just as a knife is part of a broader tool set, the built environment and our role in it are part of the broader context of living systems.

As we become open to the possibility of using different tools from our set, we can imagine a new paradigm for thriveable communities. The questions, ideas and opinions of participants from diverse backgrounds will help solve complex design issues. Since a sense of ownership is essential for building green communities that last for generations, a process in which stakeholders feel valued is as important as the design itself.

TAKING ACTION

➡ *Educate your friends and colleagues about green building standards and practices.*

➡ *Implement green building programs such as the Living Building Challenge, LEED Green Building Standard, 2010 Imperative and 2030 Challenge in your community.*

➡ *Research and purchase green building materials for home improvement projects.*

➡ *Conduct an energy audit of your home and/or workplace.*

➡ *Join a green building program in your community. If none exists, start one.*

➡ *Develop a recycling or composting program at your home and/or workplace. If you already have one in place, help your friends and colleagues start one.*

➡ *Learn about sustainable landscaping practices and implement a project at your home and/or workplace.*

FIVE

Saving Ecosystems

*If we surrendered to Earth's intelligence we could rise up rooted,
like trees.*

— RAINER MARIA RILKE

*The best life insurance for any species in an ecosystem is to
contribute usefully to sustaining the lives of other species....*

— ELISABET SAHTOURIS

ONE OF THE MOST pressing issues threatening the future of the Earth is
the decline of ecosystems and the loss of the biodiversity that under-
lies the fabric of all life on the planet. Biodiversity provides the "resilience
net" that all species, including humans, depend on to survive and thrive.
At a time of increasing pressures on the environment from overpopulation, development and globalization, conservation programs must evolve
beyond the traditional focus on preservation that led to the creation of the
national parks of the 19th and 20th centuries. We now require solutions
that balance the ecological, social and economic needs of people, many of
whom live at subsistence levels in developing countries.

Ecological decline has reached the point where conservation measures
by developed nations are essential to stem the cycle of destruction. Systems
at risk range from decimated fish stocks and coral reefs to denuded rain-
forests and polluted waterways. The destruction knows no political boundaries, and the international community, prompted by concerned citizens,
must take collective steps to deal with it.

In an increasingly crowded world, conservation efforts must balance
the needs of the poor and the needs of wildlife. Mechanisms that give poor
villagers incentives to protect wildlife are a central strategy for saving ecosystems. At the root of these efforts lies education. In the developed countries, explaining the link between the consumption of products and the
destruction of natural systems also requires public education campaigns.
Ecotourism, fair trade and cooperative initiatives are signs that socially

responsible ventures are entering the business arena. Among the new initiatives are continental conservation programs, locally managed species
protection programs, land trust initiatives and biodiversity offset programs. In addition, legislative tools such as Ecuador's constitution, which
extends the rights of natural systems, are pioneering ways of protecting
biodiversity.

Biologist E. O. Wilson estimates that the Earth is losing about one species every 20 minutes, or almost 30,000 species a year, 1,000 times faster
than normal over the history of the Earth. Scientists have called this the
planet's sixth extinction. The fifth extinction was 65 million years ago when
the dinosaurs were decimated by an asteroid impact near the Yucatan peninsula. While past extinctions had natural causes, humans are causing the
sixth, and over a relatively short period of time. How did we get to this
point? What can we do to stem the tide?

The current extinction began when humans appeared 100,000 years
ago, and the rate of destruction has increased since agricultural practices
began about 10,000 years ago. As paleontologist Niles Eldredge points out,
"Agriculture represents the single most profound ecological change in the
entire 3.5 billion-year history of life."[2] With agriculture, humans were no
longer dependent on a hunter-gatherer existence. By settling, they could
domesticate animals, grow crops and increase in population, eventually
exceeding the natural carrying capacity of the land.

E. O. Wilson uses the acronym HIPPO to explain the causes of the loss

Coastal Trees Become a "Green Wall" Against Tidal Surges in Bangladesh

Relief organizations in Bangladesh, in conjunction with the
government's Tree Plantation Movement, are assisting coastal
villagers in a campaign to plant millions of trees to reduce the
impact of storms and tidal surges. The relief group Caritas
highlights the role of "green walls" in protecting vulnerable
areas from natural calamities. Through this effort, Caritas has
intensified work begun two decades ago under its social forestry
program, which encouraged people to plant trees on fallow land
and high embankments and along roads. To get the "green wall"
program underway, the group recently distributed a quarter-
million tree saplings, mostly in Bandarban.[1]

of biodiversity: habitat loss, invasive species, pollution, population growth and overharvesting of species for consumption. If uncontrolled, these are expected to drive half the Earth's current species either to extinction or to endangered status by the end of this century.[3] These predictions are based on the current rate of devastation, which includes the severe depletion of 12 of 13 fisheries and the impact of invasive species, which account for 42 percent of all threatened and endangered species in the United States.[4] There are efforts throughout the world to restore ecosystems in decline. To succeed, solutions must take into account the economic and social issues that affect ecological problems.

Continental Conservation

Studies have shown that small protected areas lose species over time and are too small for some large mammals that require extensive tracts of land for their survival. Particular plant and animal species also may be over- or under-represented in fragmented areas. In searching to protect the Earth's biodiversity, programs have been created to protect habitats at regional and continental scales.

One innovative large-scale habitat protection program is the Wilderness Society's WildCountry Campaign in Australia. The goals of the Wild-Country Campaign are to protect remaining wilderness areas and restore critical habitats by promoting the connections linking "wildlife, habitat, climate change and people" through five landscape-scale conservation initiatives for the southern and northern sections of the continent.

WildCountry's former national coordinator Virginia Young points out, "The WildCountry vision is unashamedly ambitious. It is to protect and restore not just small patches of country, but entire ecosystems, along with ecological processes that drive and underpin them and involving every element of Australia's biodiversity, in each part of the country. So this is an inspirational vision not just for the next few years, but for the next few centuries and beyond."[5] Young combines a vision of a thriveable national future with concrete, practical steps.

The WildCountry Campaign incorporates historical, biological and cultural solutions based on the characteristics of each region. In the more heavily developed southern region, for example, restoration and habitat integrity are emphasized while in the northern region, with more wilderness areas, ecosystem conservation is the goal. Recognizing the interdependence of ecological, social and economic issues in creating a large-scale initiative,

WildCountry's strategy is to combine science with community support, public awareness and public-private partnerships.

WildCountry's education campaign introduces Australians to the rich biodiversity of their country. For example, while Australia has the world's largest number of endemic animal species, in the last 200 years 61 plant species and 54 animal species have become extinct.[6] To help the public understand the "big picture," the WildCountry team explains, for example, how monsoons in the northern region supply water to Lake Eyre in the south, which attracts breeding birds from all over the continent. WildCountry has also established partnerships with other environmental groups and government agencies to create a comprehensive vision for the region, underscoring the need to establish alliances to ensure support.

Tibet's Zone of Peace program has received less mainstream attention. When His Holiness the Dalai Lama received the Nobel Peace Prize in 1989, he called for a Zone of Peace to support the Tibetan culture and its environment. His vision would transform the Tibetan Plateau into the world's largest national park or biosphere reserve, a demilitarized zone dedicated to promoting sustainable development, peace initiatives and environmental protection. The biosphere reserve would complement UNESCO's existing World Network of Biosphere Reserves, comprising 533 reserves in 107 countries.[7] The Plateau's cultural traditions and its location between China and India could allow it to serve as a model for nonviolence and thriveable development.[8]

The Wildlands Network and the Rewilding Institute, two US-based nonprofits, aim to protect large ecosystems in North America extending from Canada to Mexico. They raise funds from philanthropic foundations and government grants. The Wildlands Network's Spine of the Continent initiative, for example, is an effort of ten conservation organizations to create a wildlife corridor from the Brooks Range in Alaska to the mountains of the Sierra Madre in Mexico. These continental efforts are based on scientific studies of the importance of habitat integrity for wildlife. Human settlements must also be considered since they often compete for the same resources.

Norman Myers introduced the biodiversity hotspots concept in the late 1980s. He emphasized identifying the world's most threatened biodiversity regions to guide environmental organizations in their conservation efforts. Subsequently, Conservation International has established a biodiversity hotspots program. Two criteria qualify a habitat as a biodiversity hotspot:

It must contain at least 1,500 species of endemic vascular plants and have lost at least 70 percent of its original habitat extent. The latest surveys show that by these criteria there are 34 hotspots, including regions of northern Mexico, the southwestern US and South America; the mountains of central Asia and Japan; South Africa; the Mediterranean basin; and Madagascar.

These 34 areas once covered almost 16 percent of the Earth's land surface but now cover only 2.3 percent. In effect, 86 percent of the planet's hotspots have already been destroyed. The 34 hotspots account for at least 150,000 endemic plant species, equivalent to 50 percent of the world's total, and 11,980 endemic terrestrial vertebrate species, or 42 percent of all terrestrial vertebrate species.[9] This raises the question of whether establishment of protected areas, many of which include settlements, is a long-term solution for preserving biodiversity. Structural solutions integrating development policies with strategies that support local habitats may yield longer-lasting benefits for communities and the environment.

A multitude of critically endangered habitats have recently been discovered. In 2006, for example, scientists from Conservation International discovered 52 new species, including 24 fish, 20 coral and 8 shrimp, in the Bird's Head Seascape off Papua in Indonesia. Threatened by fishermen who use dynamite and cyanide, this area holds nearly 600 species of reef-building coral, or 75 percent of the world's known coral.[10] Scientists who are mapping biodiversity hotspots also are challenged by climate change since species may shift their habitat range if their survival is in peril.

The hotspots approach identifies where financial resources can have the greatest impact in protecting species from extinction. The estimated cost to protect one hotspot is $160 million per year, or $5.5 billion per year for all 34 areas. This figure varies because a hotspot in a developed area is more expensive to protect than one in a developing region. Focusing on endemic species-rich areas points to the irreplaceability of the most threatened species. There must be a balance between the need to protect already devastated areas and the need to prevent future ecological decline in areas yet to be developed.

The hotspots initiatives have a list of priorities for global conservation efforts. Other conservation groups have similar programs aimed at preserving critically endangered species around the world. These include the Critical Ecosystem Partnership Fund, the World Wildlife Fund-US Global 200 Ecoregions, Birdlife International's 218 Endemic Bird Areas and the Alliance for Zero Extinction. With limited budgets, these programs must weigh the costs against the benefits associated with biodiversity protection initiatives. They must make the case, for example, that saving the greater bamboo lemur in Madagascar should matter to someone living in New York City.

Species Protection

Numerous organizations are realizing the value of local initiatives driven by individuals with a commitment to support wildlife in their community. One of these groups is the Wildlife Conservation Network (WCN), whose programs invest in individuals who empower their local communities to protect endangered species and their habitats. Cofounded in 2002 by entrepreneur Charles Knowles, WCN identifies promising conservationists around the world and provides them with financial, technical and administrative support in their efforts to protect endangered species.

WCN's team understands that the long-term success of wildlife conservation programs depends on the commitment of local people. To this

end, WCN provides local conservationists with start-up assistance in establishing nonprofit status, writing grants, developing marketing materials and fundraising. These entrepreneurs can focus on their fieldwork. They have demonstrated a willingness to implement strategies that may be difficult or risky for mainstream groups. Local entrepreneurs also adapt to working with limited budgets and their work has a direct impact on their local economy.

Children at Mokolodi Nature Reserve in Botswana, shown here with education resources and a Mokolodi educator, are raising awareness of the importance of predators in healthy ecosystems. Cheetah Conservation Botswana, a partner project of Wildlife Conservation Network, promotes the coexistence of cheetahs and local communities.

One of WCN's partner projects, Cheetah Conservation Botswana, is an example of a successful local involvement for wildlife conservation. Started in 2003, the program aims to preserve Botswana's cheetah population through research, community outreach and education and to promote the coexistence of cheetahs and local communities. Wildlife/human conflicts including cheetah killings due to livestock losses, poaching and shrinking habitat have resulted in a 90 percent drop in their population in the last 100 years to approximately 90,000 cats worldwide. Africa's population of about 10,000 cheetahs are listed as "Vulnerable" in the IUCN's Red List of Threatened Species.[11]

Cheetah Conservation Botswana changes people's perception of predators. Team members also teach local farmers and community leaders more effective farming techniques and help them explore alternative livelihoods such as a Predator Friendly Beef program. The project also works with schools to shift children's attitudes about predators. This program recognizes that humans are an integral part of preserving wildlife populations and that satisfying economic needs creates a "win-win" outcome for both villagers and wildlife.

Protecting the Land

A world away from Botswana, land conservation efforts in the United States are dealing with mounting pressures from developers. Every year the US loses about two million acres to development such as freeways, shopping centers, housing and urban sprawl. Farms, forests, wetlands and open space are destroyed for urban expansion. Land trusts, however, are making an impact through land conservation measures. There are 1,667 private land trusts in the US protecting open space, farms and woodlands in every state. In the last five years, local, state and national land trusts' conservation efforts have increased 54 percent to over 37 million acres, equal to over 16 times the size of Yellowstone National Park.[12] These small, private land trusts are taking the responsibility for permanent management of protected lands.

National land conservation groups such as The Nature Conservancy, Ducks Unlimited, The Conservation Fund and The Trust for Public Land play an important role in preserving land. In addition, hundreds of local and state volunteer groups are taking the lead in preserving lands that embody the character of their region. In 1980 the Marin Agricultural Land Trust (MALT) organized the first US agricultural land trust to protect Marin County ranches north of San Francisco. Landowners sell agricultural conservation easements to MALT, thereby gaining tax relief in exchange for prohibiting any development of their land that would reduce its agricultural value. In this way, ranchers of Marin County and elsewhere have saved their land and their livelihood from developers. Beyond the agricultural sector, land trusts in every state work with conservation groups and local agencies to protect wilderness areas, waterways and other treasured lands. The Land Trust Alliance, established in 1982, provides resources to hundreds of land trusts throughout the US.

Unfortunately, land trusts are missing in developing countries, which contain many of the world's threatened habitats but lack institutions with the financial resources and mechanisms to protect their open spaces.

Conservation Philanthropy

In addition to land trusts, the US has a legacy of individuals who have contributed to the land conservation movement through their philanthropy. Many of the national and state parks, national monuments and wilderness areas in North America were established through the generosity of individuals, families and businesses that have either acquired the land, transferred it to the public or sold conservation easements. Acadia, Grand Teton, Great Smoky Mountains and Virgin Islands National Parks are protected thanks to private philanthropy, and scores of other wildlands are preserved through the vision and commitment of individuals interested in leaving a legacy for future generations.

One of wildlands philanthropy's most celebrated examples is the creation of Baxter State Park in Maine. As governor of Maine from 1921 to 1924, Percival P. Baxter had a dream of establishing a park for all Maine's residents. He made his first purchase of 6,000 acres of land in 1930 and donated it to the state with the agreement that it would remain wild. Over the years Baxter continued purchasing land to add to the park, which today encompasses over 200,000 acres and includes the state's highest peak, Mount Katahdin.

Baxter designated a section of the park to be used as a Scientific Forest Management Area for practicing sustainable forestry. He also left a trust of $7 million to manage the park so that it would not draw from the taxpayers' general fund. To avoid potential conflicts, Baxter established a governing authority comprised of three public officials: the commissioner of Maine Inland Fisheries and Wildlife, the director of Maine State Forest Service and the state attorney general. These individuals are responsible for the park's operation and for maintaining Baxter's intent as described in his deeds of trust. The governing authority is supported by 15 citizens who make up the Baxter State Park Advisory Committee. Baxter's governing structure has ensured the successful management of the park since its inception. His vision for the people of Maine was captured in his own words:

> Man is born to die,
> His works are short-lived.
> Buildings crumble,
> Monuments decay,
> Wealth vanishes.
> But Katahdin in all its glory
> Forever shall remain
> The Mountain of the People of Maine.[13]

Baxter's words and deeds emphasize an intergenerational approach to land conservation. His perspective on the enduring value of Mount Katahdin and Maine's wilderness demonstrates an integrated approach to conservation that supports a thriveable future by connecting the people of Maine to their beloved wilderness areas.

In developing countries, where land conservation is perhaps most urgent, because of cultural perceptions of natural resources, limited history of environmental philanthropic traditions and minimal financial structures and tax incentives the tradition of wildlands philanthropy is not nearly as well established. Nevertheless, recognizing the need to make conservation efforts in the few remaining places with pristine wilderness areas, a handful of land trusts from developed countries are working internationally to preserve wilderness areas under threat of development.

In the United States, the Conservation Land Trust (CLT) has been working for the past 15 years to protect wildlands of Patagonia in southern Chile and Argentina. Founded in 1992 by entrepreneurs and philanthropists Douglas Tompkins and Kris McDivitt Tompkins, CLT aims for "the creation and/or expansion of national or provincial parks to ensure the perpetuity of their ecological and evolutionary processes with the strongest long-term protection guarantee possible…[and] supports programs for the protection of wildlife, reintroduction of locally extinct species, land restoration and programs for local development, normally involved in ecotourism, sustainable farming and environmental education."[14]

CLT has invested $150 million in two dozen properties totaling 2.2 million acres in Chile and Argentina. The demise of sheep ranching in Patagonia and the availability of pristine temperate rainforest created a window of opportunity for protecting a large wilderness area. In a way, the current situation in Patagonia is similar to that of the American west in the 19th century: large wilderness areas that remain relatively undeveloped but are under increasing pressure from developers. CLT has stepped into that crisis.

In Patagonia, CLT has protected lands devastated by fires and overgrazing and threatened by logging. However, the organization's efforts have sparked opposition and suspicion from government factions and economic interests intent on developing natural resources in Chile and Argentina. Similar opposition also was present during the establishment of the national parks in the United States. Over time, however, with understanding of the objectives behind private environmental philanthropy, there has been a gradual acceptance and support of the national parks by local residents. As Douglas Tompkins says, "It is important to understand that this local opposition is normal; it comes attached to the land itself, and in a sense, is part of the process."[15]

One CLT conservation effort that has received international attention is Pumalin Park in southern Chile. It took ten years for CLT to acquire the lands for Pumalin, and in 2005 the Chilean government declared it a national sanctuary, ensuring it added environmental protection. Although Pumalin has acquired sanctuary status, it is still threatened. Transmission lines are proposed that would cut through the wilderness to deliver energy to urban centers from dams south of the park.

Pumalin functions as a national park with public access governed by a private Chilean initiative. The park covers 738,000 acres, about the size of Yosemite National Park. It encompasses ancient conifer forests and alerce trees, fiords teeming with seabirds and sea lions, hiking trails and cabins. It is surrounded by seven agricultural demonstration farms, each in its own watershed with adjacent ranger station. These farms include native tree nurseries for restoration efforts and provide ecotourism activities. The farms support livestock, including sheep for wool and textiles, and produce local fruits such as cherries, plums, gooseberries, blueberries, red currants and raspberries. The farms have organic vegetable gardens and beehives for honey production. These working farms give visitors and residents a glimpse of the possibilities for developing a local economy in balance with its ecosystem.

CLT has sponsored other national park initiatives. Monte León National Park was donated to the Argentine National Parks Administration as the nation's first coastal national park in 2004 and Corcovado National Park was donated to the Chilean Park Service in 2005. Patagonia National Park in Chile is currently in its development phase.[16] CLT's work demonstrates the connection between the local economy and the ecosystem. How do we price natural resources? How would our perspective change if we shifted to a conservation-based economy? More significantly, what is true wealth?

Doug Tompkins, The Conservation Land Trust

Alerce trees, an endangered species that can live more than 3,000 years, are part of The Conservation Land Trust's restoration efforts in southern Chile. Land trusts play a critical role in protecting ecosystems and supporting programs in ecotourism, sustainable farming practices, education and outreach in the US and abroad.

What is Nature Worth?

There are three ways of looking at the value of land. In the first way, natural resources represent the value of what we can take from the land. In the second, real estate represents the value of what we can build on the land. In contrast, in the third way ecosystem services represent the value of what the land gives us if it is protected and restored to health.

Ecosystem services are the processes performed by nature including purifying air and water, building healthy soils, pollinating plants and detoxifying and decomposing wastes. They also include seed dispersal, erosion and pest control, carbon sequestration, flood, drought and storm protection and maintenance of habitats. Biologist Gretchen Daily defines ecosystem services as "the conditions and processes through which natural ecosystems, and the species that make them up, sustain and fulfill human life."[17] Daily makes the connection between nature's services and human well-being. In fact, ecosystem services provide the foundation for our quality of life. We have not valued them in monetary terms because they were so abundant, but this has changed.

These services are fundamental to life on the planet. They provide us with clean water and a stable climate. It is estimated that nine of the top ten medications come from natural plant products. One third of the food consumed by humans comes from plants pollinated by wild pollinators, whose services in the US are estimated at $4 billion to $6 billion every year. The 1993 floods of the Mississippi River were due in part to the destruction of wetlands along the riverbank; losses were estimated at $12 billion. Hurricane Katrina resulted in an estimated $75 billion worth of damage. The coastal impact might have been lessened by maintaining offshore barrier reefs and coastal wetlands to reduce the strength of the storm surge.[18] The Indian Ocean tsunami of 2004 showed that areas in Sri Lanka with healthy coastal mangroves received minimal wave damage, while those without them suffered. Ecosystem services maintain healthy, dynamic and resilient living systems for all species, services provided by the Earth that we are just beginning to value.

Studies by ecological economist Robert Costanza and others show that nature's services are valuable, with estimates in the trillions of dollars, but the United Nations Millennium Ecosystem Assessment team reported in 2005 that 60 percent of the world's ecosystem services are being degraded faster than they are being restored. The destruction of ecosystems is severely affecting the Earth's capacity to provide these essential services.

As the economic benefits of ecosystem services become apparent, policymakers and communities all over the world are implementing strategies to protect the environment so it can provide these services. Financing for conservation, known as Payment for Environmental Services, is gaining acceptance as a model to protect ecosystems. In New York City, for example, when the city's water quality degraded officials weighed the cost of a new water filtration plant against the cost of conserving the watershed of the Catskill Mountains. They chose the latter. The price of a new plant was $6 billion to $8 billion, compared to $660 million to restore the watershed. The city now uses its funds to purchase open space in the watershed, restrict development activities and improve the septic systems of people living in the area.

Similar decisions are being implemented elsewhere. In Seattle, instead of building new levees officials are restoring floodplains to alleviate flooding. Farmers living in Central America near the Panama Canal Zone are being paid to restore their forested lands in order to reduce soil erosion, thus minimizing the need for dredging. The restoration is funded by companies that use the canal for transporting their goods and benefit from fewer delays caused by dredging.

The Natural Capital Project is establishing mechanisms for valuing ecosystem services. Launched in 2006, it is a partnership of Stanford University, The Nature Conservancy and World Wildlife Fund. The group is led by Gretchen Daily, a Stanford biology professor and Woods Institute senior fellow, Peter Kareiva of The Nature Conservancy and Taylor Rickets of World Wildlife Fund. The Natural Capital Project is "developing tools for quantifying the values of natural capital in clear, credible, and practical ways."[19] This link between economic benefits and ecosystem services is of considerable interest to policymakers as they make decisions that affect the environment.

The Natural Capital Project has developed tools such as InVEST, which models and maps ecosystem services and biodiversity. It is compiling a Natural Capital Database to provide the public with information about conservation projects that focus on ecosystem services. Using these tools, the Natural Capital Project is working with partners to incorporate ecosystem service values into demonstration projects around the world. The primary sites include the Eastern Arc Mountains of Tanzania, the Upper Yangtze River Basin, the northern tropical Andes of Colombia and Ecuador, Sumatra, the Sierra Nevada region of California and the Hawaiian Islands. In each of these areas scientists are providing strategies for reframing the value of natural assets and ecosystem services, allowing policymakers to assess the economic value of nature's services; point to cases where policy and finance mechanisms are integrated with natural capital; and make decisions that incorporate the environmental, social and economic dimensions of resources.[20]

Conservation Finance

As tools for valuing natural assets are developed, new payment schemes and environmental markets are emerging. One of these markets came from a group of bankers, environmental activists, forest products representatives, regulators and journalists that first met in 1999 near Katoomba, Australia. From that gathering, and with the assistance of the Washington, DC, nonprofit Forest Trends, came a networking society called the Katoomba Group. One of its first initiatives was the creation of the Ecosystem Marketplace, led by its first editor-in-chief, Adam Davis. The Ecosystem Marketplace organizes information about complex programs that reward conservation. As ecosystem markets in greenhouse gases, wetlands, water pollution and endangered species develop, organizations such as the

Ecosystem Marketplace are providing information on pricing, regulations and scientific research. Such organizations will play a critical role in developing market mechanisms to manage pollutants such as carbon dioxide and sulfur dioxide.

In the United States the sulfur dioxide market began in 1990. It has become the first successful large-scale cap-and-trade scheme to reduce sulfur dioxide pollution and provides a model for market driven mechanisms that might reduce carbon dioxide emissions. These mechanisms are being explored by the Chicago Climate Exchange, the New South Wales Greenhouse Gas Reduction Scheme and Kyoto-related carbon markets. In 2005, the European Union launched the Emissions Trading Scheme as part of its cap-and-trade market to fulfill the Kyoto Protocol requirements. Global carbon markets are expected to grow to $40 billion by 2010 and reach $200 billion in the near future.[21] These growth projections point to the economic potential of markets that support restoring the Earth's ecosystems.

Other markets provide similar benefits. Water markets include US wetland and stream mitigation banks, Australia's Hunter River salinity trading program and Mexico's payment for watershed services program. Biodiversity projects include US conservation banking programs in California, Australia's biodiversity offset programs and Costa Rica's payment for forest services program. All these programs create financial mechanisms for protecting habitats.

In the US, the Clean Water Act and Endangered Species Act of the 1970s made possible more recent wetland mitigation and species banking programs, financial tools aimed at leveraging capital to protect the environment. Developers are required by law to "create, enhance or restore" an amount of land equal to or greater than the amount damaged and in a wetland of "similar function and values" in the same watershed. As a result, through what are known as wetlands banks, private for-profit groups sell "wetland credits" to developers for creating, enhancing and restoring wetlands. There are an estimated 880 permitted or planned wetland banks in the US, a market worth more than $3 billion. Similarly, species bankers are creating, enhancing and restoring habitats for endangered species and selling "species credits" to developers who plan to destroy species habitat. In California, for example, the markets have determined that Delhi Sands fly habitat is worth between $100,000 and $150,000 an acre. There are about 90 species banks in the US trading approximately $350 million worth of species credits every year.[22]

Some of the critics of conservation banking point out that it is the job of government, not of financial markets, to protect species and wetland areas. The quality of the wetlands being created as well as the long-term commitment to manage them have also been questioned. However, putting a price on wetlands, for instance, will likely make developers reconsider the impact of their activities. Because the restored wetlands may have less biodiversity than the area destroyed, developers are required to double or triple the size of the wetlands being mitigated. Early assessments of conservation banks show that with proper performance standards, enforcement and verification mechanisms, they can succeed.

Markets and Nature

The new paradigm puts a value on nature. Critics of ecosystem markets abhor commodifying the natural world and incorporating it into the economic system responsible for its demise. They question the long-term efficacy of market-based solutions and the potential slippery slope of assigning a price to nature. Who makes that determination? What, for example, is the price of beauty? These and other questions raise ethical issues about the sacredness of the natural world and our responsibility for sharing the planet with other species.

Proponents of the market-based approach to conservation point out that nature was commodified long ago by placing a monetary value on natural resources and real estate. In addition, market advocates claim that over the last 20 years conservation banks have provided a higher quality of compensatory mitigation for unavoidable impacts than any other form of regulation, and that conservation banks are important because the alternatives of fines, penalties, fees or prohibition have not worked. Rather than valuing nature once its resources are harvested and its ecosystems are degraded, these new markets value it when it is preserved and restored.

The debate surrounding ecosystem markets highlights the role of business in devising creative solutions. As Gretchen Daily says, "It's economic forces that have taken us to the brink. But we need a force that powerful to bring us away from that brink."[23] Shifting economic forces to protect rather than degrade the environment may be the only way to maintain the integrity of natural systems and, by extension, our well-being.

The rate and magnitude of global habitat loss have prompted innovative approaches to land conservation programs ranging from species protection projects to continental wilderness initiatives and conservation finance schemes. Understanding the benefits of nature's services is essential for gaining support for biodiversity and habitat protection. Recalibrating our economic system so that it more accurately reflects the true costs of resource extraction and natural processes is the beginning of a new approach to ecological economics in which human activities that regenerate natural systems will be rewarded, laying the foundation for a thriveable future.

TAKING ACTION

➡ *Join a local, national or international environmental group. Participate in one of their campaigns.*

➡ *Educate yourself and your friends about your bioregion, including your community's flora and fauna and its sources of energy, water and food.*

➡ *Volunteer with your local parks or open space department in restoration and beautification projects.*

➡ *Write a letter to your local newspaper about an environmental issue facing your community.*

➡ *Make a commitment to spend more time in nature.*

➡ *Identify native species that are endangered or indigenous to your area and protect them.*

➡ *Check if your county has an integrated pest management ordinance to reduce toxics in our waterways.*

SIX

Navigating the Confluence

All progress is precarious, and the solution of one problem brings us face to face with another problem.
— MARTIN LUTHER KING, JR.

How we will manage to uphold a decent society in the face of extraordinary change will depend on our creativity, our generosity, and our kindness, and I am confident that we can find these resources within our own hearts, and collectively in our communities.
— JAMES HOWARD KUNSTLER

As SOCIAL AND ECONOMIC networks around the world become connected, our global challenges are intensifying and their effects are more visible. Five global trends are converging: ecosystem decline, energy transition, population growth, economic disparity and climate change. Their consequences include floods, famines, high oil prices, economic upheavals, deforestation, disease outbreaks and migration from disaster zones. These challenges are interrelated and their solutions require a comprehensive approach.

Understanding the local connections to these challenges can keep us from becoming overwhelmed or apathetic and help us take action in our communities. The desire to effect change presents opportunities for simple actions at the personal and community levels, such as the actions listed at the end of each chapter. Leading by example can raise awareness and inspire change. "Thinking globally, acting locally" gives us a way to deal with these complex global trends.

Innovations are emerging in every corner of the world. Muhammad Yunus, for example, questioned the assumption that providing loans to the poor is unprofitable and unworkable. By reexamining this belief and adjusting loan mechanisms, he changed the context for microloans and his approach is now lifting millions of people out of poverty. Creative thinking, personal commitment, flexible approaches and effective action are now addressing our global challenges.

Ecosystem Decline

The decline of ecosystems involves worldwide degradation of habitats and loss of biodiversity, processes that are eroding our life-support systems. According to the IUCN Red List of Threatened Species, one in four mammals is threatened with extinction. About half the world's tropical forest habitats have been destroyed. A forested area the size of Connecticut is leveled in Indonesia every year, although 80 percent of the timber harvest is illegal. Sumatra has lost half its forest cover in the last 20 years.[2] Worldwide, forest clearing is estimated at 27.2 million hectares (272,000 square kilometers) from 2000 to 2005, representing a 2.36 percent reduction of tropical forests. Three fifths of the clearing took place in Latin America, with Brazil accounting for over 47 percent, and one third in Asia, with Indonesia accounting for over 12 percent.[3] Since most people in cities do not see the destruction, they do not make the connection between purchasing a piece of wood furniture, for example, and destroying a forest.

The world's oceans are similarly in a downward spiral. About half the Earth's fish stocks have already been fished to their limit, 30 percent are overfished and numerous fish stocks have already collapsed. Since 1950, the overfishing of large predatory fish has reduced their population by

Groovy Green Lists 100 Things You Can Do to Prepare for Peak Oil

Two recent issues of Groovy Green contain a listing developed by Sharon Astyk of "The Next One Hundred Things You Can Do To Get Ready For Peak Oil." The list is intended for practical individual action in the face of coming expensive oil, but Astyk adds that it also provides ideas for responses to "whatever else comes down the pike." Subjects under which the action steps are clustered include: home, garden, clothing, family, community and transportation. The peak oil toolkit also recommends many behavioral changes that increase in value when energy is expensive.[1]

90 percent. The reduction of wild fish stocks has led to an increase in fish farms, which already provide 42 percent of the world's seafood supply and are expected to exceed 50 percent in the next decade. Fish farming or "aquaculture" is itself damaging marine ecosystems. Overharvesting of wild fish contributes to depletion as each year 11 million metric tons of herring, sardines and mackerel are turned into food for fish farms. Pollution from manure produced by fish farms is destroying coastal areas. Fish escaped from aquaculture farms spread disease that can devastate wild fish populations.[4] These trends are becoming more pronounced as pressure to feed the world's population mounts.

The destruction of marine and terrestrial species is occurring at such a rapid rate that we remain ignorant of the diversity of species. Scientists have identified two million species, mostly birds and mammals. They identify about 15,000 new species every year. But the estimate for undiscovered species, including fish, fungi, insects and microbes, ranges from 10 to 100 million.[5] Even the low estimate shows the void in our knowledge of life on our planet.

In October 2008, a news release from the Lawrence Berkeley National Laboratory in California announced the discovery of a new species:

> The first ecosystem ever found having only a single biological species has been discovered 2.8 kilometers (1.74 miles) beneath the surface of the earth in the Mponeng gold mine near Johannesburg, South Africa. There the rod-shaped bacterium *Desulforudis audaxviator* exists in complete isolation, total darkness, a lack of oxygen, and 60-degree-Celsius heat (140 degrees Fahrenheit). *D. audaxviator* survives in a habitat where it gets its energy not from the sun but from hydrogen and sulfate produced by the radioactive decay of uranium.[6]

This discovery shows that species can live in some of the most unlikely environments. Thousands of such species that scientists have yet to catalog are in peril. They could provide medical breakthroughs, new materials or solutions to the challenges of tomorrow. As Thomas Friedman says, "Imagine a world with little or no biodiversity — a stainless-steel-and-cement world stripped bare of every plant and animal, every tree and hillside. Not only would such a world be barely livable from a biological point of view — it would be a world we would barely want to live in."[7] The alternative vision has humans as an integral part of Earth's biodiversity. Part of the solution may involve reintroducing nature to urban dwellers, many of whom suffer from what author Richard Louv calls "nature-deficit disorder."

A component of the decline of ecosystems affecting billions of people is the availability of fresh water. Sufficient water is critical for the health of ecosystems, the well-being of communities and economic development. Water usage worldwide has increased sixfold over the last century, a rate twice that of population growth, and water scarcity is a reality in many parts of the world.

- 2.8 billion people, or 40 percent of the world's population, live in areas where there is water scarcity.
- 1.1 billion people (one in six) are without access to clean water.
- 50 percent of people do not have the quality of water that Roman citizens had 2,000 years ago.
- 1.8 million children die every year from waterborne diseases — one every 15 seconds.
- Africans spend 40 billion hours every year collecting and hauling water.
- 5.3 billion people (two thirds of the world's population) will suffer water shortages by 2025.[8]

The technological solutions for safe drinking water and sanitation are available but have not reached those who need them most. The UN Development Programme points out that the water crisis involves issues of poverty, inequality, power sharing and water scarcity. Choices must be made in the allocation of water for drinking, basic sanitation, food production, hydropower, industrial production systems, river transportation and ecosystem health. Worldwide, 10 percent of water is used for household consumption while 70 percent is used for agriculture. The world's current agricultural model requires enormous quantities of water in developed nations. A single hamburger, for example, requires 10,000 liters of water, including the irrigation necessary to grow the corn to feed the cow.[9] Our rate of water consumption is reducing the water tables of major aquifers on all continents.

Initiatives to raise awareness and change water use include the End Water Poverty campaign and Blue Planet Run. The End Water Poverty campaign is a coalition of 75 African and Asian groups calling for: a global action plan for sanitation; targeting 70 percent of the aid for sanitation and water to the lowest-income countries; and protecting, effectively managing and equitably sharing water resources. Over a million people have brought water issues to the attention of policymakers.[10] In India, for example, Hindu leaders have asked their government to improve the water quality of the Ganges River, which receives 89 million liters of raw sewage daily (of which only 13 percent is treated) and threatens Indians with waterborne diseases such as typhoid, polio and jaundice.[11]

Members of the Tanzania Mission to the Poor and Disabled (PADI) pose with residents of the Songea district, Ruvuma, Tanzania. Residents built their new water access point with support from the Blue Planet Run Foundation. These and other initiatives are bringing clean water to a billion people.

Blue Planet Run (BPR) is a global relay race organized by the Blue Planet Run Foundation. The run in 2007 was the first around-the-world relay race to bring support to organizations working for safe drinking water. The foundation aims to increase global awareness of the drinking water crisis and provide safe drinking water to 200 million people by 2027. BPR supports water projects in Africa and Central America and has developed a collaborative Peer Water Exchange (PWX) program in which donors, nonprofits and observers manage and monitor each other's water projects throughout the world. The program can be scaled to meet the needs of grassroots efforts and can send experts to practitioners at all levels.[12] Blue Planet Run and End Water Poverty are leading voices calling for safe and equitable water distribution. Their relatively inexpensive safe water technology can significantly improve the well-being of a village.

Energy Transition

The shift from fossil fuels to renewable energy sources has captured the attention of politicians and the general public. Fuel prices, greenhouse gas emissions and climate change, including severe storms, floods, droughts and fires, have focused attention on energy. The crisis presents an opportunity for the US to become energy independent and to lead the world into the green economy of the 21st century.

The term "peak oil" describes the point when the maximum amount of oil has been extracted and production begins to diminish. The world's oil production will decline and its price will rise as demand for the limited supply increases. In 1956 geoscientist M. King Hubbert first predicted that the lower 48 states of the US would reach peak oil sometime between 1965 and 1970. In fact, the peak occurred between 1970 and 1971. The timing of the global peak is uncertain, but the end of "cheap oil" is upon us. Now we must prepare for a post-petroleum age.

Fossil fuels such as oil, coal and natural gas currently provide more than 85 percent of all the energy consumed in the US, including two thirds of the electricity and almost all the transportation fuels. The US imports more than 60 percent of its oil from foreign sources including Canada, Mexico, Saudi Arabia, Venezuela, Nigeria, Angola, Iraq and Algeria. Oil provides 40 percent of the total energy and coal more than half the electricity in the US.[13] With "clean coal" technology, harmful greenhouse gas emissions would be captured and stored underground. Recent calls for clean coal have revived the debate about coal-fired power plants but the technology is in its infancy, with uncertain results. The nuclear accidents at Three Mile Island and Chernobyl, construction costs, nuclear weapons proliferation and issues of safe storage of nuclear waste limit the public's enthusiasm for nuclear power schemes.

There is now a trend toward renewable sources of energy such as wind, solar, geothermal and biomass. The transition to renewables will involve creating clean technologies. Although renewable energy (excluding hydropower) is a small part of our energy supply, new renewable electricity installations in the US and the world tripled between 2000 and 2008. In 2008, renewable energy made up over 43 percent of all new grid-connected installations in the US. Installed wind energy capacity in the US, for example, increased by almost ten times between 2000 and 2008 (worldwide the increase was almost seven times). While Germany leads the world in cumulative solar PV installed capacity, the US has surpassed Germany in wind and leads the world in geothermal, biomass and CSP (concentrating solar power) installations; in the latter, mirrors are used to concentrate sunlight, collect solar energy and convert it to heat and electricity. Globally, renewables (excluding hydropower) account for 2.5 percent of the energy generated.[14] No single technology is likely to solve all the world's energy problems. Creative design and implementation of various technologies and storage for alternative energies will expand their use worldwide.

Conservation is the obvious and essential first step. It is economical and often overlooked. We are already reducing energy consumption by retrofitting existing structures, building efficient homes and commercial buildings and using insulation, energy-efficient lights, daylighting features, solar thermal and electric systems and Energy Star appliances. We now have cars and trucks with lightweight bodies, hybrid plug-ins, fuel cell and electric vehicles, alternative fuels and higher fuel efficiency standards. These are the first steps in weaning the US from its oil addiction. The cofounder of the Rocky Mountain Institute, Amory Lovins, points out, "More efficient use of oil in buildings and industry, and substituting saved natural gas and advanced biofuels, could together eliminate US oil use by the 2040s, revitalize the economy, and stop 26 percent of carbon dioxide emissions."[15] Energy use is finally on the front pages. Legislation that supports clean technologies and increased mileage standards is being enacted at the federal, state and local levels.

Awareness programs that target simple behavioral changes such as reducing thermostat settings, turning off lights and using power strips contribute to energy conservation. Over the last 35 years, for example, California's energy efficiency programs have become a world model as the state has reduced its per capita energy use to 40 percent below the national average while remaining, by some estimates, the eighth largest economy in the world.

National initiatives have outlined a path for shifting the US from fossil fuels to 100 percent renewable energy sources and achieving energy independence within ten years. Such programs include the T. Boone Pickens Plan, the Apollo Challenge and Al Gore's Generational Challenge to Repower America. The Concerto Initiative, launched by the European Commission, is a continent-wide program to promote renewable energy sources and energy efficiency. Currently about five million Europeans in 45 communities benefit from energy projects including biomass boilers, wind power, solar heating and cooling, heat pumps and district energy systems.[16] The cities of Delft, in the Netherlands, Grenoble, France, and Växjö, Sweden, have joined the SESAC (Sustainable Energy Systems in Advanced Cities) project as part of the Concerto Initiative. Such energy plans develop alliances of individuals and groups committed to energy independence.

At the municipal level, Portland, Santa Barbara, Seattle, Chicago and New York have created targets and strategies for conservation and the use of renewable energy. At the regional level, the New England Energy Alliance, a coalition of energy providers, businesses and trade organizations, is promoting strategies to ensure reliable energy supplies. The health and economic impacts of fossil fuels and climate change are on the minds of leaders and citizens everywhere.

Population Growth

Governments in all countries are facing the challenge of maintaining or improving standards of living without degrading the environment. People in developed countries are consuming resources faster than they can be replaced, while those in developing countries, where the population is growing the fastest, want to improve their standard of living.

The scarcity of natural resources threatens the environment in developing countries. Their increasing population puts added demands on necessities such as firewood, water and agricultural land. In India, for example, the threat to the Bengal tiger has been linked in part to the decline of its habitat from population pressures such as farming, logging, hunting and cattle grazing as communities encroach on protected areas.[17] Similar population pressures threaten wildlife reserves in Africa and South America.

Developed countries consume resources and produce waste at 32 times the rate of developing countries.[18] There are a billion people living in the developed world, including the US, Canada, Europe, Australia and Japan, versus 5.5 billion people in the rest of the world. The impact on the environment is best described by the equation $I = P \times A \times T$, where I stands for environmental impact, P for population size, growth and distribution, A for affluence or consumption per capita and T for level of technology. This equation emphasizes the importance of stabilizing the world's population, as the United Nations and others have recommended, in order to reduce environmental degradation.

In the US, the Numbers USA Education and Research Foundation has shown that development driven by population growth is responsible for more than half the loss of rural lands, about two million acres a year. The Weeden Foundation focuses on the impact of growing human populations on the environment. Don and Norm Weeden point out that "both sprawl and growing energy consumption are directly attributable to our rapidly growing population."[19] Environmental researcher Leon Kolankiewicz found that between 1970 and 2000 87 percent of the growth in US energy consumption and associated carbon emissions was due to population growth; only 13 percent was linked to an increase in per capita energy use. Between 2000 and 2040, greenhouse gas emissions in the US are expected to increase by 30 percent, largely because of population growth.[20]

Currently 79 million people are added to the world every year. Global population now stands at 6.8 billion and is expected to increase to 9.1 billion by 2050. Between 1987 and 1999 world population grew from five billion to six billion, an increase equal to the population of India or the combined populations of North America and Europe.[21] The US population, which reached 300 million in 2006, is expected to reach 403 million by 2050; 82 percent of this increase will come from new immigrants and their US-born descendants.[22] One encouraging population trend is the reduction in average family size, known by demographers as the total fertility rate. The average family size worldwide was 5.3 in 1950 and has dropped to about 2.7 today. It is expected to come down to 2.1 by 2050. However, the drop in average family size is countered somewhat by higher life expectancies.[23]

There are three main reasons for the increase in world population: birth rates, death rates and demographic momentum. Birth rates, particularly in developing countries, remain above replacement levels. In more than 35 developing countries, women have an average of five children each. Secondly, death rates in developing countries are declining as better health services increase life expectancy. Finally, demographic momentum is the current increase in the number of women in their reproductive years in developing countries, which in turn is the result of decades of high fertility. Thus, even if there were now replacement-level fertility (two children replacing two parents), decades of population growth have already increased the numbers of parents, as in the baby boom in the West.[24] Demographic momentum will be responsible for 49 percent of the projected population increase in developing countries, followed by unwanted pregnancies at 33 percent and family size at 18 percent.[25]

From the 1960s through the 1980s, family planning programs in developing countries have been responsible for at least 40 percent of the fertility decline. In 1970, for example, when the Thai government launched its initiative to slow population growth, it enlisted a team to distribute contraceptives throughout the country. By the late 1980s the average family size had dropped from about seven children to fewer than two, a rate below the replacement level. This program is estimated to have prevented 16 million births between 1972 and 2010, saved $11 billion in social service costs and returned $16 for every dollar invested. The 1997 Family PACT (Planning, Access, Care and Treatment) program geared to low-income women in California averted an estimated 205,000 unintended pregnancies and saved $2 billion over five years.[26] If replicated elsewhere, such voluntary family planning programs can have a substantial effect on reducing world population growth and associated environmental impacts.

Economic Disparity

Globalization has brought to light our interdependence in the world economy and the economic gap between affluent and poor countries. Although the world's economic output increased by a factor of 18 from 1900 to 2000, a fivefold increase per person, there remains a vast inequality in income distribution, with 2.5 billion people, 40 percent of the world's population, living on $2 a day or less. One out of every eight people worldwide was chronically hungry between 2001 and 2003, one in five lacked access to clean water and two in five lacked adequate sanitation.[27] Every day more than 20,000 people die from poverty, including 8,000 children dying of malaria, 5,000 adults dying of tuberculosis, 7,500 dying of AIDS, and thousands dying of diarrhea, respiratory infections and other diseases.[28] According to United Nations studies, the wealth of the top 1 percent of the world's population is equal to 40 percent of the world's net worth. The richest 10 percent own 85 percent of global assets and their holdings are increasing.[29] Thomas Homer-Dixon points out that in 1950 there were two poor people for every rich person; currently that ratio is four to one and in 2025, when the world's population is expected to reach eight billion, there will be six poor people for every rich person.[30]

This economic disparity prompts the poor to leave their homes and seek opportunities in developed countries. Our interconnected world gives the poor easy access to images of wealthy Western lifestyles through the Internet, television and print media. Thousands make the trek from Africa to Europe, from Latin America to the United States and from Southeast Asia to Australia in search of a better life for themselves and their families back home.[31] The impact of migration into developed countries is yet to be determined. Migrants provide manual labor in such areas as agriculture, construction, cleaning and food service, yet remain in the shadows as undocumented workers fearful of deportation. Their frustration became apparent in 2005 as riots broke out in poor neighborhoods in France and in 2006 tens of thousands of migrants in the US marched in cities across the country as lawmakers considered an immigration reform bill that was never passed.

Among the many initiatives seeking to change the poverty dynamics are Kiva, MicroPlace and Green for All. Some are based on the concept of microfinance, which received wide attention when Muhammad Yunus won the Nobel Prize for providing small loans to the poor through Grameen Bank. Founded in 2005 by Matt and Jessica Flannery, Kiva allows individuals to make small credit card donations online to those in need. As Forbes. com points out, "Kiva mixes the entrepreneurial daring of Google with the do-gooder ethos of Bono, lead singer of the rock band U2 [and has] managed to merge two recent socioeconomic trends — social networking and microfinance." Kiva has attracted 270,000 lenders, who have provided about $27 million in loans to 40,000 people in developing countries.[32]

The impetus for MicroPlace came from social entrepreneur Tracey Petengill who, while living in Dhaka, Bangladesh, realized the benefit of using microfinance to alleviate poverty. Launched in 2007 with the support of eBay, MicroPlace allows ordinary investors to provide loans of as little as $20 to empower the working poor to start a business, earn an income and lift themselves out of poverty. MicroPlace's investments have generated 20,000 loans to 100,000 people in dozens of countries.

Green For All was founded by Van Jones, former White House Special Advisor for Green Jobs, Enterprise and Innovation and author of *The Green Collar Economy*. Green For All seeks to build "an inclusive green economy strong enough to lift people out of poverty." To that end, it provides training and resources for green collar jobs in renewable energy, green building, green business and sustainable agriculture.

In the vanguard of green collar job training is Solar Richmond of Richmond, California (ranked in 2008 as the ninth most dangerous city in the US and the second most dangerous in California). Michele McGeoy and her team teach Richmond residents to install solar systems with the goals of creating 100 new solar jobs, delivering 50 solar installations for low-income homeowners and achieving five megawatts of solar energy in Richmond by 2010. Solar Richmond trains workers in the job skills that could lead them out of poverty. Programs that create green jobs highlight the connection between living wage jobs and climate change.

Community development banks provide financial assistance to small business owners, entrepreneurs and residents from low- and moderate-income communities. These banks include OneCalifornia Bank and its

Mindee Jeffery, Solar Richmond

Members of Solar Richmond's green jobs training program install a photovoltaic system in Richmond, California. Solar Richmond joins local city government and green businesses in creating green-collar jobs for inner-city residents. Such programs provide the skillsets for the green economy.

supporting nonprofit organization, the OneCalifornia Foundation, Grameen Bank and its sister Grameen Foundation, New Resource Bank and e3bank.

Climate Change

In 2006, Al Gore's documentary film *An Inconvenient Truth* elevated the urgency of the climate change issue and spread awareness of it to a global level. Although a minority of skeptics still doubts the cause and severity of climate change, the debate has largely shifted to how to identify and implement effective policies and strategies for curbing greenhouse gases. These heat-trapping gases, including carbon dioxide, methane and sulfur dioxide, are the result of emissions from our industrial processes, agriculture and deforestation. Events such as storms, floods, droughts, forest fires, melting icecaps and glaciers, sea-level rise and pest infestations indicate that the Earth's atmospheric temperature is rising at an alarming rate.

Before the start of the Industrial Revolution in the 1750s, the level of carbon dioxide, the main greenhouse gas, had been 280 parts per million (ppm) for the previous 10,000 years. After 1750, and especially in the last several decades, CO_2 levels have increased. They are now at 387 ppm and continue to grow at an average of 2 ppm every year.[33] Scientists are urging that to avoid the effects of climate change CO_2 levels must be reduced to 350 ppm. NASA's chief climatologist James Hansen stated in 2008 that "if humanity wishes to preserve a planet similar to that on which civilization developed and to which life on Earth is adapted, paleoclimate evidence and ongoing climate change suggest that CO_2 will need to be reduced from its current 385 ppm to at most 350 ppm."[34] The time left to reverse the climate crisis is limited. Nobel Prize winner Rajendra Pachauri says, "If there's no action before 2012, that's too late. What we do in the next two to three years will determine our future. This is the defining moment."[35]

Although some steps to curb greenhouse gas emissions have been taken, the severity of the climate crisis calls for a renewed commitment from the entire international community. In 2005 the Kyoto Protocol set binding targets for the reduction of greenhouse gas emissions for 37 industrialized countries and the European Community. The US did not sign the accord. These targets amounted to a five percent reduction below the 1990 level of greenhouse gas emissions for the period 2008–2012.[36] A subsequent conference in Bali, Indonesia, designed the Bali Roadmap for future negotiations. These will culminate in December 2009 in the Copenhagen Protocol to limit CO_2 emissions. More than any other international gathering, the Copenhagen conference may stand as the pivotal point in the international community's commitment — or lack thereof — to solving the climate crisis.[37]

Through 2008, these agreements have not included the United States, China and India, all key contributors to greenhouse gas emissions. With China building an average of one new coal power plant every other week, India rapidly industrializing and the US being the largest per capita greenhouse-gas-emitting nation, any climate change solution must include them. In a note of optimism, the Obama administration has expressed its commitment to leadership on climate change issues. The US House of Representatives voted to pass the American Clean Energy and Security Act of 2009, reducing greenhouse gas emissions by putting a price on carbon.[38] Furthermore, in 2009 the US Environmental Protection Agency declared that CO_2 and five other greenhouse gases are pollutants that threaten public health.

Programs created by government, business, communities and individuals are starting to flourish. As discussed earlier, states led by California have introduced legislation to curb greenhouse gas emissions and work toward energy independence. New programs include the Carbon Mitigation Initiative (CMI), the US Climate Action Partnership and projects from the Post Carbon Institute. In 2006, Robert Socolow and Stephen Pacala devised the CMI to reduce carbon emissions by one billion tons a year by 2054. Their systemic approach shows how the complex climate change issue can be addressed by remediating each of its components.

CMI, a partnership of Princeton University, British Petroleum and the Ford Motor Company, breaks down the climate challenge into seven "stabilization wedges" to build a "stabilization triangle" that would avoid the doubling of carbon emissions, keeping them flat for the next 50 years. CMI identifies 15 strategies currently available that if implemented on a wide scale could reduce global emissions by one billion tons a year — equal to one "wedge." The strategies target efficiency, fuel switching, carbon capture and storage, nuclear, wind, solar, biomass fuels and natural sinks:[39]

Efficiency

1. Double fuel efficiency of 2 billion cars from 30 to 60 mpg.
2. Decrease the number of car miles traveled by half.
3. Use best efficiency practices in all residential and commercial buildings.
4. Produce current coal-based electricity with twice today's efficiency.

Fuel Switching

5. Replace 1,400 coal electric plants with natural gas-powered facilities.

Carbon Capture and Storage

6. Capture AND store emissions from 800 coal electric plants.
7. Produce hydrogen from coal at six times today's rate AND store the captured CO_2.
8. Capture carbon from 180 coal-to-synfuels plants AND store the CO_2.

Nuclear

9. Add double the current global nuclear capacity to replace coal-based electricity.

Wind

10. Increase wind electricity capacity by 50 times relative to today, for a total of 2 million large windmills.

Solar

11. Install 700 times the current capacity of solar electricity.
12. Use 40,000 square kilometers of solar panels (or 4 million windmills) to produce hydrogen for fuel cell cars.

Biomass Fuels

13. Increase ethanol production 50 times by creating biomass plantations with area equal to one-sixth of world cropland.

Natural Sinks

14. Eliminate tropical deforestation AND double the current rate of new forest planting.
15. Adopt conservation tillage in all agricultural soils worldwide.

The US Climate Action Partnership grew from an alliance of for-profit and nonprofit organizations calling for legislation to "slow, stop and reverse the growth of greenhouse gas (GHG) emissions over the shortest period of time reasonably achievable." This group includes Alcoa, DuPont, Caterpillar, General Electric, Natural Resources Defense Council, Pew Center on Global Climate Change, Environmental Defense Fund and World Resources Institute. The partnership has called for action from US elected officials. Among their recommendations are enacting prompt climate change legislation; implementing a cap-and-trade program that limits greenhouse gas emissions and establishing short- and mid-term greenhouse gas emissions targets.

At the local level, the Post Carbon Institute helps communities make the transition from fossil fuels to renewable energy sources and adapt to climate change. Established in 2003 by the Meta Foundation, the Post Carbon Institute provides resources for governments and residents interested in "relocalization"; in strengthening the local economy by promoting local businesses; in food production; and in energy security. Their tools include the Oil Depletion Protocol for reducing oil consumption and their *Post Carbon Cities* guidebook, which gives communities strategies for breaking dependence on fossil fuels, stabilizing greenhouse gases and building a green economy. Several cities, counties and states in the US, Europe and Australia have taken action to reduce their oil dependence and their greenhouse gas emissions. Oakland, California, for example, completed its *Oil Independent Oakland Action Plan* in 2008. Its primary recommendation focused on alternatives in the transportation sector, where 97 percent of Oakland's oil is consumed.[40]

A Confluence of Possibilities

The convergence of these five trends — ecosystem decline, energy transition, population growth, economic disparity and climate change — presents challenges and opportunities for change. The challenges call for holistic solutions that take into account how these global problems are connected. We must understand for example, the linkages between loss of biodiversity and climate change or between poverty and the scarcity of food and potable water. We then must secure the human and financial capital to make enduring changes.

For individuals, there are many opportunities for change. Whether it is protecting local open space, creating a training program for green jobs or starting a community garden, individual initiatives support resilience in our communities. Action is rooted in the identification of achievable objectives. Then the complexity of global issues can be tackled at the personal level where we each can make the biggest difference.

TAKING ACTION

➡ Start a walking, biking or carpool program at your local school, college or workplace.

➡ Create a sustainability film series and discussion/action group through your local public library or with a nonprofit/green business.

➡ Invite neighbors to community projects such as creek restoration, vegetable gardening or a solar expo. Follow the work party with a potluck event.

➡ Design a website, blog or wiki that highlights sustainability events or projects in your community and welcomes public input.

➡ Create an ecological art space or program that celebrates our connection to the natural world.

➡ Start a study or action group on a global issue such as climate change, energy or biodiversity. Develop initiatives in your community.

➡ Support a microfinance program and share the benefits with your friends and colleagues.

SEVEN

Catalysts for Change

For it matters not how small the beginning may seem to be: what is once well done is done forever.

— Henry David Thoreau

Another world is not only possible, she is on her way. On a quiet day, I can hear her breathing.

— Arundhati Roy

Malcolm Gladwell's bestseller *The Tipping Point* describes three factors influencing social transformation: change is contagious; numerous little causes can have big effects; and change happens not slowly but in one dramatic moment. Gladwell defines the tipping point as "one dramatic moment in an epidemic when everything can change all at once...the moment of critical mass, the threshold, the boiling point."[2] In our fast-paced society, the building, education and agricultural sectors are spearheading the transformation, embracing tipping points driven by factors such as energy transition and climate change. These industries are the forerunners of other sectors that will either adapt or flounder as changes take root.

People have their own tipping points when they become motivated to act on behalf of causes greater than themselves. They may be spurred by a movie such as *An Inconvenient Truth,* which awakened millions of people to global warming and resulted in initiatives throughout the world, or by an inspiring book. Paul Hawken's *The Ecology of Commerce,* for example, inspired Interface's CEO Ray Anderson to begin greening his multinational carpet company, showing other business leaders how to shift toward sustainable practices. Environmental activist John Francis spent 17 years in silence and 20 years walking across America in support of the environment, as recounted in his book, *Planetwalker: How to Change Your World*

One Step at a Time. Such personal pilgrimages inspire us to act upon our deeply held values.

Hundreds of thousands of individuals have been working for decades on issues such as biodiversity, social justice, health, fair trade, employment, energy, agriculture and education. Now green is "in." Its infectious quality has spread its appeal, and an Internet search for the term "sustainability" now yields millions of results. Mainstream magazines and newspapers carry stories on renewable energy, climate change, hybrid and electric cars, green building, sustainable farming, biodiversity and green jobs, showing that we are rapidly approaching a tipping point, transforming interest into concrete actions for change.

The debate over the causes and implications of climate change has lasted for decades. As evidence of the human impact on climate change became indisputable, public discourse changed to finding solutions. The 2005 hurricane season, with Hurricane Katrina's devastation of New Orleans, and the 2006 debut of *An Inconvenient Truth* were catalysts for increased global awareness of climate change. Subsequent efforts, such as those by the We Campaign, 350.org and 1Sky, are coalescing into a powerful voice for action.

The case for green buildings (discussed in Chapter 4) is gaining wide acceptance because of their proven benefits such as reduced operating costs, health benefits for occupants and lower resource consumption. The green building "epidemic" is led by architects, planners, builders, students, homeowners, business leaders and administrators who recognize the benefits of green design. These individuals and their organizations are having

---

Winery's "One Bottle One Tree" Campaign
Plants One Tree Every 12 Seconds

The Trinity Oaks Vineyard in St. Helena, California, has kicked off a "One Bottle One Tree" campaign: one tree planted for every bottle of wine it sells during the next year. Collaborating with Trees for the Future, a nonprofit group that specializes in sustainable agroforestry, Trinity Oaks Vineyards will help restore tree cover to tropical landscapes throughout Africa, Latin America and Asia. Since the program began in July 2008, a tree has been planted about every 12 seconds.[1]

an impact on manufacturers as well as on local and state governments, which are increasingly incorporating green building ordinances and standards into their building codes.[3] The high cost of energy and the adoption of green building standards such as LEED and GreenPoint Rated at the municipal and state levels are leading to wider acceptance of building green. Because we have a tangible connection to the places where we live and work, we can relate more personally to green building practices than to the more abstract concept of climate change.

Greening Campuses

K-12 and higher education institutions are greening their campuses. Organizations such as the Center for Ecoliteracy, Green Schools Alliance, the Cloud Institute for Sustainability Education and Teens Turning Green are integrating sustainability education into the curriculum and operations of public and independent pre-kindergarten to grade 12 schools. Secondary schools are bringing national awareness and action to sustainability issues through peer-to-peer education and outreach programs. These programs include Teens for Safe Cosmetics, Teens Turning Green and Teens for Healthy Schools.

Colleges are offering sustainability courses, creating student "green" teams, retrofitting structures and building new high-performance facilities. This quiet revolution is well-established on college campuses and is seeding these ideas into the mainstream. Organizations such as the Association for the Advancement of Sustainability in Higher Education (AASHE) and Second Nature as well as student activists are leading the way and are influencing environmental policies well beyond their campuses.

With 18 million students enrolled in 4,000 American colleges and universities, the potential impact of higher education on thriveable practices is significant. A 2008 survey of 1,068 institutions by the National Wildlife Federation found an increase in the number of schools setting reduction targets for greenhouse gas emissions.[4] Furthermore, 660 higher education institutions are signatories to the American College & University Presidents' Climate Commitment, which establishes a process for reducing these emissions.[5] Water and energy conservation and efficiency programs are most often included. One third of the schools use off-campus renewable energy sources to meet part of their electrical, heating and cooling needs, and over 36 percent plan to generate renewable energy on their campuses.[6] Other areas for improvement include reducing the pollution and costs of commuting by students and staff and providing courses in sustainability-related fields.

One sign of the interest in greening college and university campuses is the rise in the number of sustainability coordinators, whose job involves monitoring sustainable initiatives and developing strategies for greening their institutions. AASHE, which promotes sustainability in US and Canadian colleges and universities, began in 2006 with 35 members and currently has over 600. In 2006 its first biennial national conference attracted 650 students, faculty, staff, administrators and vendors interested in the growing trend of greening campuses. By 2008 attendance had grown to over 1,700.

AASHE's standardized campus self-evaluation tool, called STARS (Sustainability Tracking, Assessment & Rating System), is providing numerous institutions with a framework for evaluating their sustainable practices. Under the guidance of Geoff Chase and Peggy Barlett, AASHE has provided sustainability education workshops throughout the US to help educators incorporate ecoliteracy in their courses. The demand for these types of workshops is increasing as campuses seek to meet the interest of students and faculty in sustainability.

The movement to green university campuses is being driven to a large extent by students. National initiatives include Recyclemania, which challenges students to reduce and recycle their waste, and Chill Out, whereby students compete for grant money by submitting projects that confront global warming. Numerous dorm energy competitions, in which students compete to reduce energy consumption, are raising awareness about resource conservation while bringing savings to their institutions. When students take ownership of their environmental impact and of their power to influence campus policies, positive changes can ripple beyond the campus community.

Initiatives such as Climate Challenge, Focus the Nation and the Energy Action Coalition are bringing youth's concerns about the climate crisis to the national stage. The Step It Up event in April 2007 attracted 1,400 demonstrations from all 50 states. Participants called for a national day of climate action and a reduction of greenhouse gases by 80 percent by 2050. In November 2007 thousands of students converged on Washington, DC, for Power Shift, a national youth summit on climate change. In January 2008 the Focus the Nation national teach-in on climate change brought together nearly a million people at 1,900 events throughout the US. Sub-

The commitment of youth to bring attention to the climate
crisis is expanding from college campuses to cities. Members
of 350.org took part in the Power Shift '09 event in which
12,000 young people called on political leaders in Washington, DC, to take action on global warming.

sequent events have sent a message to government leaders to take action
on the climate issue.[7] Power Shift '09 attracted 12,000 young activists to
Washington, DC, from across the US and a dozen countries demanding
action on climate change and clean energy. The group 350.org organized
a worldwide awareness campaign in October 2009, with over 5,200 events
in 181 countries, calling for a reduction of carbon dioxide below 350 parts
per million. These grassroots groups, strengthened by the Internet, have
formed a coalition of American and Canadian universities committed to
engaging students and their communities in finding solutions to the climate crisis.[8]

Climate change actions are occurring beyond the US and Canada. Activists have barricaded an airport taxiway in Scotland to protest the impact
of air travel and airport expansions on the climate. Others have blockaded
a ship from unloading coal in Rotterdam, the Netherlands, to protest the
construction of a new coal-fired power plant. Protestors have chained
themselves to a coal conveyor belt at a power plant in Sydney, Australia.[9]
These actions are augmenting the voices of millions calling on policymakers to deal with the climate crisis.

As of 2008, 18 colleges and universities in the United States were using renewable energy certificates to offset 100 percent of their greenhouse

gas emissions: Half a dozen others have also switched to using renewable energy for 100 percent of their energy consumption. Some 200 institutions of higher education have committed to using a paperless admissions process. The University of California system, which includes ten campuses, 220,000 students and 170,000 faculty and staff, has become a leader in sustainable practices in energy and water conservation, renewable energy, procurement, food and transportation. The UC system, along with scores of other institutions, has also adopted "climate neutral" policies with established target dates.[10]

Undergraduate and graduate programs are increasingly offering degrees in fields related to sustainability. Schools such as Antioch University, Bainbridge Graduate Institute, Presidio Graduate School, and Dominican University of California with its Green MBA program are linking commerce with the environment and social justice. Students seeking business degrees with a focus on sustainability are opting for MBA programs with course offerings such as Principles of Sustainable Management, Ecological Economics, Managerial and Environmental Accounting and Thriving Regenerative Enterprise. Undergraduate students committed to working for socially responsible organizations are signing a graduation pledge promising: "I pledge to explore and take into account the social and environmental consequences of any job I consider and will try to improve these aspects of any organization for which I work."[11] Similarly, graduate business students are taking the MBA oath, pledging to serve the greater good through responsible and ethical behavior.

College alliances are collaborating on green practices. The Eco League, for example, consists of five liberal arts colleges in the US — Alaska Public University, College of the Atlantic, Green Mountain College, Northland College and Prescott College — committed to providing environmental education. At the international level, the United Nations General Assembly established the Decade of Education for Sustainable Development 2005–2014 to promote sustainability education. The US chapter, the US Partnership for Education for Sustainable Development, is a national network of sustainability resources for sectors including higher education, grades K-12, teacher education, communities, faith groups and business. The US Partnership gives sustainability educators a platform for sharing "best practices" through phone conferences and a list server. This UN program also establishes an international mechanism for sustainability educators to connect with others and receive support for their work.

Colleges and universities are experimenting with green technologies in energy, water, green building and transportation. These campuses act as green "labs" or incubators for testing, implementing and evaluating green practices. Their students carry these experiences into their careers and throughout their lives. The community nature of a campus promotes close interactions that become a model for an active citizenry. These innovative campuses are preparing the next generation for a thriveable future.

The Food Revolution

Like the green wave on college campuses, the trend to eat organic, locally grown food has been increasing in the US. Worldwide from 2000 to 2007, organic agriculture doubled to 32 million hectares.[12] A $28 billion industry, the organic and natural foods sector has expanded from specialty stores and restaurants to national grocery store chains. Even Walmart has added organic foods to its produce section. The trend of returning to locally sourced foods was highlighted in 2007 when *The New Oxford American Dictionary* selected *locavore,* coined by residents of San Francisco to promote foods grown within a 100-mile radius, as its word of the year. In 2009 the White House planted its own organic vegetable garden, the first since Eleanor Roosevelt's World War II victory garden, to educate children about healthful local produce. As First Lady Michelle Obama pointed out, children "will begin to educate their families and that will, in turn, begin to educate our communities."[13] Planting these "education seeds" in children may establish a lifelong desire for healthful local produce for themselves and their households.

As the marketing avenues for farmers have increased, so has the public's yearning for contact with local farmers and access to local foods. The number of farmers' markets in the US grew from 1,755 in 1994 to 4,685 in 2008.[14] Similarly, the number of Community Supported Agriculture farms, in which an individual receives weekly produce from a local farmer, increased from 50 in 1990 to 2,500 in 2008.[15] Farmstands, where a single farm sells its produce, U-pick farms, which open their fields to the public, and food cooperatives have also increased in popularity.

In urban settings restaurants are promoting local foods by offering menus with selections from nearby locations. Google's Café 150 gathers its ingredients within 150 miles of its Mountain View, California, complex. Restaurants such as Chez Panisse in Berkeley, California, Cinque Terre in Portland, Maine, and Mozza in Los Angeles create seasonal menus from local food producers whenever possible: Two Blue Hill restaurants, in New York City and in Pocantico Hills, New York, grow their own food on a 20-acre plot in upstate New York; they buy less than 20 percent of their ingredients from outside their region.[16] Another variation of locally focused restaurants is Three Stone Hearth, a Community Supported Kitchen in Berkeley. Operated as a worker-owned cooperative, it provides "nutrient dense" meals from local farms to residents of the San Francisco Bay Area. Nutrient dense food uses nutritious ingredients and cooking methods that retain a high concentration of vitamins, minerals and enzymes.[17] These new ventures are reinventing how we grow, cook and distribute food.

Another approach is grocery stores that grow their own produce. Sam Mogannam, owner of Bi-Rite Market in San Francisco, for example, is determined to close the loop between farm and table. He decided to grow produce on his farm in Sonoma County and also gets produce from other local growers. As he points out, "we're committed to buying the best we can, at the fairest price to our suppliers."[18] He and his colleagues are another example in the food revolution that is contributing to a thriveable future.

In inner cities, some initiatives aimed at low-income residents are making organic food more widely available and affordable. These include the People's Grocery in Oakland, California, East New York Farms in Brooklyn, New York, and the Institute for Community Resource Development in Chicago. These programs use education, outreach and urban agriculture programs that turn empty lots into urban gardens. They hope to reinvent the urban food system by providing fresh, nutritious foods and jobs to underserved communities.

With this demand for sustainably produced local food there is a need for new farmers. In California, for example, there are only 2,900 certified farmers' market producers.[19] With 36 million residents and only 500 farmers' markets, California's gap is significant.[20] In addition, the average age of farmers in the United States is approaching 60. Two barriers that seem to deter youth from getting into farming are access to land and farming skills. Land must both be protected and made accessible to people who are interested in growing food. Land Trusts such the Marin Agricultural Land Trust have played an important role in addressing the land issues. FarmLink, in California, Washington, Pennsylvania, Connecticut and Maine, spans the generational divide by connecting older landowners with aspiring young farmers. Online communities also are helping to connect the younger tech-savvy generation with established farmers. The Green-horns, for example, is a grassroots organization creating a documentary about young farmers and writing an online guide for beginning farmers. These organizations are helping to bridge the gap between the traditional and the green economies by training a new generation of farmers.

The shift toward local, organic foods is precipitated by an unsustainable fossil-fuel-based agribusiness system that is taking its toll on the environment and on our health and well-being. The costs of the industrial food system are unsustainable as agriculture is overwhelming Earth's life-support systems. It is also responsible for 15 percent of all energy consumed in developed countries. The annual cost of soil erosion worldwide is estimated at $400 billion, and 75 percent of Africa's arable land has been degraded by erosion. In the US every year farmers use 450 million kilograms of pesticides, contaminating nearly all of the nation's waterways with chemicals known to cause cancer and birth defects.[21]

The environmental damage associated with food production is matched by health damage including cancer, heart disease, obesity and diabetes. Obesity levels in the US stand at 34 percent in adults 20 and over. Diabetes rose 13.5 percent between 2005 and 2007 to over 23 million people, or 8 percent of the population.[22] In fact, one in three Americans born in 2000 is expected to develop diabetes.[23] According to the US Department of Agriculture, healthier diets could save $71 billion a year in medical expenses.[24]

The high cost of fossil-fuel energy and the impact of climate change on crop yields are creating new opportunities for renewable energy sources such as biogas, wind and solar to be used on farms. Instead of giving farm subsidies to global agricultural companies, funds could be redirected toward smaller, sustainable farm enterprises. Efforts such as the Slow Money Alliance, led by Woody Tasch, support local food systems and local economies through a network of institutes throughout the US. Tasch describes his vision by asking, "What would the world be like if we invested 50% of our assets within 50 miles of where we live? What if there were a new generation of companies that gave away 50% of their profits? What if there were 50% more organic matter in our soil 50 years from now?"[25] These questions illustrate a vision for a thriveable future where we have local investments regenerating soil, food systems and local economies.

Several initiatives are representative of the shift toward local, organic food options. A demonstration by Italian Carlo Petrini in 1986 against the opening of a McDonald's restaurant on the Spanish Steps of Rome began the Slow Food movement. Now boasting 85,000 members and 1,000 chapters in 122 countries, Slow Food states that food "should be produced in a clean way that does not harm the environment, animal welfare or our health; and that food producers should receive fair compensation for their work."[26]

To protect traditional grains and food heritage, Slow Food has established the Slow Food Foundation for Biodiversity and the University of Gastronomic Science. In the US, Slow Food USA has planted gardens in schools and raised $50,000 to help farmers and restaurants in New Orleans recover from Hurricane Katrina.[27] The Slow Food Nation event in San Francisco in 2008 drew 85,000 people interested in supporting local farmers and food producers. This event also highlighted the City of San Francisco's Victory Gardens 2008+, a pilot program promoting food security and urban gardening by assisting 15 households to plant backyard gardens.

In the commercial sector, an encouraging partnership is the Sustainable Food Laboratory. The Lab consists of over 80 organizations committed to improving the food and agricultural systems by developing sustainable practices. The Lab was launched in 2004 by a diverse group of for-profit, nonprofit and government organizations from the Americas and Europe, including the W. K. Kellogg Foundation, Unilever, Sysco, Sadia, Oxfam, World Wildlife Fund and Brazil's Ministry of Agrarian Reform. The Lab's projects are designed to transform the relationship of food growers, distributors and consumers through leadership training; food supply chains that address poverty and environmental concerns; organizational change through in-house training; and knowledge sharing through case studies and documentation of methodologies.[28]

The Lab has undertaken myriad projects. A partnership between Unilever and Rainforest Alliance certifies that Lipton tea is sourced worldwide from Rainforest Alliance farms. A collaboration of the International Center for Tropical Agriculture, Green Mountain Coffee Roasters and Costco is improving the supply chain and distribution network of coffee and produce. A Lab purchasing guide for foodservice professionals in the US clarifies concepts such as "natural," "grass fed," "local" and "fresh."[29] These terms are widely used in the industry for marketing purposes yet many in both the industry and the general public are confused by their definitions. Clarifying their meaning sharpens communications and guards against "green washing," in which inaccurate sustainability claims are made. These projects are reestablishing the connection of farmers, sellers, distributors and the public.

The Lab is building understanding of and trust in the food system through "learning journeys." A journey to Brazil's sugarcane and soybean farms and food processing plants, for example, introduced the Lab's members to local farmers and built bonds among participants. As Peter Senge, a consultant to the Lab, points out, "Learning journeys, at their essence, are about 'sensing' (or opening awareness to the present moment), but the goal is not simply awareness for its own sake, or to only deepen relationships between key players, but doing this in the context of compelling issues about which people care deeply."[30] Strengthening relationships by meeting the farmers at the base of the supply chain of large companies is similar city dwellers connecting at farmers' markets with those who grow their produce. The Lab's learning journeys address social justice issues and the rights of farmers in developing countries. Organizations such as La Via

GREEN Foundation extension officer Ramachandrappa introduces farmer Shivanegowda to the technique of making a natural fertilizer called jeevamrutha, a mixture of cow dung, cow urine, jaggery, flour, soil and water. This rural extension education program in Karnataka, India, dubbed "Farmer Idol" after the "American Idol" television program, is successfully engaging farmers to teach each other sustainable farming practices.

Campesina, which represents small farmers from 148 organizations in 69 countries, are supporting the rights of farmers worldwide.

Another international effort aimed at increasing farmers' productivity is Digital Green, a project funded by Microsoft, which distributes instructional DVDs to farmers in a dozen Indian villages. Using local farmers trained by agricultural experts to teach their peers about successful farming practices, the locally produced DVDs have been successful in increasing agricultural productivity. Groups of farmers gather to view targeted video segments in evening screenings or watch the programs through cable networks. The segments can be testimonials and interviews with farmers, demonstrations by local farmers or experts explaining farming concepts. Extension workers engage the audience and emphasize their availability to support farmers. Because these videos feature local farmers they inspire community members to see themselves and their peers "onstage"; it has been dubbed the "Farmer Idol" program in reference to the "American Idol" television program. This participatory approach has gained wide acceptance and is a model for delivering technical advice to subsistence farmers throughout the developing world.

A similar "Farmer Idol" show in the US or Europe might help youth realize that opportunities for farming are more diverse than they were for their parents. This model broadens the definition of farmers. They don't have to live on a farm hundreds of miles from a city. Instead, they could grow food for a restaurant, lead an urban gardening program or create a school or rooftop garden. Given the aging of the farmer population in the US, introducing these ideas now is ideal.

Another part of the food system is distribution. The industrial agricultural system has streamlined the distribution of foods from around the world. It is often easier, for example, to get a tomato from Mexico than from a local farmer. A few organizations are addressing the distribution challenges and working to promote the local availability of food. La Montañita, a co-op serving New Mexico since 1976, has a distribution warehouse that provides pick-up, storage and supply services for producers and distributors of regional products to their four stores and other outlets. The co-op's role in supporting local farmers presents a model for others to emulate nationwide.

The Marin Agricultural Institute (MAI) in Marin County, California, is also working to make locally grown food more accessible in places where people work, learn and play. Collaborating with its sister organization, Marin Farmers Markets, MAI picks up hundreds of pounds of preordered fresh fruits and vegetables from the Sunday and Thursday farmers' markets and delivers them to local schools, restaurants, corporate cafeterias and catering services. Since the program began in 2006, local food worth $300,000 has been routed from over 70 local producers to 42 customers. MAI hopes to develop a model that can be shared with communities and farmers, markets throughout the country to expand the reach of locally grown food.[31]

The Green Economy

A global recession and rising unemployment provide an opportunity to develop a green economy with jobs in manufacturing hybrid cars, installing solar panels and wind turbines, retrofitting buildings, upgrading the energy grid and transportation infrastructure and restoring habitats. Van Jones, the former White House Special Advisor for Green Jobs, Enterprise and Innovation, points out, "Green collar jobs could help us conserve resources, create new sources of energy, and give the nation the power to grow the economy again. What's more, we have the chance to build this new energy economy in ways that reflect our deepest values of inclusion, diversity, and equal opportunity for everyone."[32] Green jobs support the industries that are at the forefront in tackling the climate crisis.

Marin Farmers Markets

The Sunday Marin Civic Center Farmers Market in Marin County is the third largest farmers' market in California. It brings together 200 vendors and 10,000 customers every week during the summer months. The increase in the number of farmers' markets worldwide is part of a food revolution raising awareness about the importance of a healthful diet.

Beyond the current economic crisis, the other challenges we face — ecosystem decline, energy transition, population growth and climate change — also support the restructuring of our economic system through green jobs and training programs. The number of green jobs is already rising. Worldwide there are 2.3 million jobs in the renewable energy sector; wind power employs 300,000, solar photovoltaics 170,000, solar thermal 600,000 and biofuels one million.[33]

A green economy will involve innovations in our manufacturing and service sectors. In the building industry, for example, homes and workplaces can be retrofitted with more efficient windows, lights, insulation, heating and ventilation systems and appliances to reduce energy consumption and greenhouse gas emissions and increase employment opportunities and return on investment from energy savings. The transition to the green economy will require workers to acquire skills through education programs, creating further jobs in education.

This transition is taking shape already. In Bucks County, Pennsylvania, Gamesa, a Spanish wind turbine manufacturer, employs 300 workers to make turbine blades and towers in a formerly abandoned US Steel plant. In Clinton, Illinois, Trinity, a manufacturing company from Texas, has redeveloped a freight car plant to produce wind turbine towers. In Oakley, Ohio, Cast-Fab is producing wind turbine hubs and castings. The nonprofit Envirofit has developed a retrofit kit that improves the efficiency of two-stroke engines by 30 to 50 percent and reduces emissions by up to 90 percent. There are 100 million two-stroke cars in Southeast Asia; Envirofit is working with local businesses in the Philippines to provide a microfinancing and kit-installation program and plans to offer its kit in Bangladesh, India, Pakistan and Sri Lanka.[34]

In addition to private sector initiatives, a green economy will need government leadership to provide policies, economic incentives, subsidies and investments. At the US federal level, the 2007 Green Jobs Act and the Energy Efficiency and Conservation Block Grant are government investments in green jobs. The Green Jobs Act authorized $125 million per year for a pilot program to train workers for jobs in renewable energy and energy efficiency.[35] The Energy Efficiency and Conservation Block Grant authorized $2 billion a year for local governments to implement energy and climate change measures.

In response to the US economic recession, the Obama administration's American Recovery and Reinvestment Act of 2009 includes $41 billion for renewable energy and energy efficiency programs in areas such as energy efficiency and conservation ($3.2 billion); weatherization ($5 billion); modernization of the electricity grid ($4.4 billion); high performance "green" buildings ($4.5 billion); and lithium ion and hybrid battery development ($2 billion). The stimulus package also includes nearly $20 billion in tax incentives for renewable energy and energy efficiency projects and provides $500 million for green jobs training.[36] This government investment program, enacted by the US Congress and signed by President Obama, may jump-start the US economy and support critical green industries.

At the regional level, the East Bay Green Corridor in California is a partnership of the mayors of Richmond, Emeryville, Oakland and Berkeley, the University of California at Berkeley and the Lawrence Berkeley National Laboratory. Formed in 2007, the Green Corridor wants to replicate the entrepreneurial successes of Silicon Valley by supporting emerging green industries such as renewable energy, resource conservation, green building, green business and sustainability education. This alliance is a regional model for communities worldwide to support programs that promote the green jobs of the future.

Mainstreaming Green

We have examined the transformation that is taking place in the building, education and agriculture sectors and the jobs being created in emerging green industries. These changes are the result of millions of individuals acting on their ideas for inventing a better future. Some of the mechanisms that support the rapid adoption of green practices are public awareness campaigns, prize philanthropy and open-source initiatives.

Public awareness campaigns are advancing the discourse on energy independence and climate change. The We Campaign, founded in 2006 by former Vice President Al Gore, is committed to shifting public opinion on the climate change crisis. The We Campaign already has over two million members and aims through mainstream media spots and Internet alerts to engage 10 million citizens to become climate activists. This national endeavor involves "a multi-year, commercial-scale, mainstream mobilization effort to bring public opinion past the tipping point, compelling our elected leaders to take action on climate change."[37]

Another national organization, the Apollo Alliance, takes its inspiration from John F. Kennedy's goal to land on the moon within a decade. The Alliance aims to "catalyze a clean energy revolution that will put millions of Americans to work in a new generation of high-quality, green-collar jobs."[38] The organization presented two reports in 2008, *New Apollo Program* and *Green-Collar Jobs in America's Cities*, which provide steps for developing clean energy sources and creating green-collar jobs.

The power of the Internet has been harnessed to raise public awareness of climate change through the Earth Hour event, using the simple action of turning off a light switch. Launched by World Wildlife Fund Australia and *The Sydney Morning Herald*, the 2007 campaign succeeded in having 2.2 million people turn off their lights for one hour as a symbolic gesture. In 2008 the event grew to 50 million participants from 35 official cities and 400 other cities; major landmarks such as the Golden Gate Bridge in San Francisco, the Colosseum in Rome and the CN Tower in Toronto turned off their nonessential lights. By 2009 the event reached hundreds of millions of people in over 4,000 cities in 88 countries. It introduced the Vote

Will Wilson, World Wildlife Fund

Here is the Nashville, Tennessee, skyline before (above) and after (below) the start of the 2009 Earth Hour event. Over 4,000 cities in 88 countries participated, turning off lights for one hour to symbolically vote for action on climate change.

Earth campaign, which asked participants to vote for the Earth instead of global warming. This global initiative is supported through online social communities including Facebook, Twitter, My Space, Flickr and YouTube. The campaign provides a platform for global citizens to "deliver world leaders a mandate for the right decision to be made at the United Nations Climate Summit in Copenhagen in December 2009."[39] These and numerous other public awareness initiatives are shifting our consciousness and reengaging citizens to focus on solutions.

Another popular avenue for raising awareness and seeking solutions is prize philanthropy, in which foundations, government agencies and individuals fund public competitions to solve global problems. Peter Diamandis, chairman and CEO of the X Prize Foundation, began a new era of prize philanthropy in 2004 with the Ansari X Prize; he awarded the $10 million to Scaled Composites for flying a privately funded spacecraft named SpaceShipOne into outer orbit. The X Prize Foundation has since joined with other organizations to offer prizes in genomic sequencing, the next generation of lunar landing crafts and a nonpolluting, superefficient automobile.

Since the Ansari X Prize debut, scores of other prizes have been offered. The US government is offering the $10 million H Prize for a breakthrough in the development of hydrogen technologies and the $10 million L prize to develop new lighting technology that replaces the common incandescent bulb. There is a $100,000 Buckminster Fuller Challenge for developing and implementing "a strategy that has significant potential to solve humanity's most pressing problems." The TED (Technology, Entertainment, Design) Prize provides $100,000 and the support of a network of leaders to individuals for their One Wish to Change the World. Sir Richard Branson developed the $25 million Virgin Earth Challenge for removing greenhouse gas emissions from the atmosphere. The Biomimicry Institute has a Design Challenge that asks "How would nature solve this?" to find bio-inspired solutions to any of the ten Grand Sustainability Challenges chosen by a panel of experts. The Ashoka Foundation's Changemakers competitions reward social entrepreneurs for their solutions to pressing social challenges.

Although the cost of entering some prize philanthropy contests may exclude a large number of participants, the contests bring publicity to issues and generate funding sources for the winners and visibility for groups in the selected fields. Nancy Barrand from the Changemakers health competition says, "Can I tell you that more children are being fed somewhere or health has improved [directly] because of a Changemakers competition? No.... But if you believe that change comes from making more people aware of a problem and bringing more resources to bear on that problem, then I think that Changemakers does have an impact."[40] Prize philanthropy contests are sources of inspiration and catalysts for creative ideas for a thriveable future.

Other awards are given in support of social and environmental achievements. The Right Livelihood Award, known as the "Alternative Nobel Prize," recognizes individuals "for outstanding vision and work on behalf of the planet and its people." The Goldman Environmental Prize, launched by philanthropists Richard and Rhoda Goldman in 1990, honors grassroots environmental activists from Africa, Asia, Europe, Islands and Island Nations, North America and South and Central America with international recognition and $150,000 to continue their work. Earth Island Institute's Brower Youth Awards, the Japanese Asahi Glass Foundation's Blue Planet Prize and the Heinz Family Foundation's Heinz Awards also support social and environmental leadership. These awards honor the work of people who envision a better world.

Open Source

The awards show the benefits of an "open-source" approach that spurs innovation. Open source is associated with the software industry, where the programming code is designed and modified by volunteer contributors and available free to the general public. The success of the open-source Linux computer operating system has influenced scores of other software programs for web browsing, word processing, spreadsheets and social networking and collaboration tools. Now open source is expanding into other fields.

The Internet is playing a role in this expansion by reducing the costs of creating and distributing information such as music, images, text and video and by its flexibility for developing online social networks. Wikipedia, for example, an open-source encyclopedia owned by a nonprofit foundation, has a paid staff of five people. Hundreds of thousands of daily visitors make use of the collective input of 75,000 volunteer contributors and more than 10 million articles in over 260 languages, over 2.6 million articles in English alone.[41] This remarkable reservoir of knowledge is available to people around the world for free.

Wikipedia has been faulted for inaccurate content, but this criticism was dispelled by a study in *Nature,* which compared Wikipedia to Encyclopaedia Britannica. The study concluded that "the accuracy of science in Wikipedia is surprisingly good: the number of errors in a typical Wikipedia science article is not substantially more than in Encyclopaedia Britannica, often considered the gold-standard entry-level reference work."[42] Wikipedia and other open-source initiatives have revolutionized the creation and retrieval of information. Content is now easily accessible and collaboration engenders a sense of belonging to a larger community with a broader purpose.

The Wikipedia collaborative model has inspired numerous open-source, knowledge-based networks dedicated to creating online communities and sharing resources. WiserEarth, a project of the Natural Capital Institute founded by Paul Hawken in 2007, has established an online community of 100,000 nongovernmental organizations and affiliated businesses, social entrepreneurs and individuals interested in sharing ideas and collaborating on projects. The site provides a virtual space to build alliances working "toward a just and sustainable world created by community." The Natural Capital Institute is currently developing the Wiser-Business website in support of a "global standard for responsible business behavior" and WiserGovernment for the exchange of resources for local, state and national governments.[43]

Using a global problem-solving approach, ClimatePrediction.net is harnessing the world's computer power, which is greater than that available from existing supercomputers. It is appealing to volunteers worldwide to share their personal computers in order to improve the accuracy of climate models. The project is funded by the Natural Environment Research Council, the United Kingdom's e-Science Programme and the European Union's Ensemble Programme. The Pharos Project is an open-source initiative to evaluate building materials. AskNature, a project of the Biomimicry Institute, is cataloging bio-inspired strategies, products and resources and encouraging collaboration in finding nature-based solutions. In the movement toward the freer use of ideas, two nonprofits, the Open Source Initiative and Creative Commons, are supplying the education and the tools necessary for sharing intellectual property.

The open-source approach has become a powerful tool for bringing volunteers together for a common cause. Although many global challenges face political and social obstacles, open-source initiatives inspire large numbers of like-minded people who, "in the course of working together on tasks, become bound together by trust and by shared values and understandings."[44] The resources accessible in open-source collaborations are proving the value of innovation for the common good.

Initiatives, Confluence, Scope and Approach

Oganizations and their green initiatives vary in their primary focus. Their issues include climate, population, energy, ecosystems and social justice. The scope of the projects ranges from local to regional, national and international. While some organizations take a traditional proprietary approach to tackling global issues, others use open-source cooperation to develop and deliver their products and services. (See Figure 1.)

Although many of the categories are linked, some organizations focus on climate, energy and biodiversity issues and place less emphasis on population and social justice. This discrepancy may reflect the politically volatile aspects of population and social justice issues, or perhaps their connection to the environment has yet to enter public discourse in a significant way.

The success of local and regional initiatives is often replicated at a national and international level. Modern telecommunications tools increase the capacity for this to happen. For example, the solar installation job-training program set up by Solar Richmond and the climate change tools used by CLEI's Cities for Climate Protection Campaign are being emulated by other communities throughout the world.

The open-source approach flourishes in publicly supported programs, knowledge-based projects and prize philanthropy initiatives. Government-sponsored initiatives such as New Zealand's Resource Management Act, Sweden's energy and climate plan and the UN Decade on Sustainable Development welcome public input. Similarly, the Biomimicry Institute's AskNature, the Encyclopedia of Life, WiserEarth and the US Green Building Council rely on an open-source approach for creating their knowledge base and for the innovations of their programs. Finally, awards and prizes such as the Blue Planet prize, the TED prize, Changemakers and the Virgin Earth Challenge tap into the creativity developed through an open-source approach.

Tipping Point Factors

The worldwide economic crisis, the climate crisis and the rising cost of energy are all spurring individuals and organizations toward a tipping

Figure 1: Comparison of Sustainability Organizations and Initiatives. Note: Confluence categories refer to content emphasis. Scope categories refer to geographical emphasis. The Open Source category refers to initiatives that support open-source cooperation.

Name	Year Established	Confluence					Scope				
		Climate	Population	Energy	Ecosystem	Social Justice	Local	Regional	National	International	Open Source
1SKY	2007	✓		✓					✓		
2010 Imperative	2007	✓		✓						✓	
350.org	2008	✓		✓						✓	✓
Alliance for Climate Protection	2007	✓		✓						✓	
Apollo Challenge	2003	✓		✓					✓	✓	
Architecture 2030	2005	✓		✓	✓					✓	
AskNature	2008	✓		✓	✓					✓	✓
B Corporations	2007	✓	✓	✓	✓	✓			✓	✓	
Biodiversity Hotspots	1999	✓		✓	✓					✓	
Biomimicry Design Challenge	2007	✓		✓	✓					✓	✓
Blue Planet Prize	1992	✓	✓	✓	✓	✓				✓	✓
Blue Planet Run	2002	✓	✓	✓	✓	✓				✓	
Brower Youth Awards	2000	✓	✓	✓	✓	✓				✓	
Buckminster Fuller Challenge	2007	✓	✓	✓	✓	✓				✓	
Carbon Mitigation Initiative	2000	✓		✓						✓	
Carbon Trust	2001	✓		✓	✓					✓	

Name	Year Established	Confluence					Scope				
		Climate	Population	Energy	Ecosystem	Social Justice	Local	Regional	National	Inter-national	Open Source
Changemakers	1998	✓	✓	✓	✓	✓				✓	✓
City Repair Project	1996	✓				✓	✓				
The Climate Group	2004	✓		✓	✓					✓	✓
Climateprediction.net	1999	✓		✓	✓	✓				✓	
Clinton Global Initiative	2005	✓		✓	✓	✓				✓	
Community Pulse	2008	✓	✓	✓	✓					✓	
Conservation Land Trust	2000	✓			✓					✓	
Copenhagen Climate Conference	2009	✓		✓	✓	✓				✓	✓
Creative Commons	2002	✓		✓	✓	✓				✓	✓
Digital Green	2008	✓		✓	✓	✓			✓		
e3bank	2008	✓		✓	✓	✓	✓				
Earth Hour	2007	✓		✓	✓	✓				✓	✓
ecoBUDGET	1996	✓		✓	✓	✓				✓	
EcoLeague	2003	✓	✓	✓	✓				✓		
Encyclopedia of Life	2007	✓			✓					✓	✓
Energy Action Coalition	2005	✓	✓	✓				✓			✓
Family PACT	1999		✓	✓		✓		✓			✓
FarmLink	1999	✓		✓	✓					✓	
FLOW	2006	✓	✓	✓	✓				✓	✓	
Focus the Nation	2006	✓		✓						✓	✓
GE Ecomagination	2005	✓		✓	✓					✓	

NAME	YEAR ESTABLISHED	CONFLUENCE					SCOPE				
		CLIMATE	POPULATION	ENERGY	ECOSYSTEM	SOCIAL JUSTICE	LOCAL	REGIONAL	NATIONAL	INTER-NATIONAL	OPEN SOURCE
Goldman Environmental Prize	1990	✓	✓	✓	✓	✓				✓	✓
Grameen Bank/Foundation	1976					✓			✓		
Green For All	2008	✓		✓	✓	✓			✓		✓
The Greenhorns	2007	✓	✓	✓	✓	✓			✓		
ICLEI	1991	✓	✓	✓	✓	✓				✓	
Innovation for Conservation	2008	✓	✓	✓	✓	✓				✓	
InVEST	2006	✓	✓		✓					✓	
Katoomba Group	2000	✓		✓	✓	✓				✓	
Kiva	2005					✓				✓	
LENSES	2008	✓	✓	✓	✓	✓		✓		✓	
The Long Now Foundation	1996			✓	✓	✓				✓	✓
Marin Agricultural Institute	2004					✓		✓			
MicroPlace	2007					✓				✓	
La Montañita	1976		✓	✓	✓	✓		✓			
Natural Capital Project	2006			✓	✓	✓				✓	
The Natural Step	1989	✓						✓		✓	✓
New England Energy Alliance	2005			✓						✓	

Name	Year Established	CONFLUENCE					SCOPE				
		Climate	Population	Energy	Ecosystem	Social Justice	Local	Regional	National	Inter-national	Open Source
New Resource Bank	2006	✓	✓	✓	✓	✓	✓				✓
New Zealand Resource Management Act	1991	✓	✓	✓	✓	✓			✓		✓
North American Alliance for Green Education	1997	✓	✓	✓	✓	✓			✓		
Oil Independent Oakland	2006	✓		✓	✓		✓				
OneCalifornia Bank/Foundation	2007	✓	✓	✓	✓	✓		✓		✓	
One Planet Living	2002	✓	✓	✓	✓	✓				✓	
Open Source Initiative	1998	✓	✓	✓	✓	✓				✓	✓
Pharos Project	2006	✓	✓	✓	✓	✓				✓	
Post Carbon Institute	2003	✓	✓	✓	✓	✓				✓	
Precautionary Principle	1992	✓	✓	✓	✓	✓				✓	
Resilience Alliance	1999	✓	✓	✓	✓	✓				✓	
Roots & Shoots	1991	✓	✓	✓	✓	✓				✓	
Rosetta Project	2004				✓	✓				✓	
Salmon Nation	2005	✓		✓	✓	✓		✓		✓	
Slow Food	1989			✓	✓	✓	✓				✓
Slow Money Alliance	2009				✓	✓					
Solar Richmond	2006	✓		✓	✓	✓	✓			✓	✓
Species Alliance	2005				✓					✓	

Name	Year Established	Confluence					Scope				
		Climate	Population	Energy	Ecosystem	Social Justice	Local	Regional	National	International	Open Source
Sustainable Food Lab	2004				✓					✓	
SustainLane Government	2004	✓	✓	✓	✓	✓			✓		
Sweden Energy and Climate Plan	2009	✓		✓	✓				✓		✓
TED Prize	1984	✓	✓	✓	✓	✓				✓	✓
TerraPass	2007	✓		✓						✓	
Thailand National Family Planning Program	1970		✓						✓		
Transition Towns	2006	✓	✓	✓	✓	✓	✓				✓
UN Decade on Sustainable Development	2005	✓	✓	✓	✓	✓					✓
United States Climate Action Partnership	2007	✓	✓	✓					✓		✓
US Green Building Council: LEED	1998	✓		✓	✓	✓			✓		✓
US Mayors Climate Protection Agreement	2005	✓		✓	✓	✓			✓		✓
La Via Campesina	1993	✓				✓				✓	✓
Virgin Earth Challenge	2007	✓	✓	✓	✓	✓				✓	✓
Wikipedia	2001	✓	✓	✓	✓	✓				✓	✓
WISER Projects	2007	✓		✓	✓					✓	✓
X Prize Foundation	1995	✓		✓	✓					✓	✓

point. High-performance buildings are gaining acceptance and becoming standard practice. In the educational sector, colleges and universities are laboratories for new ideas. The agribusiness model, which depletes soils and depends on petrochemicals, is giving way to local and regional organic food networks that support local economies.

As technological breakthroughs such as cell phones, computers and the Internet become more readily accessible, new possibilities are emerging for reaching people, including those in less developed regions. We are increasing our ability to deal with global social and environmental problems through alternative approaches such as open-source networks, prize philanthropy and other methods that encourage community involvement.

Ultimately our own internal tipping points have the greatest significance of all since they can move us from vision into action to improve life in our homes, our workplaces and our communities.

TAKING ACTION

➡ *Start a backyard vegetable garden or join a community garden group.*

➡ *Introduce green practices such as recycling, composting, organic gardening or energy efficiency at your local school or college.*

➡ *Create an event that honors local residents working to improve the quality of life in your town.*

➡ *Develop a program that honors the eco-heroes in your community.*

➡ *Support your local farmers' market. If you don't have one, start one.*

➡ *Support land trusts for farms in your area and create one if none exists.*

➡ *Volunteer at a local organization that is working on an issue that has meaning for you.*

EIGHT

A Thriveable Future

The future is not someplace we are going to, but one we are creating.
The paths to it are not found but created, and the activity of creating
them changes both the maker and the destination.

— JOHN SCHAAR

Imagination is more important than knowledge.

— ALBERT EINSTEIN

COMPUTER SCIENTIST Alan Kay says, "The best way to predict the future is to invent it." Now is the time to invent a thriveable future. Solving the global challenges facing humanity will require nothing less than a new worldview. The environmental, energy, population, equity and climate crises call for a reexamination of our relationship to ourselves, our neighbors and the natural world. We need to shift from a "sustainable" mindset to a "thriveable" one. This shift to thriveability can be guided by the SPIRALS framework.

While the word "sustainable" is derived from roots meaning "to uphold," the origin of "thriveable" comes from "to grasp to oneself." Sustainability separates us from nature and envisions us "getting by" by limiting our negative environmental impacts over the long term. Sustaining involves scarcity and minimalism; by contrast, thriving involves abundance and enrichment. Sustainability is shortsighted and ignores the very qualities that make us human: our passion, enthusiasm, adaptability, vision and love. Thriveability celebrates us as part of nature. We "grasp" the ability of the human spirit to prosper and flourish when we are integrated into the web of life. As mythologist Joseph Campbell reminded us, "The goal of life is to make your heartbeat match the beat of the universe, to match your nature with Nature." When we are attuned to the rhythms of nature, the possibilities are infinite. This shift from "less bad" solutions to solutions that energize us and improve our quality of life through our connections with all life forms is the essence of thriveability.

Identifying and working with leverage points will play a key role in making enduring changes. In *Leverage Points: Places to Intervene in a System,* environmentalist Donella Meadows wrote that leverage points are "places within a complex system (a corporation, an economy, a living body, a city, an ecosystem) where a small shift in one thing can produce big changes in everything.... Leverage points are points of power."[2] Examples of leverage points are taxes, standards and positive and negative feedback loops. Given the rapid rate of change in our economy, the climate, energy, population and biodiversity, making use of the right leverage points will become critical as the opportunity to intervene diminishes.

The SPIRALS Framework

The survey of sustainability principles in my previous book, *The Sustainability Revolution,* revealed themes such as stewardship, respect for limits and interdependence, bedrock values in the global conversation about sustainable practices. Beyond these values lies the need to develop criteria for effective and enduring initiatives for a thriveable future. How do we design and implement such initiatives? What should be our guideposts in developing programs from personal lifestyle changes to national environmental policies?

Italian Farm Aims to Be World's First Zero-Carbon Farm Without Offsets

A farm in the central Italian region of Umbria is aiming to cut its CO_2 emissions to zero over the course of the next year. The olive and grape farm is basing its push on a revolutionary liquid-based battery developed by the Australian company Cellstrom. Twenty-four solar panels plus a battery center will allow the farm to operate a variety of electric vehicles over a long cloudy or foggy period. Miniature tractors will use biodiesel not sourced from food-chain products. Olive-oil boilers will use wood chips from tree-thinning. By the end of 2009 the farm hopes to be the first in the world to reduce its inherent net carbon footprint to zero without using offsite offsetting.[1]

The initiatives in the current book represent a fraction of those taking place worldwide, but they indicate the diversity of approaches. The SPIRALS framework evolved from my perception of the criteria underlying initiatives that are having a positive impact. Using the SPIRALS approach as a compass, thriveable projects, which are Scalable, Place-making, Intergenerational, Resilient, Accessible, Life-affirming and involve Self-care, can be created and implemented. As in spiral shapes found in hurricanes, birds' flight patterns and galaxies, the SPIRALS characteristics are both evolving and interdependent. If an initiative is like a tree species in a forest, the criteria in the SPIRALS framework represent the ecosystem services that maintain the forest's vitality.

Scalable

Scaling initiatives for use beyond the individual or organizational level to local, regional, national and international levels requires a systems approach relying on the leverage points emphasized by Meadows. Tools that allow for the rapid scaling of products and services include standards and open-source platforms. Examples are the Internet; the interstate highway system; blogs; music, photo and text sharing tools; cell phones; ecolabels; green building and energy standards; and social networks. These innovations have spread quickly because they are easily scaled from a small town to a large city and beyond.

In certain industries, scalability requires shifting the emphasis from the product or service to the system as a whole. In the transportation sector, for example, this shift involves moving from the idea of a car as a means of independent transportation to the idea of a comprehensive mobility system. The focus remains on moving from point A to point B. Entrepreneur Shai Agassi is the founder of Better Place, a new electric vehicle service provider based in Palo Alto, California. He has launched a scalable transportation system that Thomas Friedman calls Car 2.0. Better Place provides a network of charging spots and automated battery exchange stations that support multiple types of batteries from numerous manufacturers. Instead of filling up their cars with gasoline, Better Place customers exchange used batteries for new ones, charged by many renewable energy sources, without leaving their vehicles and in less time than it would take to fill up with gasoline. Better Place customers can replenish their electric cars at charging spots throughout urban districts as well as at home.

Reducing greenhouse gas emissions from automobiles
is part of the fight against global warming. Better Place,
an electric vehicle service provider, is developing electric
vehicle charge spots, such as the one pictured here, as
well as a network of battery charge and switch stations.
These facilities make it easy for drivers to plug in and "fill
up," whether they are at home, at work or at a restaurant
or shopping mall.

Instead of selling cars, Agasi sells "mobility miles."[3] Better Place uses a
mileage-based subscription program in which customers buy or lease electric vehicles produced by Renault and Nissan with a range of 100 miles.
Customers then purchase mobility miles as they might buy minutes from
a cell phone company. The Better Place network costs six cents a mile,
about half the cost of the gasoline-based system. Better Place opened its
first charging spot and plug-in parking lots in 2008 in Israel; the electric cars and service infrastructure are scheduled to roll out in Israel and
Denmark by 2011. Australia, Canada, Japan, Hawaii and the San Francisco
Bay Area have also signed agreements with Better Place to build networks.
This model shows how a scalable approach can thrive, moving beyond our
concept of car use to an environmentally friendly, efficient transportation
system.

In the energy sector, upgrading the US energy grid will be a daunting challenge. Building a new smart grid entails developing digital technologies to reduce power consumption, accept energy from distributed sources and reduce our carbon footprint and the occurrence of blackouts. Smart meters will allow better communication between utilities and their customers as advanced sensors signal home appliances such as dishwashers and water heaters to operate during off-peak hours. The smart grid also will be capable of integrating excess energy from distributed sources such as solar panels and wind turbines.

Among the first successful pilot projects for smart grid technology is the Telegestore project. Completed in 2005, it covers over 27 million homes near Rome and other Italian cities. Using advanced metering technology, the Telegestore project's investment of €2.1 billion is yielding €500 million in annual savings, delivering more reliable service at a lower cost.[4] In the US, the cities of Austin, Texas, and Boulder, Colorado, are building smart grid technologies for home automation networks. Google and General Electric have teamed up to promote the development of a national smart grid that will support alternative energy sources and accommodate increased demand from plug-in cars. The successful scaling of initiatives requires reinventing the way we use existing systems. By reimagining how we use automobiles and energy, for example, we can devise scalable approaches for widespread adoption.

Place-making

Place-making initiatives consider the historical, cultural and biological characteristics of a community, its settlement history, values, natural cycles, environmental impacts and present concerns. Understanding these is critical for bringing together citizens to implement change. Place-making emphasizes the design, beauty and health of natural systems. David Orr points out that designers "ought to think of yourselves first as place-makers, not merely form-makers.... The first rule of place making...is to honor and preserve other places, however remote in space and culture. When you become accomplished designers...you will have mastered the integration of both making places and making them beautiful."[5] Place-making involves nourishing our connection to the cultural and ecological fabric of our community.

A sense of place encourages us to take responsibility for our neighbors and our resources. Philosopher Simone Weil reminds us that "rootedness

Joel Catchlove

Residents transform their neighborhood intersection into a public "Share-It-Square" as part of the grassroots City Repair Project in Portland, Oregon. Such initiatives bring people together and improve their quality of life.

in place is the most important and least recognized need of the human soul." For instance, understanding where our water, food and electricity come from helps us to see our interdependence with natural systems. Tracking the financial capital used to purchase goods and services reveals a community's ecological footprint, which can include its wastestream, greenhouse gas emissions, pollution and the maintenance of its buildings, roads and bridges. The social connections that evolve from "rootedness in place" form the basis for thriveable place-making projects.

One place-making initiative is the City Repair Project in Portland, Oregon. Co-director Mark Lakeman began City Repair in 1996 as a grassroots initiative, known as Intersection Repair, to convert a Portland intersection into a neighborhood public square, a Share-It-Square. The initiative started with an unpermitted tea house to bring the community together. The public square was painted in a colorful design and the tea house and an information kiosk encouraged neighbors to meet each other and reclaim their public space. When Portland officials threatened to dismantle the square, neighbors conducted a survey that showed residents welcomed the intersection changes because they encouraged greater communication with neighbors, increased safety and decreased crime.

City council members later unanimously approved an Intersection Repair ordinance, citing its support of Portland's livability goals. Over the years, Intersection Repair has expanded to 150 locations throughout Portland and the model has inspired similar efforts in dozens of cities in the US. According to the *Journal of Public Health,* crime rates at City Repair locations in Portland have dropped by as much as 10 percent; other un-"repaired" communities have had more physical and mental health problems.[6] Additional City Repair initiatives include the Village Building Convergence, a ten-day gathering of volunteers working to transform a neighborhood; City Riparian, a planting effort encouraging urban permaculture; the T-Horse, a tea house that travels through the city's neighborhoods; and the Depave project, an attempt to remove excess concrete and reduce stormwater runoff pollution.[7] The success of Portland's City Repair initiatives underscores the power of an inviting place for neighbors to meet, share their concerns and take action. Through these community efforts, residents become empowered to transform their neighborhoods.

Place-making initiatives emphasize strong social connections and built environments that complement the processes in nature. By challenging us to understand the patterns of nature and to design actions for healthy natural systems and strong neighborhoods, place-making activities encourage us to become stewards of the land and caring members of our community.

Intergenerational

The intergenerational aspect of initiatives emphasizes their long-term benefits. This perspective is often at odds with society's need for instant gratification, 24-hour news cycles, Twittering, e-mails and other technologies that increase the pace of everyday life. Daily stock fluctuations and quarterly returns from publicly traded companies add to the short-term, quick-profit mentality of much of the business sector. An intergenerational initiative is based on enduring principles that will support the well-being of future generations. The traditional Native American time-horizon evaluates current actions by their impact to the seventh generation. Similarly, we might ask, "What is our vision for our community in the next 100 or even 500 years?"

This intergenerational outlook can be seen in the Menominee Nation's sustainable forestry management practices. Situated in northeast Wisconsin and on Michigan's Upper Peninsula, the Menominee tribe traditionally lived in their forests and survived by hunting, fishing and harvesting wild rice. Since the Menominee reservation was established in 1854, the tribe's forestry practices have been a model of successful management. At the core of the 220,000-acre Menominee forest are three principles:

1. The forest must be sustainable for future generations.
2. The forest must be cared for properly to provide for the many varying needs of people over time and to support the Tribe's economy.
3. "Keep all the pieces" of the forest, to maintain diversity.[8]

Menominee Tribal Enterprises

August Corn from Menominee Tribal Enterprises loads aspen pulpwood to be delivered to a paper mill. The Menominees' intergenerational perspective and sustainable forestry practices have increased the amount of timber in their forest for the last 150 years.

These principles have given Menominee Tribal Enterprises (MTE), which manages the lumber operations, a phenomenal track record. Because of rigorous management and restoration practices, over 2 billion board-feet of timber — about 30 million board-feet per year — have been harvested from the forest since 1865 with seemingly unnoticeable changes to the land. Moreover, the amount of timber remaining in the forest has increased from 1.3 billion board-feet in 1854 to over 1.7 billion presently.[9] MTE is an example of a thriveable enterprise that goes beyond sustainable practices into regenerative ones, not merely replacing the harvested trees but enhancing the forest ecosystem. These actions are based on a perspective of abundance and their intergenerational legacy.

The Menominee tribe's Continuous Forest Inventory (CFI) monitors the health of the forest. The CFI provides information on the volume, growth and quality of the trees, which helps guide forestry management decisions. The Menominee operation has preserved 14 of 16 major forest cover types found in the region, protected the wildlife and watershed and provided the tribe with employment and economic opportunities for the last 150 years. Its success points to the integration of the ecological, social and economic aspects of the Menominees' long-term vision for their community.

This intergenerational perspective is shared by The Long Now Foundation's 10,000-year Millennium Clock, Long Bets and Longviewer projects. Founder Stewart Brand and a team of innovators and artists set out to create the Millennium Clock. It is designed to tick once a year and its cuckoo comes out every millennium — for the next 10,000 years. The prototypes of the Millennium Clock, developed by Danny Hillis, are on display at the Science Museum in London and at The Long Now Museum and Store in San Francisco. The clock, designed to synchronize with the sun, will eventually be located on a mountain in the Nevada desert near Great Basin National Park, where 5,000-year-old bristle cone pines will keep it company for a long, long time.

The Long Now Foundation's Long Bets project aims to "improve long-term thinking" by inviting people to make predictions and bets that are "societally or scientifically important." Examples include "At least one human alive in the year 2000 will be alive in 2150" and "By 2030, commercial passengers will routinely fly in pilotless planes."[10] The Long Bets project also serves as a philanthropic tool by donating the amount of the bets to charity. Longviewer, an open-source tool, provides a way to assess events over centuries and even millennia. This free software program encourages users to map time horizons and gain a long-term perspective on events and possibilities for the future.[11]

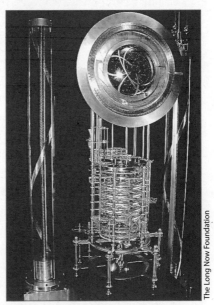

The Long Now Foundation

The first prototype of The Long Now Foundation's 10,000-year clock is designed to synchronize with the sun and keep accurate time over millennia. A monument-sized version will eventually be located on a mountaintop near Great Basin National Park, Nevada. This project highlights Long Now's commitment to maintaining an intergenerational perspective in human endeavors.

Resilient

The root of the word "resilience" comes from "resilire": to spring back or rebound. Scientist Brian Walker and his colleagues describe resilience as "the capacity of a system to absorb disturbance and reorganize while undergoing change so as to still retain essentially the same function, structure, identity, and feedbacks."[12] In the natural world, the resilience of habitats is evident in their recovery from wildfires, floods and moderate human disturbances. Resilience also applies to the capacity of our communities, with their technical and social networks, to recover from disruptions such as shortages of energy, food or water, pollution, disease, war and natural disasters.

Resilient systems have diversity, modular components, tight feedback, close social networks, redundancy and flexibility.[13] Diversity provides a community with choices. For example, a community with diversified services (high-tech, health, communications) and resources (fishing, forestry, agriculture) is better able to withstand the fluctuations of economic and ecological cycles.

Modular components concern the connections within a system. The lack of modular components in the electric grid, for example, makes it more susceptible to widespread outages. Our overconnected transportation network allows for the fast spread of diseases. In the financial realm, the 2008 collapse of the housing sector in the US economy spread to the financial and manufacturing sectors, rapidly affected developed economies and led to a worldwide economic crisis. The lack of modular components in the financial sector may have facilitated the spread of the economic crisis.

Tight feedback refers to the speed and strength of an action's results. Actions that affect the local level tend to have shorter and clearer feedback loops than those that affect distant places. Handling waste at a local landfill rather than transporting it to a distant site exposes issues associated with recycling and waste disposal. Our globalized economy is marked by long feedback loops. It is challenging for someone in the US, for example, to understand the full ecological and social impacts of buying goods grown or produced in Europe, Asia or Latin America.

Close social networks support resilient communities through the trust and human connections that neighbors extend to each other, particularly in times of need. These networks help build the social capital that makes it possible to overcome adversity. During Hurricane Katrina there were numerous examples of residents reaching out to each other. Although they could not control the impact of the hurricane, they could choose their response. The positive, flexible response they chose enhanced their resilience.

We need redundancy and flexibility when dealing with community necessities such as food, water, energy and communications networks, as well as governing structures. Having alternative sources and storage of basic resources creates a safety net. Similarly, governing structures that invite input from community members strengthen accountability and support.[14]

Efforts that incorporate community resilience strategies include ICLEI's Climate Resilient Communities Program and the Headline Climate Change Adaptation Strategy in Durban, South Africa. ICLEI's program expands the success of its Cities for Climate Protection Campaign by providing local governments with tools to assess their vulnerability to the impacts of climate change and to set priorities for adaptation, planning and action. Participating communities follow ICLEI's Five Milestones for Climate Adaptation: conduct a climate resilience study; prioritize areas for action and set goals; develop a climate resilience action plan; implement the plan; and monitor and reevaluate. The ICLEI program began in 2007 in Fort Collins, Colorado; Homer, Alabama; Keene, New Hampshire; and Miami-Dade, Florida. Homer has now developed a plan to diversify its economy so it relies less on its fishing industry. Miami-Dade County's new Climate Change Advisory Task Force is developing standards for its infrastructure, including bridges, airports, ports and buildings, to manage a rise in sea level or severe storms.[15] In Durban, city officials have developed strategies to deal with climate change by examining its effects on health, water and sanitation, coastal developments, disaster preparedness and biodiversity.[16] These communities are increasing their resilience by preparing for climate change.

David Dodman points out, "Rather than thinking about resilience as 'bouncing back' from shocks and stresses, it is perhaps more useful to think of it as 'bouncing forward' to a state where shocks and stresses can be dealt with more efficiently and successfully and with less damage to individual lives and livelihoods."[17] Resilience implies recognizing that change is inevitable and that adapting our economic and social systems to it is key to surviving and thriving. This is a new way of thinking about how we adapt to the changes we experience in our communities.

Accessible

Accessibility in initiatives focuses on developing tools and job opportunities that incorporate social and environmental justice. Social entrepreneur Van Jones champions government, business and nonprofit ventures with training programs in areas such as weatherizing homes and commercial buildings, installing solar panels, manufacturing wind turbines and making organic foods available to inner-city neighborhoods. Such programs can extend green initiatives beyond people who can presently afford them to include residents of communities in need of stable and dignified jobs. As Jones points out, "Our business and political leaders will launch tens of thousands of new green enterprises and initiatives. Each time they do, they must ask the question: How can we make this effort inclusive, ennobling and empowering to people who are disrespected in the old economy? How can this effort be used to increase the work, wealth, health, dignity and power of our society's disadvantaged?"[18] Jones emphasizes the need to expand access to thriveable initiatives to people from all socioeconomic backgrounds if the initiatives are to have a lasting impact.

The success of green initiatives hinges on empowering a wide range of individuals and communities to take part in forging the new economy. Through tax incentives, training programs and entrepreneurial ventures, green products and services can spread into the mainstream economy. In regions throughout the US, including San Francisco, Portland, Chicago, New York and Seattle, businesses and municipalities are creating green jobs and using their success to attract new industry.

Making green initiatives more accessible involves developing incentives that help residents understand their environmental impacts. In 2007 Berkeley, California, became the first city in the US to allow homeowners to pay for solar installations and other energy efficiency measures by adding the costs to their property taxes. Berkeley's Sustainable Energy Financing Program eliminates the upfront costs, one of the main barriers to the widespread adoption of solar installations. By raising capital through a bond or loan fund, Berkeley provides homeowners with the necessary funding, which is paid back over 20 years. This financing program is gaining national attention. Boulder, Colorado, and Sonoma County, California, have implemented similar programs and other municipalities are planning to follow suit.

Making information about our individual and our community's environmental impacts more accessible is a way to encourage people to make adjustments. In Sonoma County, John Garn and his team at Community Pulse have devised a web-based social marketing tool to educate residents and government agencies about their ecological footprint. Community Pulse tracks the amount of carbon dioxide emissions, energy use, water use and waste generation on an individual, community and state basis.

Residents of Cotati in Sonoma County, for example, can learn that their average per person waste generation in August 2008 was 113 pounds;

Sonoma County's was 105 pounds, and in 2006 California's was 186 pounds a month.[19] These indicators help residents and community leaders monitor their personal and community environmental actions and modify their targets as needed. They also create an incentive for community leaders to develop thriveable strategies to compete with other cities in their region. In addition, Community Pulse provides accessible resources for changing behaviors to reduce one's ecological footprint. Launched in 2008, Community Pulse is tracking several counties in California and hopes to expand its services throughout the state and eventually the nation. Whether through web-based tools such as Community Pulse or government finance programs such as Berkeley's Sustainable Energy Financing Program, accessible green initiatives can be leverage points for change.

Life-affirming

Life-affirming initiatives support long-term, regenerative activities. Biologist Janine Benyus says that "life creates conditions conducive to life." As part of the web of life, we can develop initiatives with life-affirming values: The first step is to learn from nature's evolutionary experience of 3.8 billion years. We can ask questions such as "How does nature gather energy, produce food and store water?"[20] Just as importantly we can ask, "How does nature *not* gather energy, produce food or store water?" Before we move forward with new products and technologies, we can examine the potential repercussions of our actions. The Precautionary Principle helps us evaluate these.

In 1998, a group of lawyers, scientists, policymakers and environmentalists gathered at Wingspread, the headquarters of the Johnson Foundation in Racine, Wisconsin, to discuss limiting the health and environmental impacts of human activities. One outcome of the meeting was the Wingspread Statement on the Precautionary Principle, which states: "When an activity raises threats of harm to the environment or human health, precautionary measures should be taken even if some cause and effect relationships are not fully established scientifically."[21] In essence, the Precautionary Principle places the burden of proof of an activity's safety on the initiator rather than on the public. In the face of scientific uncertainty, the principle requires the initiator to err on the side of caution, which may involve not taking any action at all. The Precautionary Principle supports a life-affirming approach by anticipating the potential harm from an action before it is too late.

When invoking the Precautionary Principle, common phrases such as "better safe than sorry" and "first do no harm" come to mind. The European Union has incorporated elements of the Precautionary Principle in its environmental policies, food laws, consumer protection policies, trade initiatives and technological developments. In the US, the City of San Francisco passed the Precautionary Principle Purchasing Ordinance in 2005. It requires officials managing the city's $600 million purchasing budget to weigh the potential environmental and health impacts of their purchases, from cleaning supplies to computers.[22] The Precautionary Principle challenges us to move slowly and assess the potential negative consequences of our actions before we "let the genie out of the bottle" by going ahead.

In addition to policies such as the Precautionary Principle, there are life-affirming initiatives seeking to restore biological diversity and the vitality of communities. The Biomimicry Institute's Innovation for Conservation program, for example, supports the conservation efforts of "bio-inspired businesses," whose designs and products are derived from natural systems. Through the program's biodiversity conservation fund, these businesses can invest a percentage of their profits in protecting the species and habitats that inspired their products. In a similar way, companies can take life-affirming actions that recognize the benefits they derive from products and services based on natural systems. The Innovation for Conservation program gives participants a way of saying "thank you" to the ecosystems we depend on for our well-being.[23]

At the individual level, Jane Goodall's Roots & Shoots program involves youth in life-affirming actions in their communities. Launched in 1991 by 16 Tanzanian students, the program engages tens of thousands of young people in service projects in over 100 countries. Participants follow the Roots & Shoots learning model: knowledge (the basis of responsible action), compassion (the engine of your project) and action (the result of learning and planning). Goodall emphasizes, "Only if we understand, can we care; Only if we care, will we help; Only if we help, shall all be saved."[24] This life-affirming approach expresses the best of the human spirit and shows how we can move toward a thriveable future.

Young people involved in Roots & Shoots participate in community service projects such as park clean-ups, habitat restoration and helping at senior centers and animal shelters. Their global campaigns include the Day of Peace, when community members make peace dove puppets from reused materials; the Trees for To-morrow Campaign to promote local tree planting efforts; and the Reusable Bag Campaign to replace plastic bags with reusable ones. Roots & Shoots combines the power of individual life-affirming actions with the needs of local communities and the environment. Life-affirming actions encourage us to look beyond our self-interest and connect with our community and with nature.

Self-care

Self-care is how we nourish and replenish ourselves. It sustains us and allows us to thrive in our attempts to make a difference in the world. We may walk in nature, make music, exercise, read, rest, paint, connect with friends and colleagues or participate in myriad hobbies.

Roots & Shoots Youth Leadership member Torri Igou and a Tanzanian member look at seedlings at a nursery in Moshi Village, Tanzania. The Roots & Shoots program involves youth from around the world in community service projects.

In nature, ecotones are the boundaries of habitats, such as the transition between a meadow and a forest or between the ocean and the shore. These zones can be very rich in species diversity and host thriving ecological communities. Similar to biological ecotones, social ecotones provide us with opportunities to flourish through our interactions with friends and colleagues. This is where our ideas meet and evolve into possibilities for change. Here we thrive through interactions that nourish our human connections. Designing spaces and activities that promote social ecotones builds community and improves our quality of life. Such ecotones include farmers' markets, festivals and gatherings with friends, neighbors and colleagues.

Whatever our source of nourishment, we benefit from identifying our needs and tapping the resources that replenish us. On an airplane we are urged to put on our oxygen masks before helping our child. Similarly, our work is most effective when we first replenish ourselves and then give to others. This is a way of greening the world from the inside out, starting with the greening of our own hearts.

Faced with the question of where to begin making a difference, perhaps it is best to ask where our interests lie. Then we can take easy steps with tangible results. These may include home, school or community projects such as replacing incandescent lights with compact fluorescent bulbs, composting, starting an organic vegetable garden, organizing carpools or bicycling. Volunteering with a local group in its environmental and community-building campaigns can provide additional resources and the camaraderie of a team of like-minded people. Organizations such as EcoTuesday, with chapters throughout the US, and Green Drinks, with international chapters, host local social gatherings for people interested in a wide range of environmental fields.

Taking personal responsibility for our financial decisions also supports a socially just and environmentally responsible world. As consumers, investors and workers, we can use our financial and human capital to affect the vitality or degradation of our communities. Understanding the impact of our purchasing and investment decisions involves screening companies. Green America, New American Dream, Business for Social Responsibility and WiserBusiness all provide resources for helping us evaluate businesses and make responsible consumer decisions.

In the political arena, an active citizenry can engage officials on issues of concern. Open meetings with elected leaders are a venue for sharing ideas on issues affecting our daily lives. The 2008 national election in the US galvanized citizens to get involved in the political process and share in the excitement of the possibility of a better future. Whether at home, in the workplace or in our communities, our individual actions flourish when we take care of ourselves. Self-care is at the root of changing the world.

Moving Toward Thriveability

The SPIRALS framework for thriveable initiatives describes a new way of meeting the challenges we face. The environmental, social and economic predicaments we find ourselves in call for a movement from sustainability to thriveability, shifting from a model of scarcity to one of abundance that taps into the spirit of possibility. Instead of a net-zero energy home, the thriveable goal is a home that generates more electricity than it uses; instead of restoring an ecosystem in decline, the thriveable goal is to regenerate it so that it teems with diverse wildlife and is integrated with flourishing human settlements. The thriveable perspective asks, "How can we satisfy basic human needs such as food, water, shelter, education, healthcare and love for all people on the planet while creating a meaningful life?"

In times of crisis throughout history, we have been able to overcome seemingly insurmountable obstacles by unifying our efforts behind a common vision. We can meet the challenges ahead with a vision in which creativity trumps knowledge and imagination is recognized as one of our most powerful assets. These timeless attributes will light our path toward a thriveable future for generations to come.

TAKING ACTION

➡ *Design a personal thriveability plan.*

➡ *Create a place-making bioregional map identifying your local foodshed, your watershed and the energy, transportation, economic and other links in your community. Share it with friends and colleagues.*

➡ *Design and implement an initiative that uses the SPIRALS framework.*

➡ *Explore how you can incorporate resilience into your network of family, friends, colleagues, workplace and community.*

➡ *Develop a green jobs training/internship program with businesses from your community.*

➡ *Develop community-building events that celebrate the talents and resources of your community members such as an arts festival, food fair, poetry reading or sports event.*

➡ *Take stock of what nourishes you. Create time and energy to implement these activities and inspire others to do the same.*

Resources

For annotated bibliography see *Thriving Beyond Sustainability* at: andresedwards.com

Organizations (in their own words)

Introduction: Drawing a Collective Map of Earth Island

Arnold Creek Productions — arnoldcreekproductions.com
The mission of Arnold Creek Productions is to create educational and inspirational media that supports the principles of sustainability and improves the lives of all people.

Bioneers — bioneers.org
Bioneers is inspiring a shift to live on Earth in ways that honor the web of life, each other and future generations. Founded in 1990, Bioneers promotes practical environmental solutions and innovative social strategies for restoring Earth's imperiled ecosystems and healing our human communities.

Buckminster Fuller Institute — bfi.org
The Buckminster Fuller Institute is dedicated to accelerating the development and deployment of solutions which radically advance human well being and the health of our planet's ecosystems.

Clinton Global Initiative — clintonglobalinitiative.org
Building on President Clinton's lifetime in public service, the Clinton Global Initiative (CGI) reflects his belief that governments need collaboration from the private sector, non-governmental organizations, and other global leaders to effectively confront the world's most pressing problems. After attending thousands of meetings during his career in which urgent needs were discussed but no action was taken to solve them, President Clinton saw a need to establish a new kind of meeting with an emphasis on results.

David Suzuki Foundation — davidsuzuki.org
Since 1990, the David Suzuki Foundation has worked to find ways for society to live in balance with the natural world that sustains us. Focusing on four program areas — oceans and sustainable fishing, climate change and clean energy, sustainability, and the Nature Challenge — the Foundation uses science and education to promote solutions that conserve nature and help achieve sustainability within a generation.

Earth Island Institute — earthisland.org
Earth Island Institute is a non-profit, public interest, membership organization that supports people who are creating solutions to protect our shared planet.

Earth Policy Institute — earth-policy.org
The Earth Policy Institute was founded by Lester Brown in May 2001 to provide a vision of a sustainable future and a plan for how to get from here to there.

Environmental Working Group — ewg.org
The mission of the Environmental Working Group (EWG) is to use the power of

public information to protect public health and the environment. EWG is a 501(c)(3) non-profit organization, founded in 1993 by Ken cook and Richard Wiles.

ERTHNXT — erthnxt.org

ERTHNXT is about all of us. And our responsibility to the planet we call home. A national non-profit committed to protecting the future of life for all species, ERTHNXT's goal is to engage young people around the world to be good stewards of our environment.

GoodGuide — goodguide.com

GoodGuide provides the world's largest and most reliable source of information on the health, environmental, and social impacts of the products in your home.

Green America — greenamericatoday.org

Green America is a not-for-profit membership organization founded in 1982. (We went by the name "Co-op America" until January 1, 2009.) Our mission is to harness economic power — the strength of consumers, investors, businesses, and the market-place — to create a socially just and environmentally sustainable society.

Green Maven — greenmaven.com

Green Maven is your gateway to the Green Web. We're a search engine that focuses on green and sustainable websites.

Green Planet Films — greenplanetfilms.org

Green Planet Films is a non-profit distributor of nature and environmental DVDs from around the globe. We promote environmental education through film.

International Institute for Sustainable Development — iisd.org

IISD is in the business of promoting change towards sustainable development. As a policy research institute dedicated to effective communication of our findings, we engage decision-makers in government, business, NGOs and other sectors in the development and implementation of policies that are simultaneously beneficial to the global economy, the global environment and to social well-being.

MBDC — mbdc.com

MBDC is a product and process design firm dedicated to revolutionizing the design of products and services worldwide. William McDonough and Dr. Michael Braungart founded MBDC in 1995 to promote and shape what they call the "Next Industrial Revolution" through the introduction of a new design paradigm called Cradle to Cradle^{SM} Design, and the implementation of eco-effective design principles.

National Wildlife Federation — nwf.org

Wildlife's ability to survive the challenges of the 21st century is becoming outpaced by the events that are transforming our world. Global warming, the loss of habitat, and people becoming more disconnected from nature than past generations are converging on a dangerous path for our planet. The work of NWF and our affiliates across the country provides answers to these challenges and will help ensure America's wildlife legacy continues for future generations.

Natural Capital Institute — naturalcapital.org

The Natural Capital Institute serves the people who are transforming the world. We are a team of researchers, teachers, students, activists, scholars, writers, social entrepreneurs, artists, and volunteers committed to the restoration of the earth and the healing of human culture. We do two things: we describe pathways of change in books and research reports, and we create tools for connecting the individuals, information, and organizations that create change.

The Natural Edge Project — naturaledgeproject.net
The Natural Edge Project (TNEP) is an independent Sustainability Think-Tank based in Australia. TNEP operates as a partnership for education, research and policy development on innovation for sustainable development.

Natural Resources Defense Council — nrdc.org
The Natural Resources Defense Council's purpose is to safeguard the Earth: its people, its plants and animals and the natural systems on which all life depends.

New American Dream — newdream.org
New American Dream helps Americans consume responsibly to protect the environment, enhance quality of life, and promote social justice.

New Dimensions Foundation — newdimensions.org
The New Dimensions Foundation is a social profit, public benefit, tax exempt, 501(c)(3) educational organization supported by listeners. Our primary activity is the independent production of broadcast dialogues and other quality programs that explore creative solutions to urgent challenges facing humankind.

New Economics Foundation — neweconomics.org
nef is an independent think-and-do tank that inspires and demonstrates real economic well-being. We aim to improve quality of life by promoting innovative solutions that challenge mainstream thinking on economic, environment and social issues. We work in partnership and put people and the planet first.

Pew Research Center for the People & the Press — people-press.org
The Pew Research Center for the People & the Press is an independent, non-partisan public opinion research organization that studies attitudes toward politics, the press and public policy issues. In this role it serves as a valuable information resource for political leaders, journalists, scholars and citizens.

Planetwork — planetwork.net
Planetwork brings a collaborative systems view rooted in conscious evolution to the intersection of sustainability & technology. We are a convening organization, gathering people from a wide variety of disciplines and vocations — science, technology, activism, business and the arts — to further the conversation about earth systems, communities and the potentially constructive role of technology.

Rocky Mountain Institute — rmi.org
Rocky Mountain Institute® (RMI), a 501(c)(3) nonprofit organization, was established in 1982 by resource analysts L. Hunter Lovins and Amory B. Lovins. What began as a small group of colleagues focusing on energy policy has since grown into a broad-based institution with approximately eighty full-time staff, an annual budget of nearly $12 million (over half of it earned through programmatic enterprise), and a global reach.

State of the World Forum — worldforum.org
The Forum was established to create a global leadership network comprised of eminent individuals — ranging from Heads of State to grass roots organizers, Nobel

Laureates to business leaders, policy makers to social activists — drawn from the governmental, business and civil society sectors, committed to discerning and implementing those principles, values and actions necessary to guide humanity wisely as it gives shape to an increasingly global and interdependent world.

Sustainable Europe Research Institute — seri.at

The Sustainable Europe Research Institute (SERI) is a Pan-European think tank exploring sustainable development options for European societies. It was set up in September 1999. Sustainability strategies must be integrated or they are not sustainable. SERI therefore takes a comprehensive view of sustainability both empirically and in its policy recommendations.

Together — together.com

Together makes it easy to take action and begin saving energy, the planet — and your hard-earned money. What's more, Together totals up the energy-savings of all of our actions and illustrates the enormous, positive impact we can have when we all pitch in. You will be joining with millions of other Americans who are also doing simple things to reduce their impact upon the planet — while simultaneously reducing their energy bills.

WiserEarth — wiserearth.org

WiserEarth is an online community space connecting the people, nonprofits and businesses working toward a just and sustainable world.

Worldchanging — worldchanging.com

Worldchanging.com is a nonprofit media organization headquartered in Seattle, WA, that comprises a global network of independent journalists, designers and thinkers. We cover the world's most innovative solutions to the planet's problems, and inspire readers around the world with stories of new tools, models and ideas for building a bright green future.

World Resources Institute — wri.org

WRI is an environmental think tank that goes beyond research to find practical ways to protect the earth and improve people's lives.... Our mission is to move human society to live in ways that protect Earth's environment and its capacity to provide for the needs and aspirations of current and future generations.

Worldwatch Institute — worldwatch.org

Worldwatch Institute delivers the insights and ideas that empower decision makers to create an environmentally sustainable society that meets human needs. Worldwatch focuses on the 21st century challenges of climate change, resource degradation, population growth, and poverty by developing and disseminating solid data and innovative strategies for achieving a sustainable society.

Wuppertal Institute for Climate, Environment, and Energy — wupperinst.org/en/home

Sustainable development requires an integrated approach to policy and science because many of the issues it raises cannot be addressed within a single department or using the tools of individual scientific disciplines. This is where the Wuppertal Institute's research programme begins — by taking an interdisciplinary approach and working towards systems understanding. Applied sustainability research is the Wuppertal Institute's stated mission.

Chapter 1: Lessons from Our Ancestors

Alaska Native Knowledge Network — ankn.uaf.edu

The Alaska Native Knowledge Network (ANKN) is an AKRSI [Alaska Rural Systemic Initiative] partner designed to serve as a resource for compiling and exchanging information related to Alaska Native knowledge systems and ways of knowing. It has been established to assist Native people, government agencies, educators and the general public in gaining access to the knowledge base that Alaska Natives have acquired through cumulative experience over millennia.

Alaska Native Science Commission — nativescience.org

The Alaska Native Science Commission (ANSC) was established in 1994 to bring together research and science in partnership with the Native community. It serves as a clearinghouse for proposed research, an information base for ongoing and past research and an archive for significant research involving the Native community. ANSC provides information, referral and networking services for researchers seeking active partners in the Native community and communities seeking research partners.

AnthroSource — anthrosource.net

AnthroSource is the premier online portal serving the needs of educators, students, researchers, and practitioners. An online service of the AAA [American Anthropological Association], AnthroSource offers access to more than 100 years of anthropological knowledge.

Canadian Arctic Resources Committee — carc.org

C.A.R.C. is a citizens' organization dedicated to the long-term environmental and social well being of northern Canada and its peoples. We believe in sustainable development and the application of the precautionary principle. Our policy and advocacy work is grounded in solid scientific and socio-economic research and experience.

The Cultural Conservancy — nativeland.org

The Cultural Conservancy is a Native American nonprofit organization dedicated to the preservation and revitalization of indigenous cultures and their ancestral lands. We are a research, education, and advocacy organization. We provide mediation, legal, information referral, and audio recording services. We also produce educational programs and materials and technical trainings on Native land conservation and land rights, cultural and ecological restoration, and traditional indigenous arts and spiritual values.

Indigenous Ways of Knowing — lclark.edu/~iwok/main.htm

Mission: To empower Tribal communities by providing educational experiences through a multicontextual process rooted in Indigenous Worldviews.

International Society for Ecology and Culture — isec.org.uk

The International Society for Ecology and Culture (ISEC) is a non-profit organisation concerned with the protection of both biological and cultural diversity. Our emphasis is on education for action: moving beyond single issues to look at the more fundamental influences that shape our lives.

Inuit Heritage Trust — ihti.ca

The Inuit Heritage Trust (IHT) is dedicated to the preservation, enrichment and protection of Inuit cultural heritage and identity embodied in Nunavut's archaeology sites, ethnographic resources and traditional place names. The Trust's activities are based on the principle of respect for the traditional knowledge and wisdom of our Elders.

The Office of Tibet, London — tibet.com
The Office of Tibet in London is an official agency of His Holiness the Dalai Lama. Established in 1981, its main function is to create a better understanding of the situation in Tibet and to draw the attention of world public opinion to the plight of the Tibetan people and the functioning of the exiled Tibetan government.

The Rosetta Project — rosettaproject.org
The Rosetta Project is a global collaboration of language specialists and native speakers working to build a publicly accessible digital library of human languages. Since becoming a National Science Digital Library collection in 2004, the Rosetta Archive has more than doubled its collection size, now serving nearly 100,000 pages of material documenting over 2,500 languages — the largest resource of its kind on the Net.

Tairona Heritage Trust — taironatrust.org
[T]he Tairona Heritage Trust [is] a small British-based NGO which, since 1990, has been working on behalf of Gonavindua Tairona. The Sierra Nevada de Santa Marta is the highest coastal mountain in the world, and the indigenous groups which live on it — the Kogi, the Arhuaco and the Assario — are the descendants of the Tairona civilization which flourished there at the time of the Spanish Invasion. Gonavindua Tairona is the political organisation founded by the Mamas (priests) of the three tribes in 1987 in order to represent their interests in the face of increasing Western pressures. The three tribes refer to themselves as "The Elder Brothers," and to Westerners as "The Younger Brother."

Tibet Environmental Watch — tew.org
This site will be used to update important Tibetan environmental information as new data becomes available and to build upon the concept of a "Zone of Peace" as presented by His Holiness the Dalai Lama.

Tibet Online — tibet.org
Tibet Online is operated by the international Tibet Support Group community, providing information on the plight of Tibet and serving as a virtual community space for the movement. This movement is dedicated to ending the suffering of the Tibetan people by returning the right of self-determination to the Tibetan people.

UNESCO: Best Practices on Indigenous Knowledge — unesco.org/most/bpindi.htm
The Netherlands Organization for International Cooperation in Higher Education/ Indigenous Knowledge (NUFFIC/IK-Unit) in co-operation with UNESCO's Management of Social Transformations Programme (MOST) has established a Database of best practices on indigenous knowledge in 1999 which initially contained 27 best practices. Through the second phase (2001–2002), 22 cases were newly added to the database.

Chapter 2: Going "Glocal"

Common Current — commoncurrent.com
Common Current provides frameworks, tools and funding mechanisms supporting goals of moving to greater sustainability. We can baseline performance data and help put systems in place to measure and report long-term results.

Community Alliance with Family Farmers — caff.org
Today's Community Alliance with Family Farmers is the result of efforts by both farmers and urban activists working together for almost 30 years. Our mission is to build a movement of rural and urban people to foster family-scale agriculture that cares for the land, sustains local economies and promotes social justice.

Conservation Economy — conservationeconomy.net
The conservation economy framework provides the basis for a wide range of training and consulting services, helping businesses, governments, and non-profits make a just and viable transition to sustainability. In order to constantly test the ideas behind a conservation economy, we also host an international "open source" Learning Network which allows people to share their insights and experiences.

Ecotrust — ecotrust.org
Ecotrust's mission is to inspire fresh thinking that creates economic opportunity, social equity and environmental well-being. Ecotrust is headquartered in Portland and is a unique organization; it integrates public and private purpose and for-profit and non-profit structures.

The E. F. Schumacher Society — smallisbeautiful.org
Founded in 1980 the mission of the Schumacher Society is to promote the building of strong local economies that link people, land, and community. To accomplish this we develop model programs, including local currencies, community land trusts, and micro-lending; host lectures and other educational events; publish papers; and maintain a library to engage scholars and inspire citizen-activists.

Global Ecovillage Network — gen.ecovillage.org
The Global Ecovillage Network is a global confederation of people and communities that meet and share their ideas, exchange technologies, develop cultural and educational exchanges, directories and newsletters, and are dedicated to restoring the land and living "sustainable plus" lives by putting more back into the environment than we take out.

ICLEI–Local Governments for Sustainability — iclei.org
ICLEI–Local Governments for Sustainability is an international association of local governments as well as national and regional local government organizations that have made a commitment to sustainable development.

LocalHarvest — localharvest.org
LocalHarvest is America's #1 organic and local food website. We maintain a definitive and reliable "living" public nationwide directory of small farms, farmers markets, and other local food sources. Our search engine helps people find products from family farms, local sources of sustainably grown food, and encourages them to establish direct contact with small farms in their local area.

New Zealand Resource Management Act — mfe.govt.nz/rma
This site is a gateway to information about the Resource Management Act 1991 (RMA), New Zealand's main piece of legislation that sets out how we should manage our environment.

One Planet Living — oneplanetliving.com
One Planet Living is a global initiative based on ten principles of sustainability developed by BioRegional and WWF.

Post Carbon Institute — postcarbon.org
Post Carbon Institute helps individuals and communities understand and respond to the environmental, societal, and economic crises created by our dependence on fossil fuels.

Resource Renewal Institute — rri.org
The Resource Renewal Institute facilitates the creation, development and implementation of practical strategies to solve the entire complex environmental problem by addressing it comprehensively. We are an incubator of transformational ideas designed to challenge and change the piecemeal way our resources are currently managed and protected.

Salmon Nation — salmonnation.com
Welcome to Salmon Nation, a community of caretakers and citizens that stretches across arbitrary boundaries and bridges urban-rural divides. We bring new meaning to the word cooperative — with unusual alliances of tribes, fishermen, farmers, ranchers, loggers, and urban-dwellers working together to improve our neighborhoods and watersheds.

Sustainability Street Institute — sustainabilitystreet.org.au
The Sustainability Street Institute has been incorporated as the body for all matters to do with the development and promulgation of the Sustainability Street Approach (SSA). The SSA was devised by Vox Bandicoot....

SustainLane — sustainlane.com
SustainLane.com is the web's largest people-powered guide to sustainable living. The hub of SustainLane Media's offerings, SustainLane.com is filled with personal accounts of how-tos, news, and local business and product reviews for sustainable living.

Transition Culture — transitionculture.org
My own thoughts led me [Rob Hopkins] to develop an approach I call "Energy Descent Action Planning (EDAP)," which works with a community to vision how they see their town 20 years in the future.... I am now looking at the wider question of how the EDAP process can evolve and be refined, as well as drawing on the experience of other communities doing similar things.... That is what I...will strive to share with you on TransitionCulture.org.

Transition Town Totnes — totnes.transitionnetwork.org
The mission of Transition Town Totnes (TTT) is two-fold. The first is to explore and then follow pathways of practical actions that will reduce our carbon emissions and dependence on fossil fuels (getting to zero carbon is increasingly seen as [a] viable response). The second is to build the town's resilience, that is, its ability to withstand shocks from the outside, to be more self reliant in terms of food, energy, employment and economics.

Western Climate Initiative — westernclimateinitiative.org
The Western Climate Initiative, launched in February 2007, is a collaboration of seven U.S. governors and four Canadian Premiers.... WCI was created to identify, evaluate, and implement collective and cooperative ways to reduce greenhouse gases in the region, focusing on a market-based cap-and-trade system.

Chapter 3: Greening Commerce

B Corporation — bcorporation.net
B Corporations are a new type of corporation which uses the power of business to solve social and environmental problems. B Corporations are unlike traditional responsible businesses because they: Meet comprehensive and transparent social and environmental performance standards; Institutionalize stakeholder interests; Build collective voice through the power of a unifying brand.

The Business Alliance for Local Living Economies — livingeconomies.org
The Business Alliance for Local Living Economies (BALLE) brings together small business leaders, economic development professionals, government officials, social innovators, and community leaders to build local living economies. We provide local, state, national, and international resources to this new model of economic development.

Business for Social Responsibility — bsr.org
Our mission is clear: work with business to create a just and sustainable world. A leader in corporate responsibility since 1992, Business for Social Responsibility (BSR) works with its global network of more than 250 member companies to develop sustainable business strategies and solutions through consulting, research, and cross-sector collaboration.

BusinessGreen.com — businessgreen.com
BusinessGreen.com is a business website that offers companies the latest news and best-practice advice on how to become more environmentally responsible, while still growing the bottom line. Companies of all sizes are coming under increasing pressure to make their operations more responsible and sustainable. Considerations of social responsibility have become important in customer satisfaction and staff retention, in the award of contracts and in stock market valuations. BusinessGreen.com is the first publication in the UK that is dedicated to green business information.

Carbon Tax Center — carbontax.org
The Carbon Tax Center ("CTC") was launched in January 2007 to give voice to Americans who believe that taxing emissions of carbon dioxide — the primary greenhouse gas — is imperative to reduce global warming.

Center for Biologically Inspired Design — cbid.gatech.edu
Georgia Tech's Center for Biologically Inspired Design brings together a group of interdisciplinary biologists, engineers and physical scientists who seek to facilitate research and education for innovative products and techniques based on biologically-inspired design solutions.

Center for Sustainable Innovation — sustainableinnovation.org
The Center for Sustainable Innovation (CSI) is a 501(c)(3) non-profit corporation created in 2004 by its founder, Mark W. McElroy. Its purpose is to conduct research, development, training, and consulting for, and with, companies around the world interested in managing and improving the sustainability of their operations.

Chicago Climate Exchange — chicagoclimatex.com
We are a financial institution whose objectives are to apply financial innovation and incentives to advance social, environmental and economic goals through the following platforms. Chicago Climate Exchange (CCX) is North America's only cap and

trade system for all six greenhouse gases, with global affiliates and projects world-wide. Chicago Climate Futures Exchange (CCFE) is a landmark derivatives exchange that currently offers standardized and cleared futures and options contracts on emission allowances and other environmental products.

Clean Edge, Inc. — cleanedge.com
Clean Edge, Inc., founded in 2000, is the world's first research and publishing firm devoted to the clean-tech sector. The company, via its publications, events, and online services, helps companies, investors, and governments understand and profit from clean technologies.

The Climate Group — theclimategroup.org
Over the next five years, The Climate Group's goal is to help government and business set the world economy on the path to a low-carbon, prosperous future. To reach this goal, we've created a coalition of governments and the world's most influential businesses — all committed to tackling climate change.

The Dictionary of Sustainable Management — sustainabilitydictionary.com
This Dictionary of Sustainable Management is an open dictionary for business leaders and students of sustainability and business-related terms. It is a project of the Presidio Graduate School. The purpose of this effort is to help people better understand how sustainability concepts are creating new understandings in the worlds of business, government, and society.

Earth Inc. — earthinc.org
Imagine the Earth as a business and you're a shareholder. We're all shareholders. Future generations are entitled to a share too. How do we maximize the benefit every shareholder receives from the Earth? How do we maximize human wellbeing? Earth, Inc. helps answer this most important question.

*faircompanies — faircompanies.com
*faircompanies is a free resource to help you act responsibly, an independent website with information and tools on sustainability. We talk about green products, ethical consumption, clean technologies, social responsibility, ethical investment, and related topics. We invite you to participate and share formulas to improve the world right now, beyond the noise of demonstrations or the imposition of ideologies.

FLOW — flowidealism.org
FLOW is an emerging movement dedicated to liberating the entrepreneurial spirit and focusing it on the goals of sustainable peace, prosperity, and happiness for all, in the next 50 years.

FreeRice — freerice.com
FreeRice is a non-profit website run by the United Nations World Food Program. Our partner is the Berkman Center for Internet & Society at Harvard University. FreeRice has two goals: 1. Provide education to everyone for free; 2. Help end world hunger by providing rice to hungry people for free. This is made possible by the generosity of the sponsors who advertise on this site.

Global Business Network — gbn.com
GBN helps organizations adapt and grow in an increasingly uncertain and volatile world. Using our leading-edge tools and expertise — scenario planning, experiential learning, networks of experts and visionaries — we enable our clients to address their

most critical challenges and gain the insight, confidence, and capabilities they need to shape the future.

GreenBiz.com — greenbiz.com
GreenBiz.com™, Business Voice of the Green Economy, is the leading source for news, opinion, best practices, and other resources on the greening of mainstream business. Launched in 2000, its mission is to provide clear, concise, accurate, and balanced information, resources, and learning opportunities to help companies of all sizes and sectors integrate environmental responsibility into their operations in a manner that supports profitable business practices.

Green Chamber of Commerce — greenchamberofcommerce.net
The Green Chamber of Commerce is dedicated to fostering the success of businesses committed to environmental and social responsibility.

Green Collar Association — greencollar.org
Our mandate is to promote employment, education, advocacy and commerce in fields that have a net benefit on the environment.

International Forum on Globalization — ifg.org
The International Forum on Globalization (IFG) is a North-South research and educational institution composed of leading activists, economists, scholars, and researchers providing analyses and critiques on the cultural, social, political, and environmental impacts of economic globalization.

The International Society for Ecological Economics — ecoeco.org
ISEE is a not-for-profit, member-governed, organization dedicated to advancing understanding of the relationships among ecological, social, and economic systems for the mutual well-being of nature and people.

Interra — interraproject.org
The Mission of Interra: To empower a community based movement of citizen consumers by providing tools for a direct alignment between daily economic activities and our deepest human values. The Goal of Interra: The Interra Project cross-cultural and intergenerational model is intended to create exponential change by inspiring, educating and rewarding local citizens for buying from socially and environmentally responsible businesses.

Kiva — kiva.org
Kiva's mission is to connect people through lending for the sake of alleviating poverty. Kiva is the world's first person-to-person micro-lending website, empowering individuals to lend directly to unique entrepreneurs around the globe.

Natural Capitalism Solutions — natcapsolutions.org
Natural Capitalism Solutions (NCS)' mission is to educate senior decision-makers in business, government and civil society about the principles of sustainability. NCS shows how to restore and further enhance the natural and human capital while increasing prosperity and quality of life.

Natural Logic — natlogic.com
Natural Logic delivers strategic sustainability consulting to companies and communities, with integrated, results-focused programs that build profit and competitive advantage while reducing your organization's environmental footprint, waste and risk.

The Natural Step — naturalstep.org
The Natural Step is an international not-for-profit organisation dedicated to education, advisory work and research in sustainable development.

OpenEco.org — openeco.org
OpenEco.org is a global on-line community that provides free, easy-to-use tools to help participants assess, track, and compare energy performance, share proven best practices to reduce greenhouse gas (GHG) emissions, and encourage sustainable innovation.

Sierra Business Council — sbcouncil.org
Sierra Business Council is a member-based organization of over 700 individuals and businesses who are committed to pioneering innovative solutions in the Sierra Nevada.

Social Venture Network — svn.org
Social Venture Network inspires a community of business and social leaders to build a just economy and sustainable planet.

Society for Organizational Learning — solonline.org
Our purpose is to discover (research), integrate (capacity development) and implement (practice) theories and practices of organizational learning for the interdependent development of people and their institutions and communities such that we continue to increase our capacity to collectively realize our highest aspirations and productively resolve our differences.

Speciesbanking.com — speciesbanking.com
Speciesbanking.com is the nation's first information clearinghouse for the species credit trading industry. Until now, there has been no centralized information resource to serve buyers, sellers, and other market participants. Basic information such as number of banks, species covered, location, availability of credits, and contact details have not been readily available.

The Story of Stuff — storyofstuff.com
From its extraction through sale, use and disposal, all the stuff in our lives affects communities at home and abroad, yet most of this is hidden from view. *The Story of Stuff* is a 20-minute, fast-paced, fact-filled look at the underside of our production and consumption patterns.

SustainableBusiness.com — sustainablebusiness.com
SustainableBusiness.com provides global news and networking services to help green business grow, covering all sectors: renewable energy, green building, sustainable investing, and organics.

TerraPass — terrapass.com
TerraPass is the brainchild of Dr. Karl Ulrich at the University of Pennsylvania. Along with 41 of his students, Karl launched TerraPass in October, 2004 as a way to help everyday people reduce the climate impact of their driving. Within its first year, TerraPass registered over 2,400 members, reduced 36 million pounds of CO_2, and earned countless national press and blog articles.

World Business Council for Sustainable Development — wbcsd.org
The World Business Council for Sustainable Development (WBCSD) is a CEO-led, global association of some 200 companies dealing exclusively with business and sustainable development.

Chapter 4: Regenerative Design

Architecture 2030 — architecture2030.org
Architecture 2030, a non-profit, non-partisan and independent organization, was established in response to the global-warming crisis by architect Edward Mazria in 2002. 2030's mission is to rapidly transform the US and global Building Sector from the major contributor of greenhouse gas emissions to a central part of the solution to the global-warming crisis.

BuildingGreen.com — buildinggreen.com
We are an independent company committed to providing accurate, unbiased, and timely information designed to help building-industry professionals and policy makers improve the environmental performance, and reduce the adverse impacts, of buildings.

Build It Green — builditgreen.org
Build It Green is a membership supported non-profit organization whose mission is to promote healthy, energy- and resource-efficient homes in California. Established in 2003, we offer a comprehensive package of local government support, professional training, collaboration forums, consumer education, and green product marketing to a range of stakeholders.

The Collaborative for High Performance Schools — chps.net
The Collaborative for High Performance Schools is leading a national movement to make schools better places to learn. CHPS' mission is to facilitate the design, construction and operation of high performance schools: environments that are not only energy and resource efficient, but also healthy, comfortable, well-lit, and containing the amenities needed for a quality education.

Development Center for Appropriate Technology — dcat.net
The Development Center for Appropriate Technology works to enhance the health of the planet and our communities by promoting a shift to sustainable construction and development through leadership, strategic relationships, and education.

ecoBUDGET — ecobudget.com
ecoBUDGET webcentre offers you the opportunity to learn everything about ecoBUDGET, the environmental management system towards sustainability, developed by ICLEI for and with local authorities.

The Encyclopedia of Earth — eoearth.org
Welcome to the Encyclopedia of Earth, a new electronic reference about the Earth, its natural environments, and their interaction with society. The Encyclopedia is a free, fully searchable collection of articles written by scholars, professionals, educators, and experts who collaborate and review each other's work.

Energy Star — energystar.gov
ENERGY STAR is a joint program of the US Environmental Protection Agency and the US Department of Energy helping us all save money and protect the environment through energy efficient products and practices.

Environmental and Energy Study Institute — eesi.org
EESI educates policymakers, builds coalitions, and develops innovative policies to protect the climate and ensure a healthy, secure, and sustainable future for America.

The Green Hive — thegreenhive.com
Created specifically to advance the movement of sustainable design and building

practices, The Green Hive is an integrated forum/marketplace that promotes community interaction, education, products and a green lifestyle.

Greensburg GreenTown — greensburggreentown.org
At 9:45 PM on May 4th, 2007 an EF5 tornado leveled the rural town of Greensburg, Kansas. Just days after the storm, the community came together and decided to rebuild sustainably, striving to become a model green town for the future. Ever since this landmark commitment was made, Greensburg GreenTown — a grassroots community-based organization — has worked side-by-side with city and county officials, business owners and local residents to incorporate sustainable principles into their rebuilding process.

Institute for the Built Environment — ibe.colostate.edu
The Institute for the Built Environment (IBE), founded in 1994 at Colorado State University, is a multidisciplinary research institute whose mission is to foster stewardship and sustainability of the built environment through a research-based, interdisciplinary educational forum.

Living Building Challenge — ilbi.org
The Living Building Challenge is a program initially launched…by the Cascadia Region Green Building Council…and has quickly become the most advanced green building rating system in the world.

Passive House Institute US — passivehouse.us/passiveHouse/PHIUSHome.html
The Passive House Institute US (PHIUS) is a consulting and research firm working to further the implementation of Passive House standards and techniques nationwide by: Constructing, measuring, and verifying performance of Passive Houses in all US climate zones; Contributing to the development of minimized mechanical systems for heating, cooling, and dehumidification; Creating design guidelines for Passive Houses in all climate zones; Providing energy calculation and consulting services; Participating in presentations, meetings, conferences, etc. regarding passive construction.

The Pharos Project — pharoslens.net
The Pharos Project seeks to define a consumer-driven vision of truly green building materials and establish a method for evaluation that is in harmony with principles of environmental health and justice. The Project's foundation is a partnership, pairing those who use building materials with those who study the products' impacts on health and the environment.

Residential Energy Services Network — natresnet.org
The Residential Energy Services Network's (RESNET®) mission is to ensure the success of the building energy performance certification industry, set the standards of quality, and increase the opportunity for ownership of high performance buildings…. RESNET Ratings provides a relative energy use index called the HERS® Index.

Sustainable Communities Network — sustainable.org
The Sustainable Communities Network is for those who want to help make their communities more livable. Here a broad range of issues are addressed and resources are provided to help make this happen. This web site is being developed to increase the visibility of what has worked for other communities, and to promote a lively exchange of information to help create community sustainability in both urban and rural areas.

U.S. Green Building Council — usgbc.org
The Washington, D.C.-based U.S. Green Building Council (USGBC) is a 501 (c)(3) non-profit organization committed to a prosperous and sustainable future for our nation through cost-efficient and energy-saving green buildings. With a community comprising…more than 20,000 member companies and organizations…USGBC… leads an unlikely diverse constituency of builders and environmentalists, corporations and non-profit organizations, elected officials and concerned citizens, and teachers and students.

Whole Building Design Guide — wbdg.org
The WBDG is the only web-based portal providing government and industry practitioners with one-stop access to up-to-date information on a wide range of building-related guidance, criteria and technology from a "whole buildings" perspective.

World Green Building Council — worldgbc.org
Through leadership collaboration, the global construction industry will transform traditional building practices and fully adopt sustainability as the means by which our environments thrive, economies prosper and societies grow to ensure the future health of our planet.

Chapter 5: Saving Ecosystems

Biodiversity Hotspots — biodiversityhotspots.org
The most remarkable places on Earth are also the most threatened. These are the Hotspots: the richest and most threatened reservoirs of plant and animal life on Earth.

Cheetah Conservation Botswana — cheetahbotswana.com
Cheetah Conservation Botswana aims to preserve the nation's cheetah population through scientific research, community outreach and education, working with rural communities to promote coexistence with Botswana's rich diversity of predator species.

The Conservation Land Trust — theconservationlandtrust.org
This website represents work we carry out at CLT. Its objective is to enable easy access to information about CLT's efforts and to the diverse projects we develop in Chile and Argentina…. CLT is dedicated to the creation and/or expansion of national or provincial parks to ensure the perpetuity of their ecological and evolutionary processes with the strongest long-term protection guarantee possible.

Ecosystem Investment Partners — ecosystempartners.com
Ecosystem Investment Partners (EIP) was founded in 2006 to provide a private funding option for important conservation properties, and to demonstrate that good conservation investment can deliver market returns to serious investors.

The Ecosystem Marketplace — ecosystemmarketplace.com
The Ecosystem Marketplace seeks to become the world's leading source of information on markets and payment schemes for ecosystem services: services such as water quality, carbon sequestration and biodiversity.

Ecosystem Valuation — ecosystemvaluation.org
This website describes how economists value the beneficial ways that ecosystems affect people — ecosystem valuation. It is designed for non-economists who need answers to questions about the benefits of ecosystem conservation, preservation or

restoration. It provides a clear, non-technical explanation of ecosystem valuation concepts, methods, and applications.

Environmental Grantmakers Association — ega.org
The mission of EGA is to help member organizations become more effective environmental grantmakers through information sharing, collaboration and networking. EGA's vision is one of an informed, diverse, collaborative network of effective grantmakers who are supporting work toward a sustainable world.

The Gund Institiute for Ecological Economics — uvm.edu/giee
The Gund Institute for Ecological Economics unites pioneering experts, leading educators, students, and others from around the world and across a wide variety of academic and environmental disciplines.

IUCN Red List of Threatened Species — iucnredlist.org
The IUCN Red List of Threatened Species™ provides taxonomic, conservation status and distribution information on plants and animals that have been globally evaluated using the IUCN Red List Categories and Criteria.

The Katoomba Group — katoombagroup.org
The Katoomba Group is an international network of individuals working to promote, and improve capacity related to, markets and payments for ecosystem services (PES). The Group serves as a forum for the exchange of ideas and strategic information about ecosystem service transactions and markets, as well as [a] site for collaboration between practitioners on PES projects and programs.

Land Trust Alliance — landtrustalliance.org
Our mission is to save the places people love by strengthening land conservation across America.

Marin Agricultural Land Trust — malt.org
Marin Agricultural Land Trust (MALT) was the first land trust in the United States to focus on farmland preservation. Founded in 1980 by a coalition of ranchers and environmentalists to preserve farmland in Marin County, California, MALT acquires agricultural conservation easements on farmland in voluntary transactions with landowners. MALT also encourages public policies that support and enhance agriculture.

Natural Capital Project — naturalcapitalproject.org
Our mission is to align economic forces with conservation by mainstreaming natural capital into decisions.

The Nature Conservancy — nature.org
The mission of The Nature Conservancy is to preserve the plants, animals and natural communities that represent the diversity of life on Earth by protecting the lands and waters they need to survive.

The Rewilding Institute — rewilding.org/rewildit
The Rewilding Institute (TRI) has three broad goals: (1) To effectively integrate conservation biology and wildlands and wildlife conservation. (2) To provide a long-term, hopeful vision for conservation in North America. (3) To create a North American Wildlands Network Vision and a strategy to implement it.

The Sonoran Institute — sonoraninstitute.org
The nonprofit Sonoran Institute, founded in 1990, works across the rapidly chang-

ing West to conserve and restore natural and cultural assets and to promote better management of growth and change. The Institute's community-based approach emphasizes collaboration, civil dialogue, sound information, local knowledge, practical solutions and big-picture thinking.

Wildlands Network — twp.org
Wildlands Network represents networks of people protecting networks of land. Our focus is to restore, protect and connect North America's best wild places. Our international network of conservation partners and individuals work[s] to make sure Nature has enough "room to roam," to survive for the long-term. But our protected lands are in short supply, and our mission is urgent.

Wildlife Conservation Network — wildlifeconservationnetwork.org
Wildlife Conservation Network is dedicated to protecting endangered species and preserving their natural habitats. We support innovative strategies for people and wildlife to co-exist and thrive.

Chapter 6: Navigating the Confluence

350.org — 350.org
350.org is an international campaign dedicated to building a movement to unite the world around solutions to the climate crisis — the solutions that science and justice demand. Our mission is to inspire the world to rise to the challenge of the climate crisis — to create a new sense of urgency and of possibility for our planet.

The Alliance for Climate Protection — climateprotect.org
Our mission is to persuade the American people — and people elsewhere in the world — of the importance and urgency of adopting and implementing effective and comprehensive solutions for the climate crisis.

Apollo Challenge — apollochallenge.org
Fundamentally, the Apollo Challenge aims to ensure that our nation makes ambitious investments in clean energy and efficiency that will allow America — within 10 years — to achieve energy independence, and create 3 million good jobs here at home.

Blue Planet Network (formerly Blue Planet Run Foundation — blueplanetnetwork.org
Our Mission: Unlock the global capacity and creativity of individuals, philanthropies, businesses and expert water organizations to solve the global safe drinking water crisis. Our Vision: Blue Planet Network envisions a world where every human can draw from their well or turn on their tap, safely drink the water, and have access to health and economic advancement as a result.

Carbon Mitigation Initiative — cmi.princeton.edu
The mission of the Carbon Mitigation Initiative (CMI) is to lead the way to a compelling and sustainable solution of the carbon and climate change problem.... CMI aims to identify the most credible methods of capturing and sequestering a large fraction of carbon emissions from fossil fuels in order to establish which, if any, of these methods will: Have the desired effect on atmospheric carbon and climate; Be safe and reliable, with minimal negative environmental impact; Involve neither prohibitive economic costs nor prohibitive disruption of patterns of energy consumption.

Climate Counts — climatecounts.org
Climate Counts is a collaborative effort to bring consumers and companies together

in the fight against global climate change. We are a nonprofit organization funded by Stonyfield Farm, Inc. and launched in collaboration with Clean Air-Cool Planet.

Climate Progress — climateprogress.org
Climate Progress is dedicated to providing the progressive perspective on climate science, climate solutions, and climate politics. It is a project of the Center for American Progress Action Fund, a nonprofit, nonpartisan organization.

Copenhagen Climate Conference 2009 — unfccc.int/2860.php *and* en.cop15.dk
(The official websites of the United Nations and the Danish government for the Climate Change Conference in Copenhagen COP 15/CMP 5, 7–15 December 2009) In 2012 the Kyoto Protocol to prevent climate changes and global warming runs out. To keep the process [in] line there is an urgent need for a new climate protocol. At the conference in Copenhagen 2009 the parties of the UNFCCC [United Nations Framework Convention on Climate Change] meet for the last time on [the] government level before the climate agreement need[s] to be renewed.

e3bank — e3bank.com
e3bank is being created for the growing ranks of consumers who are beginning to understand what it really means to be green and who are hungry for a different kind of bank — one that aligns with their values and "walks the talk."

End Water Poverty — endwaterpoverty.org
The global crisis in sanitation and water requires an extraordinary effort to tackle it. End Water Poverty is an international campaign, driven by a growing coalition of like-minded organisations, calling for immediate action.

Energy Bulletin — energybulletin.net
EnergyBulletin.net is a clearinghouse for information regarding the peak in global energy supply.

Energy Information Administration — eia.doe.gov
At the Energy Information Administration, we provide policy-neutral data, forecasts, and analyses to promote sound policy making, efficient markets, and public understanding regarding energy and its interaction with the economy and the environment.

Global Footprint Network — footprintnetwork.org
At Global Footprint Network our programs are designed to influence decision makers at all levels of society and to create a critical mass of powerful institutions using the Footprint to put an end to ecological overshoot and get our economies back into balance.

Grameen Foundation — grameenfoundation.org
Grameen Foundation's mission is to enable the poor, especially the poorest, to create a world without poverty.

MicroPlace — microplace.com
MicroPlace's mission is to help alleviate global poverty by enabling everyday people to make investments in the world's working poor.

New England Energy Alliance — newenglandenergyalliance.org
The time to act is now. The New England Energy Alliance was formed to advocate for the actions necessary to encourage development of new energy infrastructure

and the continued operation of existing infrastructure that may face retirement for a number of reasons.

New Resource Bank — newresourcebank.com
Founded by renowned entrepreneurs, business leaders and highly experienced bankers, we understand how excellent banking can empower businesses, organizations and individuals to make greater impact on their efforts.

OneCalifornia Foundation — onecalfoundation.org
OneCalifornia Foundation engages in charitable and educational activities that primarily support the goals of OneCalifornia Bank, FSB. Included are programs and initiatives to help eliminate discrimination, encourage affordable housing, alleviate economic distress, stimulate community development and increase financial literacy.

Pew Center on Global Climate Change — pewclimate.org
The Pew Center on Global Climate Change brings together business leaders, policy makers, scientists, and other experts to bring a new approach to a complex and often controversial issue. Our approach is based on sound science, straight talk, and a belief that we can work together to protect the climate while sustaining economic growth.

Real Climate Economics — realclimateeconomics.org
The Real Climate Economics website offers a reader's guide to the real economics of climate change, an emerging body of scholarship that is consistent with the urgency of the problem as seen from a climate science perspective.

SESAC — concerto-sesac.eu
The European Sustainable Energy Systems in Advanced Cities (SESAC) project aims at showing how the local economy is able to thrive at the same time as less CO_2 is emitted. This is being translated into innovative energy measures in both new building development projects and the renovation of existing buildings.

Solar Energy International — solarenergy.org
Our mission is to provide education and technical assistance so that others will be empowered to use renewable energy technologies.

United States Climate Action Partnership — us-cap.org
USCAP is an expanding alliance of major businesses and leading climate and environmental groups that have come together to call on the federal government to enact legislation requiring significant reductions of greenhouse gas emissions.

US Department of Energy: Office of Energy Efficiency and Renewable Energy — www1.eere.energy.gov
EERE works to strengthen the United States' energy security, environmental quality, and economic vitality in public-private partnerships.

WaterAid — wateraid.org/uk
WaterAid is an international charity. Our mission is to overcome poverty by enabling the world's poorest people to gain access to safe water, sanitation and hygiene education.

World of Good Development Organization — worldofgood.org
World of Good Development Organization aims to substantially improve economic and social conditions for millions of workers and their families living at or below

the poverty level in the developing world. We strive to create systemic change in the buying practices of U.S. companies through advocacy, monitoring, & worker's rights training that will result in bridging the gap between the global north and south.

Chapter 7: Catalysts for Change

1BOG — 1bog.org

Homeowners looking to buy solar panels face a few problems: It's expensive. It's complicated. They don't know which installer they should trust. 1BOG (1 Block Off The Grid) organizes people in a community to go through the process together. This approach has several benefits: An organized community can buy solar in bulk, so 1BOG negotiates with installers to get about 15% off for each homeowner in the collective. We make the process much more simple and painless, as well as use our deep solar energy expertise to educate consumers throughout the process. We offer safety in numbers because everyone gets the same pricing from a top quality installer, and everything is transparent.

1Sky — 1sky.org

1Sky was created in 2007 to focus the power of millions of concerned Americans on a single goal: bold federal action by 2010 that can stem global warming. The 1Sky Solutions are grounded in scientific necessity — they are the bottom line of what's needed to dramatically reduce carbon emissions while maximizing energy efficiency, renewable energy and breakthrough technologies.

3Degrees — 3degreesinc.com

The 3Degrees team is committed to the company's stated mission: reducing the magnitude of climate change. We share this passion with our partners by building strong relationships that enable them to effectively and accurately develop climate strategies and highlight our combined achievements in moving toward a post-carbon economy.

Alliance for Climate Protection — climateprotect.org

Our mission is to persuade the American people — and people elsewhere in the world — of the importance and urgency of adopting and implementing effective and comprehensive solutions for the climate crisis.

American College & University Presidents' Climate Commitment — presidentsclimatecommitment.org

The American College & University Presidents' Climate Commitment is a high-visibility effort to address global warming by garnering institutional commitments to neutralize greenhouse gas emissions, and to accelerate the research and educational efforts of higher education to equip society to re-stabilize the earth's climate.

Ask Nature — asknature.org

…AskNature [is] the online inspiration source for the biomimicry community. Think of it as your home habitat — whether you're a biologist who wants to share what you know about an amazing organism, or a designer, architect, engineer, or chemist looking for planet-friendly solutions. AskNature is where biology and design cross-pollinate, so bio-inspired breakthroughs can be born.

Association for the Advancement of Sustainability in Higher Education — aashe.org

AASHE is an association of colleges and universities that are working to create a sustainable future. Our mission is to empower higher education to lead the sustainability transformation. We do this by providing resources, professional development, and a network of support to enable institutions of higher education to model and advance sustainability in everything they do, from governance and operations to education and research.

Blue Planet Prize — af-info.or.jp/en/blueplanet/about.html
In 1992, the year of the Earth Summit, the Asahi Glass Foundation established the Blue Planet Prize, an award presented to individuals or organizations worldwide in recognition of outstanding achievements in scientific research and its application that have helped provide solutions to global environmental problems. The Prize is offered in the hopes of encouraging efforts to bring about the healing of the Earth's fragile environment.

Bread for the Journey — breadforthejourney.org
For twenty years, Bread for the Journey's model of grassroots micro-granting has helped to make communities more just, vital, and whole. In 1988, we began our first Bread for the Journey chapter over a spaghetti dinner in Santa Fe, New Mexico. Today, Bread for the Journey's 20 volunteer chapters — like brilliant points of light — are bringing healing and transformation to communities across North America through Neighborhood Philanthropy.

The Buckminster Fuller Challenge — challenge.bfi.org
Each year a distinguished jury awards a $100,000 prize to support the development and implementation of a strategy that has significant potential to solve humanity's most pressing problems.

California FarmLink — californiafarmlink.org/joomla/index.php
Our mission is to build family farming and conserve farmland in California by linking aspiring and retiring farmers; and promoting techniques and disseminating information that facilitate intergenerational farm transitions.

Campaign for Environmental Literacy — fundee.org
The Campaign for Environmental Literacy was formally established in February 2005 as a response to the environmental education (EE) community's most vital political need: concerted support from the federal government.

Carbon Trust — carbontrust.co.uk
The Carbon Trust's mission is to accelerate the move to a low carbon economy by working with organisations to reduce carbon emissions now and develop commercial low carbon technologies for the future.

Carrotmob — carrotmob.org
Carrotmob is a method of activism that leverages consumer power to make the most socially-responsible business practices also the most profitable choices. Businesses compete with one another to see who can do the most good, and then a big mob of consumers buys products in order to reward whichever business made the strongest commitment to improve the world. It's the opposite of a boycott.

Center for Ecoliteracy — ecoliteracy.org
The Center for Ecoliteracy is dedicated to education for sustainable living. We provide information, inspiration, and support to the vital movement of K-12 educators, parents, and other members of the school community who are helping young people gain the knowledge, skills, and values essential to sustainable living.

Center for Food Safety — centerforfoodsafety.org
The Center for Food Safety (CFS) is a non-profit public interest and environmental advocacy membership organization established in 1997 by its sister organization, International Center for Technology Assessment, for the purpose of challenging harmful food production technologies and promoting sustainable alternatives.

Climate Protection Campaign — climateprotectioncampaign.org
Our mission is to create a positive future for our children and all life by inspiring action in response to the climate crisis. We advance practical, science-based solutions for achieving significant greenhouse gas reductions.

Climateprediction.net — climateprediction.net
Climateprediction.net is a distributed computing project to produce predictions of the Earth's climate up to 2080 and to test the accuracy of climate models. To do this, we need people around the world to give us time on their computers — time when they have their computers switched on, but are not using them to their full capacity.

The Cloud Institute for Sustainability Education — sustainabilityed.org
The mission of The Cloud Institute is to ensure the viability of sustainable communities by leveraging changes in K-12 school systems to prepare young people for the shift toward a sustainable future.

The College Sustainability Report Card — greenreportcard.org
GreenReportCard.org is the first interactive website to provide in-depth sustainability profiles for hundreds of colleges in all 50 US states and in Canada. Information is based on extensive research conducted for the *College Sustainability Report Card.*

Community Pulse — communitypulse.org
Community Pulse is an interactive social marketing tool that helps people align their behavior and take action to steadily reduce their own, and by extension, their community's environmental impact. It utilizes multiple forms of media to provide personal, localized footprints for CO_2, energy, water, and waste.

Digital Green — digitalgreen.org
Digital Green (DG) is a research project that seeks to disseminate targeted agricultural information to small and marginal farmers in India through digital video. The Digital Green system sustains relevancy in a community by developing a framework for participatory learning. The system includes a digital video database, which is produced by farmers and experts. The content within this repository is of various types, and sequencing enables farmers to progressively become better farmers.

Earth Hour — earthhour.org
Earth Hour began in Sydney in 2007, when 2.2 million homes and businesses switched off their lights for one hour. In 2008 the message had grown into a global sustainability movement, with 50 million people switching off their lights. Global landmarks such as the Golden Gate Bridge in San Francisco, Rome's Colosseum, the Sydney Opera House and the Coca Cola billboard in Times Square all stood in darkness.

East New York Farms — eastnewyorkfarms.org
East New York Farms is a collaborative project whose mission is to organize youth and adult residents to address food issues in their community by promoting local and regional sustainable agriculture and community-based economic development.

Ecoagriculture Partners — ecoagriculture.org
"Ecoagriculture" is a term coined in 2000 (by Sara Scherr and Jeffrey McNeely, authors of the Future Harvest-commissioned report *Common Ground, Common Future: How Ecoagriculture Can Help Feed the World and Save Wild Biodiversity*) to convey a vision of rural communities managing their resources to jointly achieve three broad goals at a landscape scale — what we refer to as the "three pillars" of ecoagriculture: Enhance rural livelihoods; Conserve or enhance biodiversity and ecosystem services; and Develop more sustainable and productive agricultural systems.

The Eco League — ecoleague.org
The Eco League is the only college consortium in the United States dedicated to environmental learning and the active pursuit of environmental studies. Eco League colleges offer semester exchange programs that allow students of one school to study at another, giving them access to ecosystems throughout the nation via their studies at: Alaska Pacific University (Alaska); College of the Atlantic (Maine); Green Mountain College (Vermont); Northland College (Wisconsin); Prescott College (Arizona). These small liberal arts institutions all share similar missions and value systems based on environmental responsibility, social change, and educating students to build a sustainable future.

Ecological Farming Association — eco-farm.org
The Ecological Farming Association nurtures healthy and just farms, food systems, communities and environment by bringing people together for education, alliance building and advocacy.

Encyclopedia of Life — eol.org
The Encyclopedia of Life (EOL) is an ambitious, even audacious project to organize and make available via the Internet virtually all information about life present on Earth. At its heart lies a series of Web sites — one for each of the approximately 1.8 million known species — that provide the entry points to this vast array of knowledge. The entry-point for each site is a species page suitable for the general public, but with several linked pages aimed at more specialized users. The sites sparkle with text and images that are enticing to everyone, as well as providing deep links to specific data.

Energy Action Coalition — energyactioncoalition.org
Founded in June 2004 by youth climate leaders, the Energy Action Coalition unites a diversity of organizations in an alliance that supports and strengthens the student and youth clean and just energy movement in North America.

Facing the Future — facingthefuture.org
We empower teachers with the resources they need to ignite their students' interest in complex global issues while helping them achieve academically. Our approach is positive and solutions-oriented, and our business model is systemic and leveraged: Facing the Future programming reaches hundreds of thousands of students each year at a cost of less than $2 per student.

Focus the Nation — focusthenation.org
Through education, engagement and action, Focus the Nation empowers young leaders to accelerate the transition to a more just and prosperous clean energy future.

Gen We — gen-we.com
Millennials are the largest generation in American history. Born between 1978 and

2000, they are 95 million strong, compared to 78 million Baby Boomers. They are independent — politically, socially, and philosophically — and they are spearheading a period of sweeping change in America and around the world.

Global Energy Network Institute — geni.org
GENI's mission is to conduct research and to educate world leaders and the public about the critical viability of the interconnection of electric power networks between nations and continents, with an emphasis on tapping abundant renewable energy resources, what we call "the GENI Initiative." Our research shows that linking renewables between all nations will mollify conflicts, grow economies and increase the quality of life and health for all. This is a strategy rooted in the highest priority of the World Game simulation developed by Dr. Buckminster Fuller three decades ago.

Goldman Environmental Prize — goldmanprize.org
The Goldman Prize continues today with its original mission to annually honor grassroots environmental heroes from the six inhabited continental regions: Africa, Asia, Europe, Islands and Island Nations, North America, and South and Central America. The Prize recognizes individuals for sustained and significant efforts to protect and enhance the natural environment, often at great personal risk. Each winner receives an award of $150,000, the largest award in the world for grassroots environmentalists.

The Greenhorns — thegreenhorns.net
Our mission, as a small grass-roots nonprofit based in the Hudson Valley of New York, is to support, promote and recruit young farmers in America.

Green Schools Alliance — greenschoolsalliance.org
The mission of the GSA is to galvanize pre-K to grade 12 schools' individual concerns about climate change and the environment into collective action to protect our shared future.

Green Science Policy Institute — greensciencepolicy.org
The Green Science Policy Institute provides unbiased scientific data to government, industry, and non-governmental organizations to facilitate more informed decision-making about chemicals used in consumer products.

Holistic Management International — holisticmanagement.org
HMI provides, promotes and teaches holistic land management, which works in concert with natural processes. Holistic Management has been proven effective in restoring damaged grasslands to health and sustainability, and at increasing the productivity and profitability of ranches and farms.

Institute for Community Resource Development
4429 W. Fulton Street and
200 N. Kenneth Avenue
Chicago, Illinois, USA
Telephone: (773) 261-7339
The mission of the Institute for Community Resource Development (ICRD) in Chicago, Illinois is to rebuild the local food system. ICRD projects include: building grocery stores that bring access to sustainable products to urban communities of color, organizing farmers markets, converting vacant lots to urban farm sites, and distributing locally grown produce to restaurants.

The Land Institute — landinstitute.org
When people, land, and community are as one, all three members prosper; when they relate not as members but as competing interests, all three are exploited. By consulting Nature as the source and measure of that membership, The Land Institute seeks to develop an agriculture that will save soil from being lost or poisoned while promoting a community life at once prosperous and enduring.

Locavores — locavores.com
We are a group of concerned culinary adventurers who are making an effort to eat only foods grown or harvested within a 100 mile radius of San Francisco for an entire month. We recognize that the choices we make about what foods we choose to eat are important politically, environmentally, economically, and healthfully. In 2005, we challenged people from the bay area (and all over the world) to eat within a 100 mile radius of their home for the month of August....

Marin Agricultural Institute — marinagriculturalinstitute.org
Marin Farmers Markets, founded in 1987 and developed into a non-profit 501(c)(5) agricultural membership organization, launched MAI, its sister organization in 2004 to further the public benefit goals of MFM.

Marin Farmers Markets — marinfarmersmarkets.org
Our mission is to promote a viable food system, to educate the public about the benefits of buying fresh and locally grown food, and to bring farmers and communities together. Marin Farmers Markets operates seven markets in the Bay area, four in Marin County (Sunday and Thursday Civic Center, Novato and Fairfax) and three in Alameda County (Oakland-Grand Lake, Newark and Hayward).

Mayors Climate Protection Center — usmayors.org/climateprotection
Douglas H. Palmer, Mayor of Trenton and President of The US Conference of Mayors and Conference Executive Director Tom Cochran officially launched The US Conference of Mayors Climate Protection Center on February 20, 2007 in recognition of an increasingly urgent need to provide mayors with the guidance and assistance they need to lead their cities' efforts to reduce the greenhouse gas emissions that are linked to climate change.

La Montañita Co-op — lamontanita.coop
La Montañita Co-op is a community-owned, consumer cooperative with two locations in Albuquerque, one in Santa Fe and one in Gallup. All stores offer fresh organic produce, bulk foods, local organic beef, lamb and other meats and cheeses, fair trade products and a wide variety of natural and organic groceries, freshly prepared deli foods, natural body care, vitamins and supplements.

National Wildlife Federation: Campus Ecology Program — nwf.org/campusEcology
The National Wildlife Federation's Campus Ecology® program promotes climate leadership and sustainability among colleges and universities by providing resources and technical support, creating networking opportunities and organizing education events.

New Leaders Initiative — newleadersinitiative.org
The New Leaders Initiative (NLI) grows environmental leadership by raising the profile of young emerging environmental leaders in North America, celebrating their

achievements, and providing them with the skills, resources, and relationships to lead effective campaigns and projects. NLI honors the legacy of David Brower — firebrand environmentalist, community activist, and founder of Earth Island Institute. NLI is home to the Brower Youth Awards, the premier North American awards honoring bold young environmental leaders.

North American Alliance for Green Education — naage.org
The North American Alliance for Green Education is a student-inspired consortium of environmental colleges and organizations with a commitment to environmental studies programs. Our mission is to combine institutional strengths to maximize educational opportunities for students and faculty.

Open Source Initiative — opensource.org
The Open Source Initiative (OSI) is a non-profit corporation formed to educate about and advocate for the benefits of open source and to build bridges among different constituencies in the open-source community.

People's Grocery — peoplesgrocery.org
People's Grocery is a community-based organization in West Oakland that develops creative solutions to the health problems in our community that stem from a lack of access to and knowledge about healthy, fresh foods. Our mission is to build a local food system that improves the health and economy of the West Oakland community.

Reos Partners — reospartners.com
Reos Partners is an international organisation dedicated to supporting and building capacity for innovative collective action in complex social systems. We organise, design and facilitate results-oriented multi-stakeholder partnerships, within and across business, government and civil society organisations.

Second Nature — secondnature.org
Second Nature's mission is to accelerate movement toward a sustainable future by serving and supporting senior college and university leaders in making healthy, just, and sustainable living the foundation of all learning and practice in higher education.

Slow Food — slowfood.org
Slow Food is a non-profit, eco-gastronomic member-supported organization that was founded in 1989 to counteract fast food and fast life, the disappearance of local food traditions and people's dwindling interest in the food they eat, where it comes from, how it tastes and how our food choices affect the rest of the world. Today, we have over 100,000 members in 132 countries.

Slow Money Alliance — slowmoneyalliance.org
Slow Money. It's a new economic vision. It's an emerging network of investors, donors, farmers, and activists committed to building local food economies. It's about the soil of the economy. It's the beginning of the "nurture capital" industry.

Solar Richmond — solarrichmond.org
Solar Richmond promotes and inspires the use of solar power and energy efficiency in order to bring the economic benefits of the green economy to Richmond, and serves the community through solar installation training, empowering a new "green-collar" workforce and opening doors to employment.

Stone Soup Leadership Institute — soup4world.com
The Stone Soup Leadership Institute is a 501 (c)(3) educational organization that develops tools, programs and community initiatives that honor everyday heroes and train future and emerging leaders to work together to build a better world. Founded in 1997 on the island of Martha's Vineyard, the Institute moved to Larkspur in 2000. The Institute brings the Stone Soup fable to life, inspiring people to give their gifts — so together we can feed the hunger in our souls and the hunger in the world.

Sustainable Food Lab — sustainablefood.org
The mission of the Sustainable Food Lab is to accelerate the shift of sustainable food from niche to mainstream. We define a sustainable food and agriculture system as one in which the fertility of our soil is maintained and improved; the availability and quality of water are protected and enhanced; our biodiversity is protected; farmers, farm workers, and all other actors in value chains have livable incomes; the food we eat is affordable and promotes our health; sustainable businesses can thrive; and the flow of energy and the discharge of waste, including greenhouse gas emissions, are within the capacity of the earth to absorb forever.

Technology, Entertainment, Design — ted.com
TED stands for Technology, Entertainment, Design. It started out (in 1984) as a conference bringing together people from those three worlds. Since then its scope has become ever broader. The annual conference now brings together the world's most fascinating thinkers and doers, who are challenged to give the talk of their lives (in 18 minutes).

Teens Turning Green — teensturninggreen.org
Teens Turning Green is a national movement of youth transforming the world by investigating and eliminating toxic exposures in daily lives, schools and communities; advocating for change in policy and habits to protect our health, and educating peers and the community about greener alternatives. Through collaborative change, these young leaders inspire us all to work toward healthy people and a sustainable future.

UN Decade of Education for Sustainable Development — gdrc.org/sustdev/un-desd/index.html
The United Nations Decade of Education for Sustainable Development (DESD, 2005–2014), for which UNESCO is the lead agency, seeks to integrate the principles, values, and practices of sustainable development into all aspects of education and learning, in order to address the social, economic, cultural and environmental problems we face in the 21st century.

The US Partnership for Education for Sustainable Development — uspartnership.org
The US Partnership consists of individuals, organizations and institutions in the United States dedicated to education for sustainable development (ESD). It acts as a convener, catalyst, and communicator working across all sectors of American society.

La Via Campesina — viacampesina.org
The principal objective of La Via Campesina is to develop solidarity and unity among small farmer organizations in order to promote gender parity and social justice in fair economic relations; the preservation of land, water, seeds and other natural resources; food sovereignty; [and] sustainable agricultural production based on small and medium-sized producers.

Virgin Earth Challenge — virginearth.com
The Virgin Earth Challenge is a prize of $25m for whoever can demonstrate to the judges' satisfaction a commercially viable design which results in the removal of anthropogenic, atmospheric greenhouse gases so as to contribute materially to the stability of Earth's climate.

We, The World — wetheworld.org
Our mission is to maximize social change on a global scale. Our programs and events are designed to Inspire, Inform and Involve increasing numbers of people in the growing global movement that has the transformative consciousness of peace and service to people and the planet at its core.

X PRIZE Foundation — xprize.org
The mission of the X PRIZE Foundation is to bring about radical breakthroughs for the benefit of humanity. We do this by creating and managing prizes that drive innovators to solve some of the greatest challenges facing the world today.

Zero Emissions Research and Initiatives — zeri.org
Zero Emissions Research and Initiatives (ZERI) is a global network of creative minds seeking solutions to world challenges. The common vision shared by the members of the ZERI family is to view waste as resource and seek solutions using nature's design principles as inspiration.

Chapter 8: A Thriveable Future

Aldo Leopold Leadership Program — leopoldleadership.stanford.edu
The mission of the Leopold Leadership Program at Stanford University's Woods Institute for the Environment is to advance environmental decision making by providing academic environmental scientists with the skills and connections they need to be effective leaders and communicators.

Better Place — betterplace.com
Founded in October 2007 on $200 million of venture capital, Better Place, in its first six months, announced cooperative agreements with Israel and Denmark to transform their transportation infrastructure from oil-based to renewable energy and significantly reduce harmful emissions. Better Place's model means consumers subscribe to transportation as a service, much like they do today with mobile phones. Auto companies make the electric cars that plug in to the Better Place electric recharge network of charging stations and battery swap stations. Energy companies provide the network's power through growing renewable energy projects. And Better Place provides the batteries to make owning an electric car affordable and convenient.

Biomimicry Institute — biomimicryinstitute.org
The Biomimicry Institute is a not-for-profit organization whose mission is to nurture and grow a global community of people who are learning from, emulating, and conserving life's genius to create a healthier, more sustainable planet.

Chaordic Commons — chaordic.org
The Chaordic Commons is a global network of individuals and organizations committed to pioneering new ways to organize, based on the discovery and expression of deep common purposes and essential principles of right relationship. Working around the world in every sector of today's rapidly evolving societies, owning mem-

bers of the Commons are pathfinders developing, disseminating, and implementing new concepts of organization that result in more equitable sharing of power and wealth, improved health, and greater compatibility with the human spirit and biosphere.

City Repair — cityrepair.org
City Repair began in Portland, Oregon with the idea that localization — of culture, of economy, of decision-making — is a necessary foundation of sustainability. By reclaiming urban spaces to create community-oriented places, we plant the seeds for greater neighborhood communication, empower our communities and nurture our local culture.

Conservation Psychology — conservationpsychology.org
Conservation psychology is the scientific study of the reciprocal relationships between humans and the rest of nature, with a particular focus on how to encourage conservation of the natural world.

Green Drinks International — greendrinks.org
Every month people who work in the environmental field meet up at informal sessions known as Green Drinks. We have a lively mixture of people from NGOs, academia, government and business. Come along and you'll be made welcome. Just say, "are you green?" and we will look after you and introduce you to whoever is there. It's a great way of catching up with people you know and also for making new contacts. Everyone invites someone else along, so there's always a different crowd, making Green Drinks an organic, self-organising network.

The Jane Goodall Institute — janegoodall.org
The Jane Goodall Institute advances the power of individuals to take informed and compassionate action to improve the environment for all living things.

The Long Now Foundation — longnow.org
The Long Now Foundation was established in 1996 to develop the Clock and Library projects, as well as to become the seed of a very long term cultural institution. The Long Now Foundation hopes to provide counterpoint to today's "faster/cheaper" mind set and promote "slower/better" thinking. We hope to creatively foster responsibility in the framework of the next 10,000 years. (The Long Now Foundation uses five digit dates; the extra zero is to solve the deca-millennium bug which will come into effect in about 8,000 years.)

Menominee Tribal Enterprises — mtewood.com
Menominee Tribal Enterprises is committed to excellence in the sustainable management of our forest, and the manufacturing of our lumber and forest products providing a consistently superior product while serving the needs of our forest, employees, wood products customers, tribal community, and future generations.

Project for Public Spaces — pps.org
Imagine a plaza or town square bustling with people who are greeting each other, buying, selling, and exchanging ideas. For everyone striving to make public spaces better, PPS is that town square. Our vision is to act as the central hub of the global Placemaking movement, connecting people to ideas, expertise, and partners who share a passion for creating vital places.

Resilience Alliance — resalliance.org

The Resilience Alliance is a multidisciplinary research group that explores the dynamics of complex social-ecological systems (SESs) in order to discover foundations for sustainability. Established in 1999, the RA is supported by an international network of member institutions that includes universities, government, and non-government agencies. It has two main activities — a Science Program and a Communications and Outreach Program.

Roots & Shoots — rootsandshoots.org

Mission: To foster respect and compassion for all living things, to promote understanding of all cultures and beliefs and to inspire each individual to take action to make the world a better place for people, animals and the environment.

Science & Environmental Health Network — sehn.org

SEHN was founded in 1994 by a consortium of North American environmental organizations (including the Environmental Defense Fund, the Environmental Research Foundation, and OMB Watch) concerned about the misuse of science in ways that failed to protect the environment and human health. Granted 501(c)(3) status in 1999, SEHN operates as a virtual organization, currently with six staff and seven board members working from locations across the U.S.

Stockholm Resilience Centre — stockholmresilience.org

The Stockholm Resilience Centre is a new international centre that advances transdisciplinary research for governance of social-ecological systems with a special emphasis on resilience — the ability to deal with change and continue to develop.

Thrivability Institute — honoringalllife.org/ThrivabilityInstitute.php

The mission of the Thrivability Institute (Thriv'In) is to establish itself as a highly respected research institute, think tank, learning organization and global resource center for an emergent new culture inspired by principles of sustainability, integrative systems design, quantum science, and heart-centered intelligence.

Zerofootprint — zerofootprint.net

The Zerofootprint group of companies empowers communities, businesses, and organizations to live ingeniously in a low carbon world. We do green. The group is currently comprised of three distinct but related organizations: Zerofootprint Not-for-Profit, Zerofootprint Software and Zerofootprint Carbon.

Online Publications (in their own words)

Ecology and Society — ecologyandsociety.org

Ecology and Society is an electronic, peer-reviewed, multi-disciplinary journal devoted to the rapid dissemination of current research. Manuscript submission, peer review, and publication are all handled on the Internet. Software developed for the journal automates all clerical steps during peer review, facilitates a double-blind peer review process, and allows authors and editors to follow the progress of peer review on the Internet.

Environmental Building News — buildinggreen.com/ecommerce/ebn.cfm?

Environmental Building News (EBN) is a monthly newsletter featuring comprehensive, practical information on a wide range of topics related to sustainable building — from energy efficiency and recycled-content materials to land-use planning and indoor air quality.

Future 500 Newsletter — future500.org
Mission: To forge relationships between corporations and NGOs to advance the "triple bottom line."

Good — good.is
GOOD is the integrated media platform for people who want to live well and do good. We are a company and community for the people, businesses, and NGOs moving the world forward. GOOD's mission is to provide content, experiences, and utilities to serve this community.

GreenSource — greensource.construction.com
GreenSource is made in a collaborative process that is similar to a well-designed sustainable building. We are separate companies that meet frequently to collaborate and create this…magazine and its Web site.

Grist — grist.org
Grist is the nation's favorite independent source of green news and views. Since 1999, Grist has provided incisive and irreverent information that connects readers to the environmental issues that are part of everyday life, like food, energy, climate, politics, consumption, and pop culture.

Ode Magazine — odemagazine.com
Ode is a print and online publication about positive news, about the people and ideas that are changing our world for the better.

People and Place — peopleandplace.net
Some relationships are long familiar. Boy meets girl. Summer turns to fall. Other connections are newly recognized or scarcely affirmed. The DNA we share. The biosphere that supports all life. What are the ties that draw people together and to place? How have these connections — and our understandings — evolved over time? What social-ecological relationships support a more reliable prosperity? How is meaningful change accelerated? Part weblog, part web-based journal, People and Place hosts an inquiry on ideas that connect us.

Resilience Science — rs.resalliance.org
The Resilience Science weblog is operated by Garry Peterson, a professor in Geography and the School of the Environment at McGill University in Montreal, Canada. It was started in early 2005 by Garry Peterson and Marco Janssen as an experiment to communicate recent work by and of interest to those interested in resilience in social ecological systems.

Resurgence Magazine — resurgence.org
The Resurgence Trust publishes Resurgence magazine to promote ecological sustainability, social justice and spiritual values.

The Solutions Journal — thesolutionsjournal.com
The aim of Solutions is to encourage and publish integrative solutions to the world's most pressing problems: climate disruption, loss of biodiversity, poverty, energy descent, overfishing, and human population growth, to name a few.

Sustainable Industries — sustainableindustries.com
Sustainable Industries caters to sustainable business leaders on the West Coast, the most dynamic region of the world for sustainable business innovation, and beyond. Our growing community of thought leaders has been fostering the innovations

chronicled in Sustainable Industries for many years, and as such we are able to offer a more sophisticated dialogue and higher level of analysis than can be found in other media outlets covering similar topics.

Transition Towns WIKI — transitiontowns.org
This site is home to Transition Initiatives and the Transition Network. It's a WIKI for use by all the communities that have adopted the Transition Model for responding positively and creatively to the twin challenges of Peak Oil and Climate Change.

TreeHugger — treehugger.com
TreeHugger is the leading media outlet dedicated to driving sustainability mainstream. Partial to a modern aesthetic, we strive to be a one-stop shop for green news, solutions, and product information. At TreeHugger we know that variety is the spice of life, so you can find all you need to go green in our up to the minute blog, weekly and daily newsletters, weekly video segments, weekly radio show and our user-generated blog, Hugg.

Trim Tab — cascadiagbc.org/news/announcing-trim-tab
Welcome to a new era of communication at Cascadia: Trim Tab! Every three months, you will receive this online magazine awash with provocative articles, interviews and news on the issues, designs, and people that are truly transforming the built environment. Our mission with Trim Tab is to incite deep discussion and inspire the real solutions that our industry must undertake to address the global challenges we face.

Utne Reader — utne.com
Utne Reader and *Utne.com* are digests of independent ideas and alternative culture. Not right, not left, but forward thinking. We're most interested in creating a conversation about everything from the environment to the economy, politics to pop culture.

World Watch Magazine — worldwatch.org/taxonomy/term/41
World Watch is an internationally known and award-winning magazine focused on people, the environment, and how they relate to each other.

YES! Magazine — yesmagazine.org
YES! Magazine is an award-winning, ad-free, nonprofit publication that supports people's active engagement in building a just and sustainable world.

Notes

Introduction: Drawing a Collective Map of Earth Island

1. Jared Diamond. *Collapse: How Societies Choose to Fail or Succeed.* Viking/Penguin, 2005, pp. 3, 6, 79–119. AbsoluteAstronomy.com. *Easter Island* [Cited August 23, 2009] absoluteastronomy.com/topics/Easter_Island and "Easter Island." *Encyclopedia Britannica* [Cited August 23, 2009] britannica.com/EBchecked/topic/176886/Easter-Island. Also Easter Island Foundation. *Easter Island History* [Cited August 23, 2009] islandheritage.org/eihistory.html.

2. Robin McKie."Isle of Plenty." *The Observer,* September 21, 2008 [Cited August 15, 2009] guardian.co.uk/environment/2008/sep/21/renewableenergy.alternativeenergy. Also Jean-Marie Macabrey. "If you build it, tourists, politicians and the media will come." *The New York Times,* March 25, 2009 [Cited August 23, 2009] nytimes.com/cwire/2009/03/25/25climatewire-if-you-build-it-tourists-politicians-and-the-10276.html. For additional information about Samsø Island, see Elizabeth Kolbert. "The Island in the Wind." *The New Yorker,* July 7, 2008 [Cited February 13, 2009] newyorker.com/reporting/2008/07/07/080707_fact_kolbert

3. Water: Water Aid [Cited February 17, 2009] wateraid.org/international/what_we_do/statistics/default.asp. Species extinction: World Resources Institute [Cited February 17, 2009] rainforestweb.org/Rainforest_Information/Species_Extinction. Oil consumption: Energy Information Administration [Cited September 9, 2009] eia.doe.gov/basics/quickoil.html. Grant Smith and Christian Smollinger. *Crude Oil Rises From A Seven-Week Low After Equities Recover.* Bloomberg Press, February 13, 2009 [Cited February 17, 2009] bloomberg.com. Use Search News to find title. Carbon emissions: Personal communication with T. J. Blasing, Carbon Dioxide Information Analysis Center, on February 18, 2009. Estimated data from 1950–2005. Carbon Dioxide Information Analysis Center. *Global Fossil-Fuel CO_2 Emissions* [Cited February 18, 2009] cdiac.ornl.gov/trends/emis/tre_glob.html. Also World Resources Institute. *Climate and Atmosphere* [Cited February 17, 2009] earthtrends.wri.org. Click on Climate and Atmosphere/Searchable Database.

Chapter 1: Lessons from Our Ancestors

1. *About Santa Fe Living Treasures* [Cited September 28, 2009] sflivingtreasures.org/index.php/about.html. Cited in Sustainable Practices #359, August 8, 2008. See Karen Nilsson Brandt and Sharon Niederman. *Living Treasures: A Celebration of the Human Spirit, Volume I.* Western Edge Press, 1997 and Richard McCord. *Santa Fe Living Treasures: Our Elders, Our Hearts, Volume II, 1994–2008.* Sunstone Press, 2009.

2. Government of Canada. *Bioindicators.* Biobasics [Cited August 23, 2009] biobasics.gc.ca/english/View.asp?x=740.

3. International Campaign for Tibet. "Tibet: The World's 'Third Pole.'" Excerpt from the ICT report *Tracking the Steel Dragon: How China's Economic Policies and the Railway Are Transforming Tibet* [Cited August 26, 2009] savetibet.org/media-center/stories-interviews/tibet-the-world's-'third-pole'.

4. Tenzin P. Atisha. *The Tibetan Approach to Ecology*. The Office of Tibet, 1996 [Cited January 18, 2008] tibet.com/Eco/eco7.html.

5. For more information see Robert Z. Apte and Andrés R. Edwards. *Tibet: Enduring Spirit, Exploited Land*. 2nd ed., AuthorHouse, 2004, pp. 24–26. Also Melvyn C. Goldstein and Cynthia M. Beall. *Nomads of Western Tibet: The Survival of a Way of Life*. University of California Press, 1990.

6. Robert B. Ekvall. *Fields on the Hoof: Nexus of Tibetan Nomadic Pastoralism*. Waveland Press, 1968, pp. 61–65.

7. Robert A. F. Thurman. "An Outline of Tibetan Culture." *Cultural Survival Quarterly*, vol. 12, no.1, 1988.

8. The Balinese. *The Goddess and the Computer: Anthropology and Real Life Problems* [Cited February 8, 2008] anthro4n6.net/bali/watertemples.html.

9. J. Stephen Lansing. *Perfect Order: Recognizing Complexity in Bali*. Princeton University Press, 2006, p. 9.

10. Ibid., pp. 12–15.

11. Alaska Native Science Commission. *What is Traditional Knowledge? Traditional Knowledge Systems in the Arctic* [Cited February 8, 2008] nativescience.org. Click on Key Issues: Traditional Knowledge.

12. AbsoluteAstronomy.com. *Inuit* [Cited August 23, 2009] absoluteastronomy .com/topics/Inuit and "Eskimo People." *Encyclopedia Britannica* [Cited August 23, 2009] britannica.com/EBchecked/topic/192518/Eskimo. Also *Inuit*. The Free Dictionary [Cited August 23, 2009] encyclopedia.farlex.com/Inuit+people. Also J. Sydney Jones. *Inuit*. Countries and Their Cultures [Cited August 23, 2009] everyculture.com/multi/Ha-La/Inuit.html.

13. Henry P. Huntington and Nikolai I. Mymrin. *Beluga Whale TEK: Traditional Ecological Knowledge of Beluga Whales*. Arctic Studies Center, Inuit Circumpolar Conference [Cited January 18, 2008] mnh.si.edu/arctic/html/tek.html.

14. Daniel Nettle and Suzanne Romaine. *Vanishing Voices: The Extinction of the World's Languages*. Oxford University Press, 2000, p. 16.

15. Stephen Ferry. "Keepers of the World." *National Geographic Magazine*, October 2004, p. 54.

16. The Nature Conservancy. *Colombia: Places We Protect — Sierra Nevada de Santa Marta* [Cited August 20, 2009] nature.org/wherewework/southamerica/colom bia/work/art5303.html. Also Louis Mejia. *Kogi: Lost Tribe of Pre-Colombian America*. Labyrinthina [Cited August 20, 2009] labyrinthina.com/kogi.htm.

17. Alan Ereira. *The Elder Brothers: A Lost South American People and Their Message About the Fate of the Earth*. Random House, 1990, pp. 196–197.

18. Ibid., p. 225.

19. Convention on Biological Diversity. *Article 8(j): Traditional Knowledge, Innovations and Practices* [Cited February 15, 2008] cbd.int/traditional.

20. For access to World Intellectual Property Organization (WIPO) reports, see *Intellectual Property Needs and Expectations of Traditional Knowledge Holders* [Cited October 12, 2009] wipo.int/tk/en/tk/ffm/report/index.html.

21. World Intellectual Property Organization. *Traditional Knowledge, Genetic Resources and Traditional Cultural Expressions/Folklore* [Cited August 23, 2009] wipo.int/tk/en; *Traditional Knowledge* [Cited August 23, 2009] wipo.int/tk/en/ tk; *Genetic Resources* [Cited August 23, 2009] wipo.int/tk/en/genetic. Also Convention on Biological Diversity. *About the TKIP Portal* [Cited August 23, 2009] cbd.int/tk/about.shtml and *Background Material* [Cited August 23, 2009] cbd. int/tk/material.shtml.

22. International Work Group for Indigenous Affairs. *Background Information on the Declaration on the Rights of Indigenous Peoples* [Cited February 15, 2008] iwgia.org/sw356.asp.

23. Daniel Nettle and Suzanne Romaine. *Vanishing Voices,* pp. 4–7, 18.

24. Ibid., pp. 13–14.

25. For more details see The Rosetta Project [Cited February 15, 2008] rosettaproj ect.org.

Chapter 2: Going "Glocal"

1. "Club adds to gas tax." Tribtown.com, May 31, 2008 [Cited August 20, 2009] tribtown.com/news/gas-8216-tax-oil.html. Cited in Sustainable Practices #360, June 6, 2008.

2. For further information about Rob Hopkins' work and to download *Kinsale 2021: An Energy Descent Action Plan* see Transition Culture [Cited August 20, 2009] transitionculture.org.

3. For details about Transition Towns Initiatives, see Rob Hopkins. *The Transition Handbook: From Oil Dependency to Local Resilience.* Chelsea Green Publishers, 2008 or visit Transition Towns WIKI [Cited March 21, 2008] transitiontowns.org.

4. *Transition Culture: An Evolving Exploration into the Head, Heart and Hands of Energy Descent* [Cited August 20, 2009] trinifar.wordpress.com/2007/08/06/ energy-descent-action-plan.

5. Information for "The 12 Steps to Transition" is adapted from Rob Hopkins. *The Transition Handbook,* pp. 148–175 and from Transition Towns WIKI. *12 Key Steps to embarking on your transition journey* [Cited March 21, 2008] transition towns.org/TransitionNetwork/12Steps.

6. For additional information on open-space technology see Rob Hopkins. *The Transition Handbook,* pp. 162, 168–169. Also Harrison Owen. *Open Space Technology: A User's Guide.* Barrett-Koehler Publishers, 2008.

7. Vox Bandicoot. *Sustainability Street* [Cited July 10, 2009] voxbandicoot.com.au/ sustainability_street.html.

8. Sustainability Street. *About North Melbourne Sustainability Street* [Cited September 23, 2009] northmelbourness.com. Click on About Us.

9. Sustainability Street. *Evaluations and Results* [Cited September 23, 2009] sustain abilitystreet.org.au. Click on Evaluations and Results. For additional information about community-based social marketing, see Fostering Sustainable Behavior [Cited August 20, 2009] cbsm.com.

10. Salmon Nation. *About Salmon Nation* [Cited April 17, 2007] salmonnation.com/ about/faq.html.

11. Salmon Nation. *The Values* [Cited August 16, 2007] salmonnation.com/about/ sn_values.pdf.

12. Bruce Hill. *Saving the Kitlope.* Ecotrust, 1997 [Cited February 23, 2009] ecotrust. org/news/SavingKitlope_1997.html.

13. Ian Gil. *An Easy Million.* Ecotrust, 1994 [Cited August 22, 2009] ecotrust.org/ news/Kitlope_EasyMillion.html. Source: *The Georgia Straight,* vol. 28, no. 1391, August 19, 1994.

14. Craig Jacobson. *Welcome Home: G'psgolox Pole Returns Home to Kitimaat Village After 80 Years.* Ecotrust [Cited February 23, 2009] ecotrust.org/nativepro grams/gpsgolox_totem_pole.html. Also Ecotrust. *Kitlope Ecosystem, British Columbia.* Adapted from *Natural Sense: The Conservation Economy Emerges, 1991–2001* [Cited February 23, 2009] ecotrust.org/publications/ns_kitlope.html.

15. California Environmental Protection Agency. California Climate Action Team. *Executive Summary. Climate Action Team Report to Governor Schwarzenegger and the California Legislature, March 2006,* p. i [Cited September 19, 2009] climatechange.ca.gov/climate_action_team/reports/2006report/2006-04-03_FINAL_CAT_REPORT_EXECSUMMARY.PDF. Also Office of the Governor. "Gov. Schwarzenegger Signs Landmark Legislation to Reduce Greenhouse Gas Emissions." Press release, September 27, 2006 [Cited August 21, 2009] gov.ca.gov/press-release/4111.

16. California Environmental Protection Agency. California Climate Action Team. *Executive Summary. Climate Action Team Report,* pp. i, vi. Also The White House. *Energy & Environment* [Cited August 21, 2009] whitehouse.gov/agenda/energy_and_environment.

17. California Environmental Protection Agency. California Climate Action Team. *Executive Summary. Climate Action Team Report,* p. iii.

18. Office of the Governor. "Governor Schwarzenegger Celebrates 3rd Anniversary of AB 32." Press release, September 24, 2009 [Cited September 29, 2009] gov.ca.gov/press-release/13354. Also Office of the Governor. "Gov. Schwarzenegger Signs Executive Order to Advance State's Renewable Energy Portfolio Standard to 33 Percent by 2020." Press release, September 15, 2009 [Cited September 29, 2009] gov.ca.gov/press-release/13273.

19. California Planning and Development Report. *SB 375 is Now Law — But What Will It Do?* October 1, 2008 [Cited February 23, 2009] cp-dr.com/node/2140. Also Office of the Governor. "Governor Schwarzenegger Signs Sweeping Legislation to Reduce Greenhouse Gas Emissions through Land-Use." Press release, September 30, 2008 [Cited August 21, 2009] gov.ca.gov/press-release/10697.

20. Pew Center on Global Climate Change. *Western Climate Initiative* [Cited September 28, 2009] pewclimate.org/WesternClimateInitiative. Also Western Climate Initiative [Cited September 28, 2009] westernclimateinitiative.org.

21. Legislative Assembly of British Columbia. *BILL 44 — 2007 Greenhouse Gas Reduction Targets Act* [Cited August 21, 2009] leg.bc.ca/38th3rd/1st_read/gov44-1.htm.

22. John Vidal. "Sweden plans to be the first oil free economy." *The Guardian,* February 8, 2006 [Cited September 28, 2009] guardian.co.uk/environment/2006/feb/08/frontpagenews.oilandpetrol.

23. Ben Block. *Sweden Prepares to Lead EU on Climate.* Worldwatch Institute, March 18, 2009 [Cited March 19, 2009] worldwatch.org/node/6039. Also Government Offices of Sweden. *A sustainable energy and climate policy for the environment, competitiveness and long-term stability.* 2009, pp. 2–3 [Cited October 6, 2009] sweden.gov.se/sb/d/2031/a/120088.

24. Government Offices of Sweden. *Energy Policy* [Cited September 28, 2009] sweden.gov.se/sb/d/5745/a/19594. Also Government Offices of Sweden. Ministry of the Environment, Ministry of Enterprise, Energy and Communications. *An eco-efficient future — an overview of Swedish climate and energy policy.* 2009, pp. 3–9 [Cited September 28, 2009] sweden.gov.se/sb/d/574/a/129935. Also Government Offices of Sweden. *A sustainable energy and climate policy for the environment, competitiveness and long-term stability,* pp. 2–3.

25. David Wiles. *The road to Sweden's oil-free future.* Sweden.se, March 31, 2006 [Cited September 19, 2009] sweden.se/eng/Home/Work-live/Sustainability/

Reading/The-road-to-Swedens-oil-free-future. Also Government Offices of Sweden. *A sustainable energy and climate policy for the environment, competitiveness and long-term stability,* pp. 1–5.

26. Helen Clark. *Launch of emissions trading scheme.* beehive.govt.nz, September 20, 2007 [Cited August 21, 2009] beehive.govt.nz/node/30691.

27. Resource Renewal Institute. *Green Plans in Action: New Zealand: History* [Cited February 29, 2008] rri.org/newzealand_history.html.

28. Resource Renewal Institute. *Green Plans in Action: New Zealand: Measuring Success* [Cited August 23, 2009] rri.org/newzealand_measuring.html.

29. Destination Lake Taupo. *Facts & Figures* [Cited August 23, 2009] laketauponz .com/lifestyles/business/taupo-facts-figures.html. Also AbsoluteAstronomy .com. *Lake Taupo* [Cited August 23, 2009] absoluteastronomy.com/topics/Lake_ Taupo. Also New Zealand Department of Conservation: Parks & Recreation. *Tongariro/Taupo* [Cited August 23, 2009] doc.govt.nz/parks-and-recreation/ places-to-visit/tongariro-taupo/turangi-taupo-area/lake-taupo-area.

30. Taupo-nui-a-Tia 2020. *2020 Taupo-nui-a-Tia Action Plan: An Integrated Sustainable Development Strategy for the Lake Taupo Catchment* [Cited August 21, 2009] taupoinfo.org.nz/default.asp. Click on The 2020 Taupo-nui-a-Tia Action Plan (2020 TAP) is available.

31. Ibid., pp. 7–8.

32. Taupo-nui-a-Tia 2020. *2006/07 Annual Report of the 2020 Taupo-nui-a-Tia Joint Management Group on progress towards implementing the 2020 Taupo-nui-a-Tia Action Plan* [Cited August 21, 2009] taupoinfo.org.nz/pdf/2007_annual_report .pdf and taupoinfo.org.nz/happening.asp.

33. Resource Renewal Institute. *Green Plans in Action: European Union: Measuring Success* [Cited September 30, 2009] rri.org/eu_measuring.html.

34. Ibid.

35. Cisco. "Network as the Next Utility for 'Intelligent Urbanisation.'" Press release, February 12, 2009 [Cited April 29, 2009] newsroom.cisco.com/dlls/2009/prod_ 021209c.html.

36. ICLEI–Local Governments for Sustainability. *A Worldwide Movement of Local Governments* [Cited August 21, 2009] iclei.org. Click on Programs.

37. For the latest figures contact ICLEI–Local Governments for Sustainability USA at 436 14th Street, Suite 1520, Oakland, CA 94612, (510) 844-0699, iclei-usa@ iclei.org. See also ICLEI. *2008 Annual Report* [Cited September 28, 2009] iclei -usa.org/about-iclei/annual-reports.

38. For additional information see: SustainLane [Cited September 10, 2009] sustain lane.com; Common Current [Cited September 10, 2009] commoncurrent.com; and Alternative Channel. *Warren Karlenzig: Sharing Initiatives.* June 30, 2008 [Cited September 10, 2009] alternativechannel.tv/communication-durable videos/ACIDD-TIC1/Warren-Karlenzig-sharing-initiatives/1071. See also Warren Karlenzig. *How Green is Your City? The SustainLane US City Rankings.* New Society Publishers, 2007.

Chapter 3: Greening Commerce

1. Fiona Harvey. "Shoppers count the carbon." *Financial Times,* August 12, 2007 [Cited August 26, 2009] us.ft.com/ftgateway/superpage.ft?news_id=ft00812200 71533588709. Cited in Sustainable Practices #351, August 17, 2007.

2. Andrew W. Savitz with Karl Weber. *The Triple Bottom Line: How Today's Best-Run Companies Are Achieving Economic, Social, and Environmental Success—and How You Can Too.* Jossey-Bass, 2006, p. xiii.
3. For additional details, see International Forum on Globalization [Cited May 12, 2008] ifg.org.
4. Websites: Boutelle.com [Cited August 21, 2009] boutell.com/newfaq/misc/sizeofweb.html. E-mails: About.com [Cited August 21, 2009] email.about.com/od/emailtrivia/f/how_many_email.htm. Cell phones: Infoplease [Cited August 21, 2009] indexmundi.com/world/telephones_mobile_cellular.html. Television sets: *Business Week* [Cited August 21, 2009] businessweek.com/magazine/content/05_06/b3919124_mz063.htm. For additional information see Nielsen Media Research [Cited May 12, 2008] nielsenmedia.com.
5. For details see *The Story of Stuff* [Cited August 21, 2009] storyofstuff.com.
6. For details see FreeRice [Cited August 21, 2009] freerice.com. Also British Broadcasting Corporation. *Web Game Provides Rice for Hungry.* November 10, 2007 [Cited August 21, 2009] news.bbc.co.uk/2/hi/europe/7088447.stm.
7. For a description of the steps involved in Dell's manufacturing of laptop computers see Thomas L. Friedman. *The World is Flat: A Brief History of the Twenty-First Century.* Farrar, Straus and Giroux, 2005, pp. 414–419.
8. *Ford Encourages Suppliers to Turn Industry Crisis Into an Opportunity for Restructuring.* Reuters, August 7, 2009 [Cited September 28, 2009] reuters.com/article/pressRelease/idUS175022+07-Aug-2009+PRN20090807.
9. Andrew W. Savitz with Karl Weber. *The Triple Bottom Line*, p. 63.
10. John Elkington. "Enter the Triple Bottom Line" in Adrian Henriques and Julie Richardson, eds. *The Triple Bottom Line: Does It All Add Up?* Earthscan Publications, 2004, p. 6.
11. For additional information, see Biomimicry Institute. *What Do You Mean by the Term Biomimicry? A Conversation with Janine Benyus, author of Biomimicry: Innovation Inspired by Nature* [Cited September 23, 2009] biomimicryinstitute.org/about-us/what-do-you-mean-by-the-term-biomimicry.html. Also Treehugger. *Janine Benyus on Biomimicry in Design on TH Radio* [Cited September 23, 2009] Part One: treehugger.com/files/2008/12/the-th-interview-janine-benyus-1.php and Part Two: treehugger.com/files/2009/01/the-th-interview-janine-benyus-2.php. Also Personal Life Media. Living Green. *Biomimicry: Janine Benyus is Honored by TIME* [Cited September 23, 2009] Part One, Episode 26: personallifemedia.com/podcasts/224-living-green/episodes/3351-biomimicry-janine-benyus-honored and Part Two, Episode 27: personallifemedia.com/podcasts/224-living-green/episodes/3354-biomimicry-janine-benyus-honored-time.
12. Paul Hawken. *Blessed Unrest: How the Largest Movement in the World Came into Being and Why No One Saw It Coming.* Viking, 2007, p. 182.
13. Indigo Development. *The Industrial Symbiosis at Kalundborg, Denmark* [Cited August 21, 2009] indigodev.com/Kal.html. Also Smart Communities Network. *Eco-Industrial Parks* [Cited August 23, 2009] smartcommunities.ncat.org/business/ecoparks.shtml and AbsoluteAstronomy.com. *Kalundborg* [Cited August 23, 2009] absoluteastronomy.com/topics/Kalundborg.
14. Gregory C. Unruh. "The Biosphere Rules." *Harvard Business Review,* February 2008, p. 112.
15. Helmar.org. *Bill McDonough: Making business sustainable* [Cited August 21, 2009] helmar.org/index.php?id=88. Source: *FastCompany,* June 1998.

16. Texas Commission on Environmental Quality. *TCEQ List of Computer-Equipment Manufacturers* [August 21, 2009] tceq.state.tx.us/assistance/P2Recycle/electronics/manufacturer-list.html.

17. European Commission. *End of Life Vehicles* [Cited August 21, 2009] ec.europa.eu/environment/waste/elv_index.htm.

18. James Gustave Speth. *The Bridge at the Edge of the World: Capitalism, the Environment, and Crossing from Crisis to Sustainability.* Yale University Press, 2008, p. 170.

19. Thomas L. Friedman. "The Inflection Is Near?" *The New York Times,* March 7, 2009 [Cited August 21, 2009] nytimes.com/2009/03/08/opinion/08friedman.html.

20. Bill McKibben. *Deep Economy: The Wealth of Communities and the Durable Future.* Time Books, 2007, p. 12. See also Clive Crook. "The Height of Inequality." *The Atlantic,* September 2006 [Cited September 28, 2009] theatlantic.com/doc/200609/crook-inequality.

21. Steve Shifferes. *World Inequality Rises.* BBC News, January 17, 2002 [Cited August 16, 2009] news.bbc.co.uk/1/hi/business/1763410.stm. For the original study, see Branko Milanovic. "True World Income Distribution, 1988 and 1993: First Calculation Based on Household Surveys Alone." *The Economic Journal,* vol. 112, iss. 476, January 2002 [Cited September 28, 2009] res.org.uk/economic/ejtoc.asp?ref=0013-0133&vid=112&iid=476&oc=-9999.

22. World Wildlife Fund (WWF) and Global Footprint Network. *Living Planet Report 2006 outlines scenarios for humanity's future* [Cited August 23, 2009] footprintnetwork.org/newsletters/gfn_blast_0610.html.

23. Millennium Ecosystem Assessment. *Overview of the Millennium Ecosystem Assessment* [Cited August 23, 2009] millenniumassessment.org/en/About.aspx.

24. Thomas L. Friedman. "The Inflection Is Near?"

25. James Gustave Speth, *The Bridge at the Edge of the World,* p. 149.

26. Bill McKibben. *Deep Economy,* pp. 41–42.

27. Patagonia. *Environmentalism: What We Do* [Cited May 20, 2008] patagonia.com.

28. 1% For The Planet. *A Quick Guide,* p. 1 [September 19, 2009] onepercentfortheplanet.org/en/files/Onepercent_Quick_Guide.pdf.

29. Dean's Beans. *Communication on Progress 2007/2008. United Nations Global Compact,* p. 1 [Cited August 22, 2009] deansbeans.com/coffee/page/un_global_compact.

30. Dean's Beans. *Nicaragua: Landmines, Coffee and Hope* [Cited August 22, 2009] deansbeans.com/coffee/people_centered/nic_cafe.html.

31. Dean's Beans. *Dean's Beans Organic Coffee: 2008 Carbon Dioxide Emissions Report,* pp. 2–3 [Cited September 23, 2009] deansbeans.com/coffee/page/carbon_neutral_initiative.

32. Peter Senge, Bryan Smith et al. *The Necessary Revolution: How Individuals and Organizations Are Working Together to Create a Sustainable World.* Doubleday, 2008, p. 327.

33. Sean McFadden. "Organic Growth." *Boston Business Journal,* February 2, 2007 [Cited August 22, 2009] deansbeans.com/coffee/in_the_news/detail.html?newsid=18.

34. Super Eco. *Seventh Generation* [March 13, 2009] supereco.com/company/seventh-generation.

35. Seventh Generation. *Spheres of Influence: Seventh Generation 2007 Corporate Consciousness Report,* p. 5 [Cited August 22, 2009] seventhgeneration.com/corporate-responsibility/2007.

36. Ibid., pp. 3, 5.
37. Jeffrey Hollender. *Has Seventh Generation Sold Out by Working with Walmart?* GreenBiz.com, October 28, 2009 [August 22, 2009] greenbiz.com/blog/2008/10/28/has-seventh-generation-sold-out-working-wal-mart.
38. Peter Senge, Bryan Smith et al. *The Necessary Revolution,* p. 350. Also Seventh Generation. *Spheres of Influence,* pp. 10–12. Also personal communication with Dave Rapaport of Seventh Generation on March 18, 2009.
39. Sean McFadden. "Organic Growth."
40. Bryan Walsh."How to Save the Planet and Make Money Doing It." *Time Magazine,* April 20, 2008 [Cited August 22, 2009] time.com/time/health/article/0,85 99,1732518,00.html. See also "Farmers enter carbon trading through biogas use." *The Times of India,* May 14, 2008 [Cited September 19, 2009] timesofindia.india times.com/news/environment/developmental-issues/Farmers-enter-carbon-trading-through-biogas-use/articleshow/3039614.cms. For additional details on Chicago Climate Exchange see [Cited September 19, 2009] chicagoclimatex .com. "US House of Representatives Committee Approves Climate Change Legislation." *Voice of America News,*May 22, 2009 [Cited May 27, 2009] voanews .com/english/2009-05-22-voa17.cfm. At the time of writing, the US Senate has yet to vote on the American Clean Energy and Security Act of 2009.
41. Sierra Business Council. *Sierra Nevada Wealth Index: Summary* [Cited August 22, 2009] sbcouncil.org/Summary.
42. Building Alliances for Local Living Economies. *A Local Living Economy* [Cited August 22, 2009] livingeconomies.org. Click on Entrepreneurs/A Living Economy.
43. For additional information, visit FLOW [Cited August 22, 2009] flowidealism .org.
44. DuPont. *An Expanded Commitment* [Cited August 22, 2009] www2.dupont .com/Sustainability/en_US/Newsroom/speeches/coh_101006.html.
45. Mike Hewitt. *Why I Believe in Felt Leadership.* Dupont Consulting Services, June 18, 2007 [Cited August 22, 2009] www2.dupont.com/Consulting_Services/en_ US/news_events/article20070618.html.
46. Whole Foods Market. *About Whole Foods Market* [Cited August 22, 2009] whole foodsmarket.com/company/index.php.
47. John Mackey. *Detailed Reply to Pollan Letter.* The CEO's Blog, June 26, 2006 [Cited August 22, 2009] www2.wholefoodsmarket.com/blogs/jmackey/2006/06/26/ detailed-reply/#more-15.
48. Swiss Re. *Our position and objectives* [Cited August 22, 2009] swissre.com. Click on About Us/Knowledge & expertise/Top Topics/Climate change/Our position and objectives.
49. Swiss Re. *Our commitments* [Cited August 22, 2009] swissre.com. Click on About Us/Knowledge & expertise/Top Topics/Climate change/Our commitments.
50. CNNMoney.com/Fortune. *10 Green Giants: Swiss Re* [August 22, 2009] money .cnn.com/galleries/2007/fortune/0703/gallery.green_giants.fortune/9.html.
51. Swiss Re. *Tackling our own footprint* [Cited August 22, 2009] swissre.com. Click on About Us/Knowledge & expertise/Top Topics/Climate change/Tackling our own footprint.
52. Allianz. *Fireman's Fund wins California environmental award.* November 27, 2008 [Cited August 22, 2009] allianz.com/en/press/news/business_news/insur ance/news_2008-11-27.html.

53. Grist. *The Birth of Blue: Adam Werbach calls for a new movement of a billion consumers*. April 12, 2008 [Cited August 22, 2009] gristmill.grist.org/article/the-birth-of-blue. Also personal communication with Kory Lundberg of Walmart on March 20, 2009.

54. Walmart. *Climate and Energy* [Cited August 22, 2009]walmartstores.com/Sustainability/7673.aspx. Also Walmart. *2009 Global Sustainability Report*, pp. 20–23 [Cited September 28, 2009] walmartstores.com/sites/sustainabilityreport/2009.

55. Walmart. *Zero Waste* [Cited August 22, 2009] walmartstores.com/Sustainability/7762.aspx. Also Walmart. *2009 Global Sustainability Report*, pp. 20–23.

56. Grist. *The Birth of Blue*. Also Walmart. *2009 Global Sustainability Report*, pp. 20–23.

57. Walmart. *2009 Global Sustainability Report*, p. 87.

58. Lester R. Brown. *Plan B 4.0: Mobilizing to Save Civilization*. W. W. Norton and Company, 2009, p. 246. Also Earth Policy Institute. "The Great Mobilization" in *Plan B 4.0: Mobilizing to Save Civilization*, Part III [Cited September 29, 2009] earth-policy.org/index.php?/books/pb4.

59. Ibid., p. 249.

60. Ibid., pp. 244–245.

61. Peter Barnes, Robert Costanza et al. *Creating an Earth Atmospheric Trust*. Grist, January 2, 2008 [Cited August 23, 2009] grist.org/article/creating-an-earth-atmospheric-trust. See also Earth Inc. *An Earth Atmospheric Trust: A proposal to stop global warming and end poverty* [Cited August 23, 2009] earthinc.org.

62. Ceres. *Global Reporting Initiative (GRI)* [Cited August 23, 2009] ceres.org/Page.aspx?pid=435.

63. For further information, see Natural Capital Solutions. *Climate Protection Manuals* [Cited August 23, 2009] climatemanual.org and natcapsolutions.org/ClimateProtectionManual.htm.

64. Bay Area Green Business Program. *About the Green Business Program* [Cited August 23, 2009] greenbiz.ca.gov/AboutUs.html.

65. Tata Group. *Being a Tata person* [Cited August 23, 2009] tata.com/company/Articles/inside.aspx?artid=YoUkRmtLqXQ=.

Chapter 4: Regenerative Design

1. Biomimicry Institute. *Termite-Inspired Air Conditioning* [Cited August 23, 2009] biomimicryinstitute.org/case-studies/case-studies/termite-inspired-air-conditioning.html. Cited in Sustainable Practices #369, November 7, 2008.

2. US Green Building Council. *Green Building Research* [Cited August 23, 2009] usgbc.org/displaypage.aspx?cmspageid=1718. Also US Green Building Council. *Green Building Facts: Green Building by the Numbers*. January 2009 [Cited October 10, 2009] usgbcaz.org/storage/usgbcaz/documents/USGBC_Publications/gbf_green_building_by_the_numbers_2009.pdf.

3. Michael Renner, Sean Sweeney et al. *Green Jobs: Working for People and the Environment*. Worldwatch Report 177, p. 16 [Cited August 23, 2009] worldwatch.org/node/5925. See also United Nations Environment Programme. *Buildings and Climate Change: Status, Challenges and Opportunities*. UNEP, 2007, p. v [Cited October 11, 2009] unep.org/publications/search/pub_details_s.asp?ID=3934.

4. For additional information see Sim Van der Ryn and Stuart Cowan. *Ecological Design: Tenth Anniversary Edition*. 2nd ed., Island Press, 2007, pp. 168–183.

5. Stephen R. Kellert. *Building for Life: Designing and Understanding the Human-Nature Connection.* Island Press, 2005, p. 93.
6. William McDonough and Michael Braungart. *Cradle to Cradle: Remaking the Way We Make Things.* North Point Press, 2002, p. 78.
7. Stephen R. Kellert. *Building for Life,* p. 96.
8. John Tillman Lyle. *Regenerative Design for Sustainable Development.* John Wiley & Sons, 1994, pp. 10–11.
9. Regenesis. *Regenerative Development* [Cited August 23, 2009] regenesisgroup.com/RegenerativeDevelopment.
10. For details on Regenerative Development see: Integrative Design Collaborative [Cited October 5, 2009] integrativedesign.net and Ben Haggard, Bill Reed et al. *Regenerative Development* [Cited August 23, 2009] integrativedesign.net/resources.
11. Congress for the New Urbanism. *Charter of the New Urbanism* [Cited August 16, 2009] cnu.org/charter.
12. Congress for the New Urbanism. *Charter of the New Urbanism.* Also Congress for the New Urbanism. *Project Database* [Cited August 23, 2009] cnu.org/search/projects. Also Robert Steuteville and Philip Langdon. "The New Urbanism: A better way to plan and build 21st Century communities." *New Urban News,* July 24, 2009 [Cited August 24, 2009] newurbannews.com/AboutNewUrbanism.html.
13. Urban Strategies. *Principles of Intelligent Urbanism* [Cited August 24, 2009] urbanstrategies-networks.blogspot.com/2008/04/principles-of-intelligent-urbanism.html. Also AbsoluteAstronomy.com. *Principles of Intelligent Urbanism* [Cited August 24, 2009] absoluteastronomy.com/topics/Principles_of_Intelligent_Urbanism.
14. US Green Building Council. *About USGBC* [Cited September 21, 2009] usgbc.org/ShowFile.aspx?DocumentID=5960. See also US Green Building Council *.LEED 2009 Vision & Executive Summary* [online.] [Cited August 23, 2009] usgbc.org/ShowFile.aspx?DocumentID=4121.
15. International Living Building Institute. *The Standard* [Cited August 23, 2009] ilbi.org/the-standard.
16. Architecture 2030. *The 2030 Challenge* [Cited August 23, 2009] architecture2030.org. Click on The 2030 Challenge.
17. Energy Star. *History of Energy Star* [Cited August 23, 2009] energystar.gov/index.cfm?c=about.ab_history.
18. TE Studio. *Passive House History* [Cited September 21, 2009] timeian.com/blog/?page_id=391. See also Passive House Institute US [Cited September 21, 2009] passivehouse.us/passiveHouse/PHIUSHome.html.
19. For additional information on the Pharos Framework see *Pharos: Signaling the Future of Material Selection* [Cited August 22, 2009] pharoslens.net.
20. Institute for the Built Environment. *LENSES* [Cited October 12, 2009] ibe.colostate.edu/projects/lenses.htm. See also "Building for People: Integrating Social Justice into Green Design." *Environmental Building News,* vol. 18, no. 10, October 2009 [Cited October 12, 2009] buildinggreen.com.
21. Thomas L. Friedman. "A Green Dream in Texas." *The New York Times,* January 8, 2006 [Cited August 23, 2009] select.nytimes.com/2006/01/18/opinion/18friedman.html?_r=1. Also Paul Westbrook. *Sustainability at Texas Instruments.* Texas Instruments, 2007 [Cited August 23, 2009] ti.com/corp/docs/rennerroadfab/

rfab_tour.pdf. Also personal communication with Paul Westbrook of Texas Instruments on March 31, 2009.

22. Global Ecovillage Network. *Find Ecovillages* [Cited March 25, 2009] gen.eco village.org/index.html.

23. Stephen R. Kellert. *Building for Life*, pp. 26–27.

24. One Planet Living [Cited September 22, 2009] oneplanetliving.org/index.html. See also Pooran Desai and Paul King. *One Planet Living: A Guide to Enjoying Life on Our One Planet*. Alastair Sawday Publishing Company, 2006.

25. BioRegional. *BedZED* [Cited August 23, 2009] bioregional.com/what-we-do/ our-work/bedzed.

26. Peabody. *Factsheets: BedZED* [Cited August 23, 2009] peabody.org.uk/media -centre/factsheets/bedzed.aspx.

27. *Greensburg: Sustainable Comprehensive Plan, 05.19.08* [Cited August 23, 2009] greensburgks.org. Click on Recovery Planning/Sustainable Comprehensive Master Plan.

28. David Wiles. *Sweden's Green Role Model City.* Sweden.se, May 18, 2007 [Cited August 23, 2009] swedense/eng/Home?Work-live/Sustainability/Reading/Swe dens-green-role-model-city. Also Biopact. *A look at Växjö, Europe's greenest city* [Cited August 23, 2009] biopact.com/2007/09/look-at-vxj-europes-greenest -city.html.

29. For more information, see *Environmental Programme: City of Växjö, 2006-05-18* [Cited August 23, 2009] vaxjo.se/english. Click on Sustainable Development and the Environmental Programme. For information on ecoBudget, see ecoBudget Webcentre [Cited August 23, 2009] ecobudget.com.

30. For more information on Masdar City see *WWF, Abu Dhabi unveil plans for sustainable city.* World Wildlife Fund [Cited August 23, 2009] panda.org/index .cfm?uNewsID=121361. For information on Huangbaiyu see "Building in Green." *Newsweek,* September 26, 2005 [Cited August 23, 2009] newsweek.com/id/1045 98. For information on Vauban and Quarry Village see Elizabeth Rosenthal. "In German Suburb, Life Goes On Without Cars." *The New York Times,* May 11, 2009 [Cited August 23, 2009] nytimes.com/2009/05/12/science/earth/12suburb .html?.

Chapter 5: Saving Ecosystems

1. *Caritas Helps Build "Green Wall" to Protect People from Natural Calamities.* UCANews.com, July 8, 2008 [Cited August 23, 2009] ucanews.com/2008/07/08/ caritas-helps-build-green-wall-to-protect-people-from-natural-calamities. Cited in Sustainable Practices #368, October 31, 2008.

2. Niles Eldredge. *The Sixth Extinction.* Action Bioscience [Cited August 23, 2009] actionbioscience.org/newfrontiers/eldredge2.html.

3. E. O. Wilson. *TED Wish Address, 8 March 2007.* The Encyclopedia of Life [Cited August 23, 2009] eol.org/files/pdfs/edward_wilson_ted_speech.pdf. See also *2007 TED Prize winner E. O. Wilson on TEDTalks.* TED Blog [Cited August 23, 2009] blog.ted.com/2007/04/2007_ted_prize_2.php.

4. Niles Eldredge, *The Sixth Extinction.*

5. Tein McDonald. "The Wilderness Society's 'WildCountry' Program: An interview with its National Coordinator, Virginia Young." *Ecological Management & Restoration,* vol 5, no. 2, August 2004, pp. 87–97 [Cited August 23, 2009] wilder ness.org.au/pdf/Ecological_Management_Restoration-JournAug04.pdf.

6. The Wilderness Society. *WildCountry: A New Vision for Nature* [Cited August 23, 2009] wilderness.org.au/files/WildCountry-a_new_vision_for_nature2005.pdf.

7. UNESCO. *FAQ — Biosphere Reserves?* [Cited August 24, 2009] unesco.org/mab/doc/faq/brs.pdf. Also Andrew C. Revkin. "U.N. Names 22 New Biosphere Reserves." *The New York Times,* Science, May 26, 2009 [Cited August 24, 2009] dotearth.blogs.nytimes.com/2009/05/26/un-names-22-new-biosphere-reserves.

8. For additional information on Zones of Peace see Tibet Environmental Watch. *Zone of Peace* [Cited August 23, 2009] tew.org/zop/index.html. Also Zones of Peace International Foundation. *Definition of a Zone of Peace* [Cited August 24, 2009] zopif.org/zop-definition.htm.

9. Conservation International. *Biodiversity Hotspots: Hotspots Science, Key Findings* [Cited August 24, 2009] biodiversityhotspots.org/Pages/default.aspx. Click on Hotspots Science and then on Key Findings.

10. "New Species Found Off Indonesia." *The New York Times,* Science, September 19, 2006 [Cited September 9, 2009] nytimes.com/2006/09/19/science/19shark.html.

11. Cheetah Conservation Botswana [Cited September 19, 2008] cheetahbotswana.com.

12. Land Trust Alliance. *Executive Summary* [Cited August 11, 2009] landtrustalliance.org/about-us/land-trust-census/executive-summary.

13. Baxter State Park, Maine. *A Brief History of Our Park* [Cited August 24, 2009] baxterstateparkauthority.com/aboutus/history.html.

14. The Conservation Land Trust. *Our Mission* [Cited September 25, 2008] theconservationlandtrust.org/eng/mision_introduccion.htm.

15. Douglas Tompkins. *Worldwide Experience in the Creation of Areas for Conservation.* The Conservation Land Trust [Cited August 24, 2009] theconservationlandtrust.org/eng/mision_conflictos_articulo_1.htm.

16. For additional information see *The Conservation Land Trust: The First Ten Years 1992–2002.* The Conservation Land Trust, 2002.

17. Heather Tallis and Peter Kareiva. "Ecosystem Services." *Current Biology,* vol. 15, iss. 18, September 20, 2005 [Cited August 24, 2009] sciencedirect.com. Enter one author's full name in Quick Search.

18. Ibid.

19. Natural Capital Project. *About The Natural Capital Project* [Cited September 21, 2009] naturalcapitalproject.org/about.html.

20. I am indebted to Gretchen Daily for additional information about the Natural Capital Project and the InVEST tool, obtained through personal communication on June 30, 2009.

21. Ecosystem Marketplace. *About Ecosystem Marketplace* [Cited August 24, 2009] ecosystemmarketplace.com. Click on About.

22. Latest statistics are available at Speciesbanking.com [Cited March 24, 2009] speciesbanking.com. See also Ricardo Bayon. "Banking on Biodiversity" in Worldwatch Institute. *State of the World 2008: Innovations for a Sustainable Economy.* W. W. Norton and Company, 2008, pp. 126–131, or Worldwatch Institute [Cited August 24, 2009] worldwatch.org/node/5568.

23. E. B. Boyd. *Earth For Hire.* Common Ground, April 2008 [Cited August 24, 2009] commongroundmag.com/2008/04/earthforhire0804.html.

Chapter 6: Navigating the Confluence

1. Sharon Astyk. "The Next One Hundred Things You Can Do To Get Ready For Peak Oil." *Groovy Green,* March 5, 2007 [Cited August 24, 2009] groovygreen. com/groove/?p=2270. Cited in Sustainable Practices #306, May 25, 2007.

2. Thomas Homer-Dixon. *The Upside of Down: Catastrophe, Creativity, and the Renewal of Civilization.* Island Press, 2006, p. 143.

3. Matthew C. Hansen, Stephen V. Stehman et al. "Humid tropical forest clearing from 2000 to 2005 quantified by using multitemporal and multiresolution remotely sensed data." *Proceedings of the National Academy of Sciences of the United States of America,* vol. 105, no. 27 (July 8, 2008): 9439–9444. Also at PNAS [Cited August 24, 2009] pnas.org/content/105/27/9439.full.

4. Brian Halwell. *Farming Fish for the Future. Summary.* Worldwatch Report 176 [Cited October 22, 2008] worldwatch.org/node/5880.

5. Brian Handwerk. "Team Races to Catalog Every Species on Earth." *National Geographic News,* March 5, 2002 [Cited October 22, 2008] news.nationalgeo graphic.com/news/2002/03/0305_0305_allspecies.html.

6. "Bold Traveler's Journey Toward the Center of the Earth." Berkeley Lab, News release, October 9, 2008 [Cited September 20, 2009] newscenter.lbl.gov/press-releases/2008/10/09/bold-traveler%e2%80%99s-journey-toward-the-center-of-the-earth.

7. Thomas L. Friedman. *Hot, Flat, and Crowded: Why We Need A Green Revolution — and How It Can Renew America.* Farrar, Straus and Giroux, 2008, p. 142.

8. Rick Smolan and Jennifer Erwitt. *Blue Planet Run: The Race to Provide Safe Drinking Water to the World.* Earth Aware Editions, 2007, pp. 6–15.

9. Ger Bergkamp and Claudia W. Sadoff. "Water in a Sustainable Economy" in *State of the World 2008: Innovations for a Sustainable Economy.* W. W. Norton and Company, 2008, pp. 109–112. Also available at Worldwatch Institute [Cited August 24, 2009] worldwatch.org/node/5561#toc.

10. End Water Poverty. *The issue* [Cited August 24, 2009] endwaterpoverty.org/ the_issue.

11. Ben Block. *Water Advocates Speak Out for Improved Sanitation.* Worldwatch Institute, August 8, 2008 [Cited August 24, 2009] worldwatch.org/node/5845.

12. Blue Planet Run Foundation [Cited October 23, 2008] blueplanetrun.org. For further information see Peer Water Exchange [Cited October 23, 2008] peer water.org.

13. US Department of Energy. *Energy Sources* [Cited August 24, 2009] energy.gov/ energysources/index.htm.

14. US Department of Energy: Energy Efficiency & Renewable Energy. *2008 Renewable Energy Data Book.* July 2009 [Cited September 21, 2009] www1.eere.energy. gov//maps_data/pdfs/eere_databook.pdf. For information on CSP, see US Department of Energy: Energy Efficiency & Renewable Energy. *Concentrating Solar Power* [Cited September 20, 2009] www1.eere.energy.gov/solar/csp.html.

15. Amory B. Lovins. *Reinventing the Wheels: The Automotive Efficiency Revolution.* America.gov, May 9, 2008 [Cited September 20, 2009] america.gov/st/energy -english/2008/May/20080520182338WRybakcuH1.032656e-02.html. Source: July 2006 edition of *eJournal USA.*

16. Concerto [Cited October 23, 2008] concertoplus.eu. See also *What is SESAC? Sustainable Energy Systems in Advanced Cities* [Cited August 24, 2009] concerto-sesac.eu. Click on About SESAC/What is SESAC?

17. Somini Sengupta. "At Indian Preserves, Tigers Remain King as People Are Coaxed Out." *The New York Times,* April 16, 2008 [Cited August 24, 2009] nytimes.com/2008/04/16/world/asia/16tiger.html?scp=4&sq=tigers%20india&st=cse.
18. Jared Diamond. "What's Your Consumption Factor?" *The New York Times,* January 2, 2008 [Cited August 12, 2009] nytimes.com/2008/01/02/opinion/02diamond.html?.
19. Don Weeden and Norm Weeden. *Immigration, Population and the Environment: Connecting the Dots.* Population Media Center, September 6, 2007 [Cited October 23, 2008] populationmedia.org/2007/09/page/2.
20. Ibid.
21. United Nations Department of Economic and Social Affairs, Population Division. *World Population Prospects: The 2008 Revision* [Cited September 28, 2009] esa.un.org/unpp. Also Don Weeden and Norm Weeden. *Immigration, Population and the Environment* and US Census Bureau. *World POPclock Projection* [Cited September 28, 2009] census.gov/ipc/www/popclockworld.html.
22. Pew Hispanic Center. *US Population Projections: 2005–2050.* February 11, 2008 [Cited February 19, 2009] pewhispanic.org/reports/report.php?ReportID=85. See also Mary M. Kent and Mark Mather. "What Drives US Population Growth?" *Population Bulletin,* vol. 57, no. 4, December 2002 [Cited August 24, 2009] prb.org/Source/57.4WhatDrivesUSPopulation.pdf. Also M. Munson and P. Sutton. "Births, marriages, divorces, deaths: provisional data for 2003." *National Vital Statistics Reports,* vol. 52, no. 22, June 10, 2004.
23. J. Joseph Speidel, Deborah C. Weiss et al. "Family Planning and Reproductive Health: The Link to Environmental Preservation." *Population & Environment,* vol. 28, nos. 4–5, May 2007, p. 248.
24. Thomas Homer-Dixon. *The Upside of Down,* pp. 62–63.
25. J. Joseph Speidel, Deborah C. Weiss et al. "Family Planning and Reproductive Health," p. 250.
26. Ibid., p. 252.
27. Gary Gardner and Thomas Prugh. "Seeding the Sustainable Economy" in *State of the World 2008: Innovations for a Sustainable Economy.* W. W. Norton and Company, 2008, pp. 4, 8–9. Also Worldwatch Institute [Cited August 24, 2009] worldwatch.org/node/5561#toc.
28. Jeffrey D. Sachs. *The End of Poverty: Economic Possibilities for Our Time.* Penguin Press, 2005, p. 1.
29. Jerry Mander, ed. *Manifesto on Global Economic Transitions.* The International Forum on Globalization, The Institute for Policy Studies and Global Project on Economic Transitions, September 2007, p. 19 [Cited August 24, 2009] ifg.org/pdf/manifesto.pdf.
30. Thomas Homer-Dixon. *The Upside of Down,* p. 65.
31. Ibid., pp. 65–69.
32. *When Small Loans Make A Big Difference.* Forbes.com, Knowledge@Wharton, June 3, 2008 [Cited August 24, 2009] forbes.com/2008/06/03/kiva-microfinance-uganda-ent-fin-cx_0603whartonkiva.html. Also Kiva [Cited August 24, 2009] kiva.org.
33. Thomas L. Friedman. *Hot, Flat, and Crowded,* pp. 119–120. Also *350 Science.* 350.org [Cited October 31, 2008]350.org/en/about/science.
34. Bill McKibben. "Civilization's Last Chance: The planet is nearing a tipping point

on climate change, and it gets much worse, fast." *The Los Angeles Times,* May 11, 2008 [Cited August 16, 2009] latimes.com/news/opinion/la-op-mckibben11 -2008may11,0,7434369.story.

35. Ibid.

36. United Nations Framework Convention on Climate Change. *Kyoto Protocol* [Cited October 31, 2008] unfccc.int/kyoto_protocol/items/2830.php.

37. At the time of writing, the Climate Conference, Copenhagen 2009 is forthcoming.

38. At the time of writing, the American Clean Energy and Security Act of 2009 has not yet moved to the US Senate for a vote.

39. Princeton University. *CMI: Carbon Mitigation Initiative* [Cited October 7, 2009] cmi.princeton.edu. Also Princeton University. CMI. *Stabilization Wedges Introduction* [Cited October 7, 2009] cmi.princeton.edu/wedges/intro.php; R. Socolow, R. Hotinski et al. "Solving the Climate Problem: Technologies Available to Curb CO_2 Emissions." *Environment,* vol. 46, no. 10, 2004, pp. 8–19 [Cited October 7, 2009] princeton.edu/~cmi/resources/CMI_Resources_new_files/En viron_08-21a.pdf; and Princeton University. CMI. *Stabilization Wedges Game* [Cited October 7, 2009] cmi.princeton.edu/wedges/game.php.

40. City of Oakland. *Oil Independent Oakland (OIO) By 2020 Task Force* [Cited September 29, 2009] oaklandnet.com/Oil/default.html. Also Post Carbon Cities. *Government responses to peak oil (sub-national)* [Cited September 29, 2009] postcarboncities.net/peakoilactions.

Chapter 7: Catalysts for Change

1. Trinity Oaks Vineyards [Cited August 25, 2009] onebottleonetree.com. Cited in Sustainable Practices #365, September 19, 2008.

2. Malcolm Gladwell. *The Tipping Point: How Little Things Can Make a Big Difference.* Back Bay Books, 2002, pp. 9, 12.

3. For additional information on greening building codes, see Development Center for Appropriate Technology [Cited August 25, 2009] dcat.net.

4. National Wildlife Federation: Campus Ecology. *Campus Environment 2008: A National Report Card on Sustainability in Higher Education* [Cited August 25, 2009] nwf.org/campusEcology/docs/CampusReportFinal.pdf.

5. American College & University Presidents' Climate Commitment [Cited August 25, 2009] presidentsclimatecommitment.org.

6. National Wildlife Federation: Campus Ecology. *Executive Summary. Campus Environment 2008: A National Report Card on Sustainability in Higher Education,* p. 6 [Cited September 9, 2009] nwf.org/campusEcology/docs/Executive SumFinal.pdf.

7. Power Shift '09 [Cited March 20, 2009] powershift09.org and *Focus the Nation 2008.* Focus the Nation [Cited August 25, 2009] focusthenation.org/focus-nat ion-2008-0.

8. For additional information see [Cited October 13, 2009]: Recyclemania: recy clemaniacs.org, Chill Out: nwf.org/campusecology/chillout, Climate Challenge: climatechallenge.org, Step It Up 2007: stepitup2007.org, Power Shift '09: power shift09.org, Focus the Nation: focusthenation.org and 350.org: 350.org.

9. Ben Block. *Climate Protests Escalate Worldwide.* Worldwatch Institute, November 19, 2008 [Cited August 16, 2009] worldwatch.org/node/5939. Also Severin Carrell. "Climate change protest disrupts flights at Aberdeen." *The Guardian,*

March 3, 2009 [Cited August 16, 2009] guardian.co.uk/environment/2009/mar
/03/aberdeen-airport-climate-protest.

10. Lea Hartzog and Michael Fox, eds. "Cool Crowd, Organic food? Check. Solar power, biodiesel buses, and composting? Check, check, check. Colleges
large and small get their green on." *Sierra Magazine,* September/October 2008
[Cited August 25, 2009] sierraclub.org/sierra/200809/coolschools/cool-ideas
-list.asp.

11. Graduation Pledge Alliance [Cited August 16, 2009] graduationpledge.org.

12. Alice McKeown. *Organic Agriculture More Than Doubled Since 2000.* Worldwatch Institute, July 23, 2009 [Cited August 25, 2009] worldwatch.org/node/
6199.

13. Marian Burros. "Obamas to Plant Vegetable Garden at White House." *The New
York Times,* March 20, 2009 [Cited August 16, 2009] nytimes.com/2009/03/20/
dining/20garden.html.

14. US Department of Agriculture: Agricultural Marketing Services. *Farmers Market Growth: 1994–2009* [Cited August 25, 2009] ams.usda.gov/AMSv1.0. Click
on Farmers Markets and Local Food Marketing, then on Farmers Markets and
then on Farmers Market Growth: 1994–2009.

15. Local Harvest. *A Short Glossary of Direct Marketing Avenues* [Cited August 25,
2009] localharvest.org/descriptions.jsp.

16. John Cloud. "Eating Better Than Organic." *Time,* March 2, 2007 [Cited August
25, 2009] time.com/time/magazine/article/0,9171,1595245,00.html.

17. Three Stone Hearth [Cited August 25, 2009] threestonehearth.com.

18. For more details see Bonnie Azab Powell. "The Bi-Rite Stuff." *Edible San Francisco,* iss. 14, October/November 2008 [Cited August 25, 2009] ediblecommunit
ies.com/sanfrancisco/index.php?/Issue-14/the-bi-rite-stuff.html. Also Bi-Rite
Market [Cited June 16, 2009] biritemarket.com.

19. California Department of Food and Agriculture. *Certified Farmers Market Program* [Cited August 25, 2009] cdfa.ca.gov/is/i_&_c/cfm.html.

20. US Department of Agriculture. The Census of Agriculture. "Table 1. Historical
Highlights: 2007 and Earlier Census Years." *2007 Census Report* [Cited August
25, 2009] agcensus.usda.gov/Publications/2007/Full_Report. Click on US by
Table and then on Table 1.

21. Claire Hope Cummings. *Essay — Ripe for Change: Agriculture's Tipping Point.*
Worldwatch Institute [Cited August 25, 2009] worldwatch.org/node/4119.

22. Centers for Disease Control and Prevention. *Overweight and Obesity Trends
Among Adults* [Cited August 25, 2009] cdc.gov/nccdphp/dnpa/obesity/trend/
index.htm. Also American Diabetes Association. *Diabetes Statistics* [Cited August 25, 2009] diabetes.org/diabetes-statistics.jsp.

23. BBC News. *One in three will have diabetes.* October 7, 2003 [Cited August 25,
2009] news.bbc.co.uk/2/hi/health/3171140.stm.

24. Claire Hope Cummings. *Essay — Ripe for Change.*

25. Slow Money Alliance. *Principles* [Cited September 22, 2009] slowmoneyalliance
.org/principles.html.

26. Slow Food. *Our Philosophy* [Cited August 25, 2009] slowfood.com. Click on
About us/Our philosophy.

27. Kim Severson. "Slow Food Savors Big Moment." *The New York Times,* July 23,
2008 [Cited August 25, 2009] nytimes.com/2008/07/23/dining/23slow.html.

28. Sustainable Food Laboratory. *Frequently Asked Questions* [Cited August 13,
2009] sustainablefoodlab.org/faq.

29. Sustainable Food Laboratory. *Frequently Asked Questions.* Also Sustainable Food Laboratory. *The Changing Vocabulary of Food Purchasing: A Guide for Food Service Professionals* [Cited August 13, 2009] sustainablefoodlab.org/article/articleview/17174/1/2373.

30. Peter Senge, Bryan Smith et al. *The Necessary Revolution: How Individuals and Organizations Are Working Together to Create a Sustainable World.* Doubleday, 2008, pp. 249–250, 259–262.

31. Personal communication with Amelia Spilger of Marin Farmers Markets on June 16, 2009. For details visit Marin Agricultural Institute [Cited August 25, 2009] marinagriculturalinstitute.org. Also Marin Farmers Markets [Cited June 16, 2009] marinfarmersmarkets.org.

32. Van Jones. *The Green Collar Economy: How One Solution Can Fix Our Two Biggest Problems.* HarperOne, 2008, p. 11.

33. Michael Renner, Sean Sweeney et al. *Green Jobs: Working for People and the Environment.* Worldwatch Report 177, 2008, p. 5 [Cited August 25, 2009] worldwatch.org/node/5825.

34. Ibid., pp. 12, 21.

35. Green For All. *Green Jobs Act FAQ* [Cited September 22, 2009] greenforall.org/files/faq-greenjobsact07.pdf/view.

36. Michael Grabell and Christopher Weaver. *The Stimulus Plan: A Detailed List of Spending.* ProPublica, February 13, 2009 [Cited August 25, 2009] propublica.org/special/the-stimulus-plan-a-detailed-list-of-spending#stim_energy; also Panama Bartholomy. *The Stimulus Package: Impacts on Green Building and California.* US Green Building Council, Northern California [Cited August 25, 2009] usgbc-ncc.org/index.php?option=com_content&task=view&id=170&Itemid=210. Also US Department of Labor. "US Department of Labor announces $500 million for 5 grant solicitations to train workers for green jobs." News release, June 24, 2009 [Cited September 22, 2009] dol.gov/opa/media/press/eta/eta20090725.htm.

37. *The Alliance for Climate Protection and the We Campaign: Fact Sheet* [Cited August 16, 2009] wecansolveit.org/content/new. Click on We Campaign fact sheet.

38. Apollo Alliance. *Mission* [Cited September 28, 2009] apolloalliance.org/about/mission.

39. AbsoluteAstronomy. *Earth Hour* [Cited September 29, 2009] absoluteastronomy.com/topics/Earth_Hour. Also Earth Hour. *Vote Earth* [Cited September 29, 2009] earthhour.org/whos-voting; Earth Hour. *Earth Hour's Countdown to Copenhagen* [Cited September 29, 2009] earthhour.org/media-centre; and Earth Hour. *Copenhagen Businesses to Switch Off During Climate Summit* [Cited September 29, 2009] earthhour.org/media-centre. At the time of writing, the Global Climate Conference in Copenhagen is forthcoming.

40. Dahlia Fahmy. *Charity Prize Fight.* Portfolio.com, June 12, 2008 [Cited August 25, 2009] portfolio.com/news-markets/national-news/portfolio/2008/06/12/Prize-Philanthropy.

41. Paul Hawken. *Blessed Unrest: How the Largest Movement in the World Came into Being and Why No One Saw It Coming.* Viking, 2007, pp. 157–158.

42. "Wiki's Wild World." *Nature,* no. 438, December 15, 2005, p. 890 [Cited August 25, 2009] nature.com/nature/journal/v438/n7070/full/438890a.html.

43. WiserEarth. *About WiserEarth* [Cited August 25, 2009] wiserearth.org/article/About. Also Natural Capital Institute. *WISER* [Cited August 25, 2009] naturalcapital.org/wiser.htm.

44. Thomas Homer-Dixon. *The Upside of Down: Catastrophe, Creativity and the Renewal of Civilization.* Island Press, 2006, p. 295.

Chapter 8: A Thriveable Future

1. Duncan Kennedy. *Italy aims for carbon-neutral farm.* BBC, October 18, 2008 [Cited August 25, 2009] news.bbc.co.uk/2/hi/europe/7669522.stm. Cited in Sustainable Practices #368, October 31, 2008.
2. Donella H. Meadows. *Leverage Points: Places to Intervene in a System.* Sustainability Institute, 1999 [Cited August 16, 2009] sustainer.org/pubs/Leverage_ Points.pdf.
3. Thomas L. Friedman. "While Detroit Slept." *The New York Times,* December 10, 2008 [Cited January 9, 2009] nytimes.com/2008/12/10/opinion/10friedman .html?em.
4. National Energy Technology Laboratory. *Modern Grid Benefits.* August 2007, p. 15 [Cited August 25, 2009] netl.doe.gov/moderngrid/resources.html. Click on Modern Grid Benefits.
5. David Orr. "Our Great Work." *Resurgence,* no. 248, May/June 2008, pp. 26–28. See also [Cited January 15, 2009] resurgence.org.
6. City Repair. *The City Repair Project's Placemaking Guidebook: Neighborhood Placemaking in the Public Right-of-Way.* 2nd ed., City Repair, 2006, pp. 19–21, 139–143. Also personal communication with Mark Lakeman of City Repair, March 9, 2009.
7. City Repair. *Projects* [Cited August 25, 2009] cityrepair.org/about/projects.
8. Menominee Tribal Enterprises. *Concept of Sustainable Forestry on the Menominee Reservation* [Cited August 25, 2009] mtewood.com/concept-sustainable-forestry.htm.
9. Personal communication with Bill Schmidt of Menominee Tribal Enterprises on July 28, 2009. Also see Fred Hillman. "Menominee Tribe Wins Award for Logging Practices Harvesting Timber Balanced with Preserving Wildlife." *Wausau Daily Herald,* April 15, 1996. See [Cited August 25, 2009] mtewood.com/award .htm.
10. The Long Now Foundation. *Long Bets* [Cited August 25, 2009] longbets.org/ bets.
11. For additional information, see: The Long Now Foundation: longnow.org. The 10,000-year clock: longnow.org/projects/clock. Long Bets: longbets.org. Longviewer: longnow.org/about/longview.php. [All Cited August 25, 2009].
12. B. Walker, C.S. Holling et al. "Resilience, Adaptability and Transformability in Social–ecological Systems." *Ecology and Society,* vol. 9, iss. 2, art. 5, 2004 [Cited August 25, 2009] ecologyandsociety.org/vol9/iss2/art5.
13. For additional background see Brian Walker. "Resilience Thinking." *People and Place,* vol. 1, iss. 2, November 24, 2008 [Cited August 25, 2009] peopleandplace. net/featured_voices/2008/11/24/resilience_thinking. Also Rob Hopkins. *The Transition Handbook: From Oil Dependency to Local Resilience.* Chelsea Green Publishing, 2008.
14. Mark J. Maggio. "Hurricane Katrina: Resiliency, The Other Side of Tragedy." *Federal Probation,* vol. 70, no. 3, December 2006 [Cited September 23, 2009] uscourts.gov/fedprob/December_2006/hurricane.html. Also American Psychological Association. APA Help Center. *Resilience: After a Hurricane* [Cited September 23, 2009] apahelpcenter.org/articles/article.php?id=113.

15. ICLEI–Local Governments for Sustainability. *Five Milestones for Climate Adaptation* [Cited August 25, 2009] iclei-usa.org/programs/climate/Climate_Adaptation/five-milestones-for-climate-adaptation. See also ICLEI. *Climate Adaptation Planning Success Stories* [Cited August 25, 2009] iclei-usa.org/success-stories/climate-adaptation/climate-adaptation.

16. Worldwatch Institute. *State of the World 2009: Into a Warming World.* W. W. Norton and Company, 2009, p. 161 and [Cited August 25, 2009] worldwatch.org/node/5982. Also *Case Study: Durban adapts to climate change.* id21insights [Cited August 25, 2009] id21.org/insights/insights71/art05.html.

17. Worldwatch Institute. *State of the World 2009,* p. 168.

18. Van Jones. *The Green Collar Economy: How One Solution Can Fix Our Two Biggest Problems.* HarperOne, 2008, p. 71.

19. Personal communication with John Garn of Community Pulse on September 22, 2009. Community Pulse. *Providing Indicators for Action* [Cited January 28, 2009] communitypulse.org. Also Joy Lanzendorfer. *Doing the Math: Community Pulse project takes consumption numbers and makes them real.* Metroactive, September 19, 2007 [Cited September 22, 2009] metroactive.com/bohemian/09.19.07/news-0738.html.

20. For additional information about Janine Benyus and biomimicry, see TED Global. Talks. *Janine Benyus: Biomimicry in Action.* July 2009 [Cited September 23, 2009] ted.com/index.php/talks/janine_benyus_biomimicry_in_action.html. Also Sara Stroud. *Evolution Meets Creation in Biomimicry.* Reuters/Sustainable Industries [Cited September 23, 2009] reuters.com/article/mnGreenBuildings/idUS177480475020090728 or sustainableindustries.com/technology/51788452.html.

21. Science and Environmental Health Network. *The Precautionary Principle: A Common Sense Way to Protect Public Health and the Environment.* January 2000 [Cited August 25, 2009] mindfully.org/Precaution/Precautionary-Principle-Common-Sense.htm.

22. Bay Area Working Group on the Precautionary Principle. *The Precautionary Principle in Action: Bay Area Working Group Action locally and regionally.* Taking Precaution.org [Cited August 25, 2009] takingprecaution.org/inact_bayarea.html.

23. Biomimicry Institute. *Innovation for Conservation: Conservation Inspired by Nature's Genius* [Cited September 23, 2009] biomimicryinstitute.org/innovation-4-conservation/innovation-for-conservation/protecting-inspiration.html.

24. Roots & Shoots. *About Us* [Cited August 25, 2009] rootsandshoots.org/aboutus/model.

Index

About the Author

ANDRÉS R. EDWARDS is an educator, author, media designer and sustainability consultant. He is founder and president of EduTracks a firm specializing in developing education programs and consulting services on sustainable practices for green building and business initiatives. His work includes developing sustainability plans as well as training and awareness programs for municipalities, colleges and businesses. He has worked as producer, exhibit developer, and consultant for projects in natural history, biodiversity and sustainable  community for companies and towns throughout the US and abroad. He is the author of *The Sustainability Revolution: Portrait of a Paradigm Shift* (2005), selected by Apple as an electronic book example for the education market, and co-author with Robert Z. Apte of *Tibet: Enduring Spirit, Exploited Land* (2004). Mr. Edwards has given radio and television interviews and lectured and presented seminars about his work at conferences, universities, and for business and community organizations. He lives in northern California. For further information visit: andresedwards.com.

If you have enjoyed *Thriving Beyond Sustainability*,
you might also enjoy other

Books to Build a New Society

Our books provide positive solutions for people who
want to make a difference. We specialize in:

Sustainable Living ✦ Ecological Design and Planning

Natural Building & Appropriate Technology ✦ New Forestry

Environment and Justice ✦ Conscientious Commerce

Progressive Leadership ✦ Resistance and Community

Nonviolence ✦ Educational and Parenting Resources

New Society Publishers

ENVIRONMENTAL BENEFITS STATEMENT

New Society Publishers has chosen to produce this book on recycled
paper made with 100% post consumer waste, processed chlorine free,
and old growth free.

For every 5,000 books printed, New Society saves the following
resources:[1]

25	Trees
2,264	Pounds of Solid Waste
2,491	Gallons of Water
3,249	Kilowatt Hours of Electricity
4,115	Pounds of Greenhouse Gases
18	Pounds of HAPs, VOCs, and AOX Combined
6	Cubic Yards of Landfill Space

[1]Environmental benefits are calculated based on research done by the
Environmental Defense Fund and other members of the Paper Task Force who study
the environmental impacts of the paper industry.

For a full list of NSP's titles, please call 1-800-567-6772 or check out our web site at:

www.newsociety.com

NEW SOCIETY PUBLISHERS